CURT PIRES & DAVID RUBÍN WITH MICHAEL GARLAND

THE FICTION ™

BOOM! STUDIOS

THE FICTION, April 2016. Published by BOOM! Studios, a division of Boom Entertainment, Inc. The Fiction is ™ & © 2016 Curt Pires. Originally published in single magazine form as THE FICTION No. 1-4. ™ & © 2015 Curt Pires. All rights reserved. BOOM! Studios™ and the BOOM! Studios logo are trademarks of Boom Entertainment, Inc., registered in various countries and categories. All characters, events, and institutions depicted herein are fictional. Any similarity between any of the names, characters, persons, events, and/or institutions in this publication to actual names, characters, and persons, whether living or dead, events, and/or institutions is unintended and purely coincidental. BOOM! Studios does not read or accept unsolicited submissions of ideas, stories, or artwork.

A catalog record of this book is available from OCLC and from the BOOM! Studios website, www.boom-studios.com, on the Librarians page.

BOOM! Studios, 5670 Wilshire Boulevard, Suite 450, Los Angeles, CA 90036-5679. Printed in China. First Printing.

ISBN: 978-1-60886-858-2, eISBN: 978-1-61398-529-8

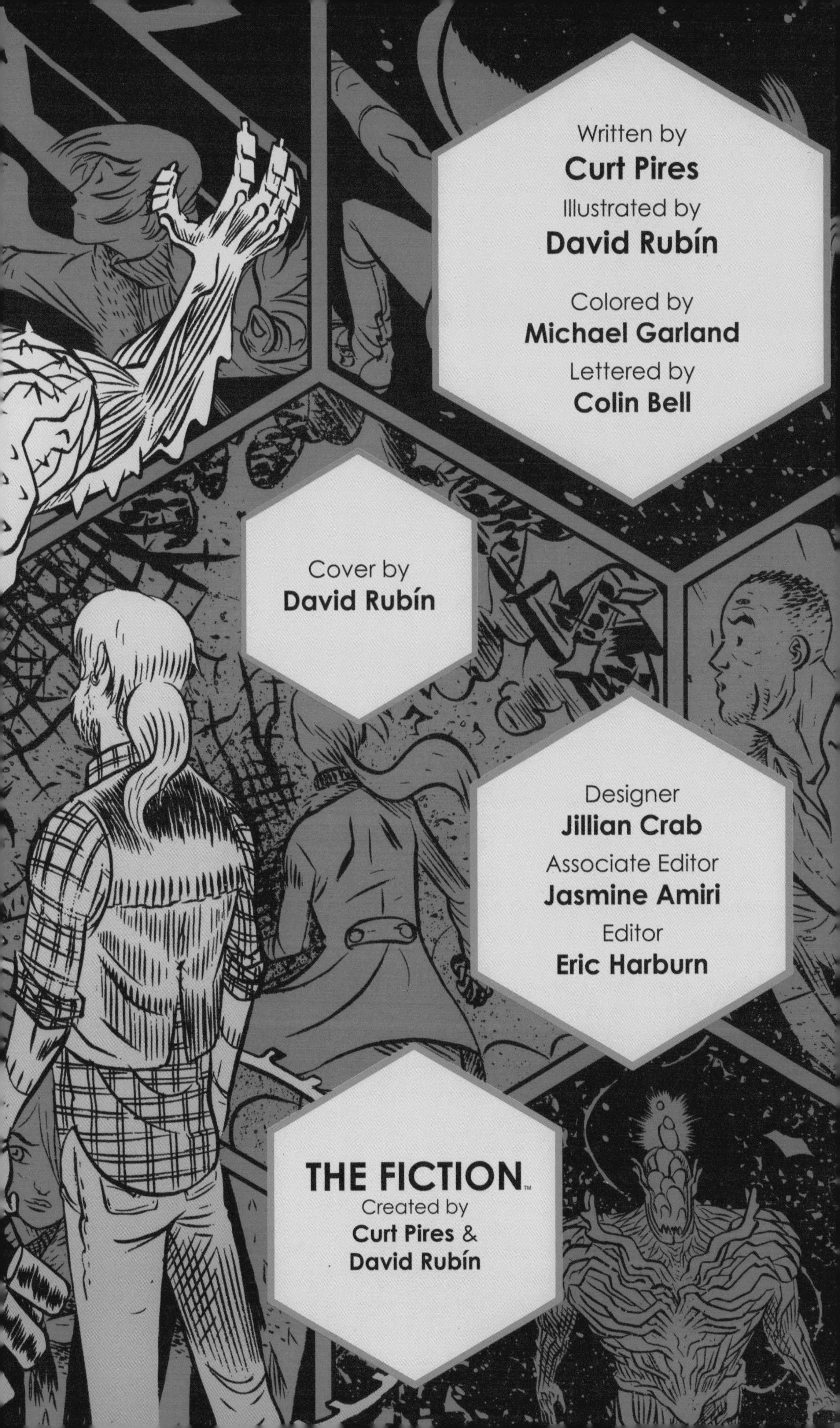

Written by
Curt Pires
Illustrated by
David Rubín

Colored by
Michael Garland
Lettered by
Colin Bell

Cover by
David Rubín

Designer
Jillian Crab
Associate Editor
Jasmine Amiri
Editor
Eric Harburn

THE FICTION™

Created by
Curt Pires &
David Rubín

CHAPTER I
The Story of Everything

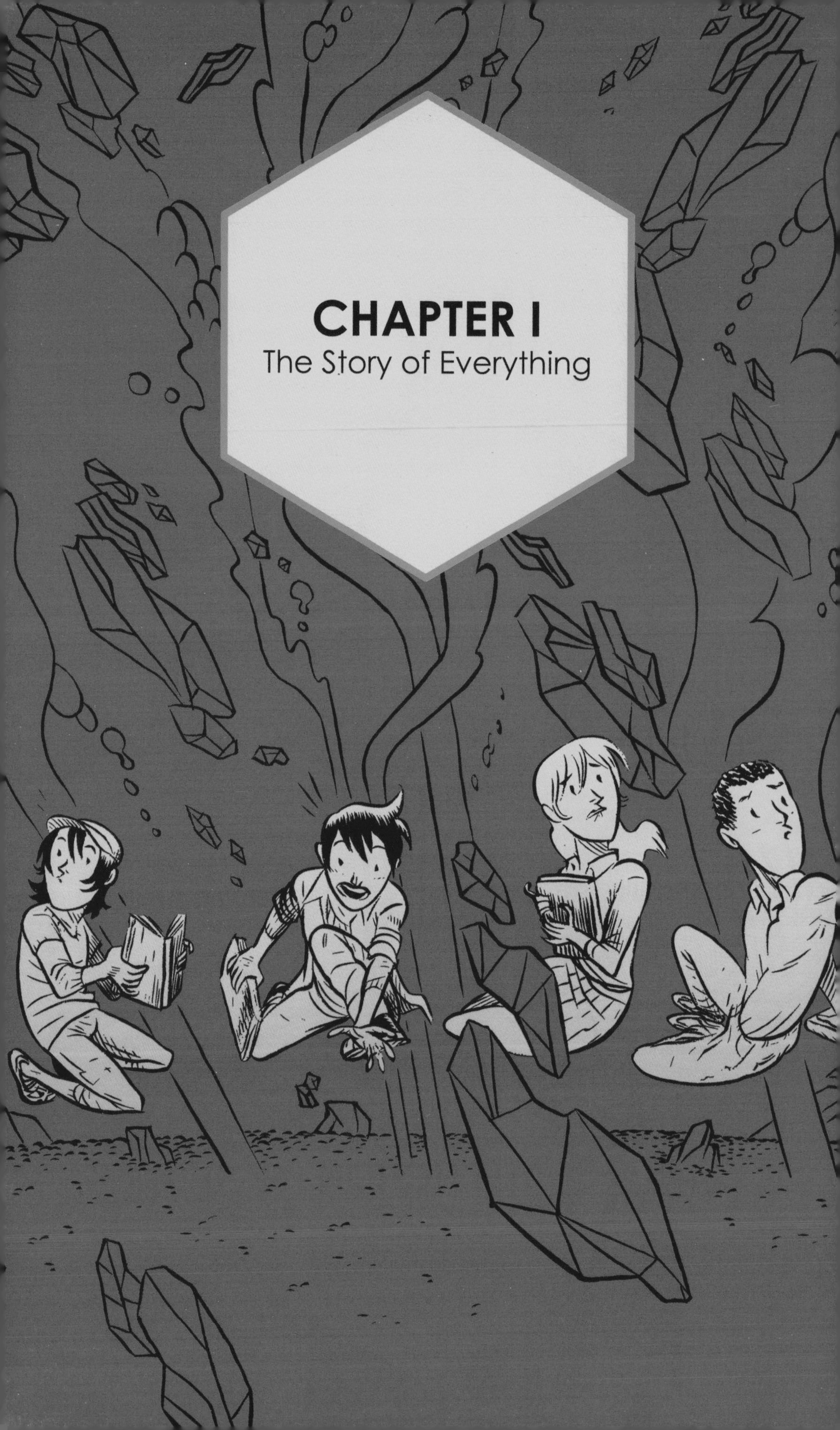

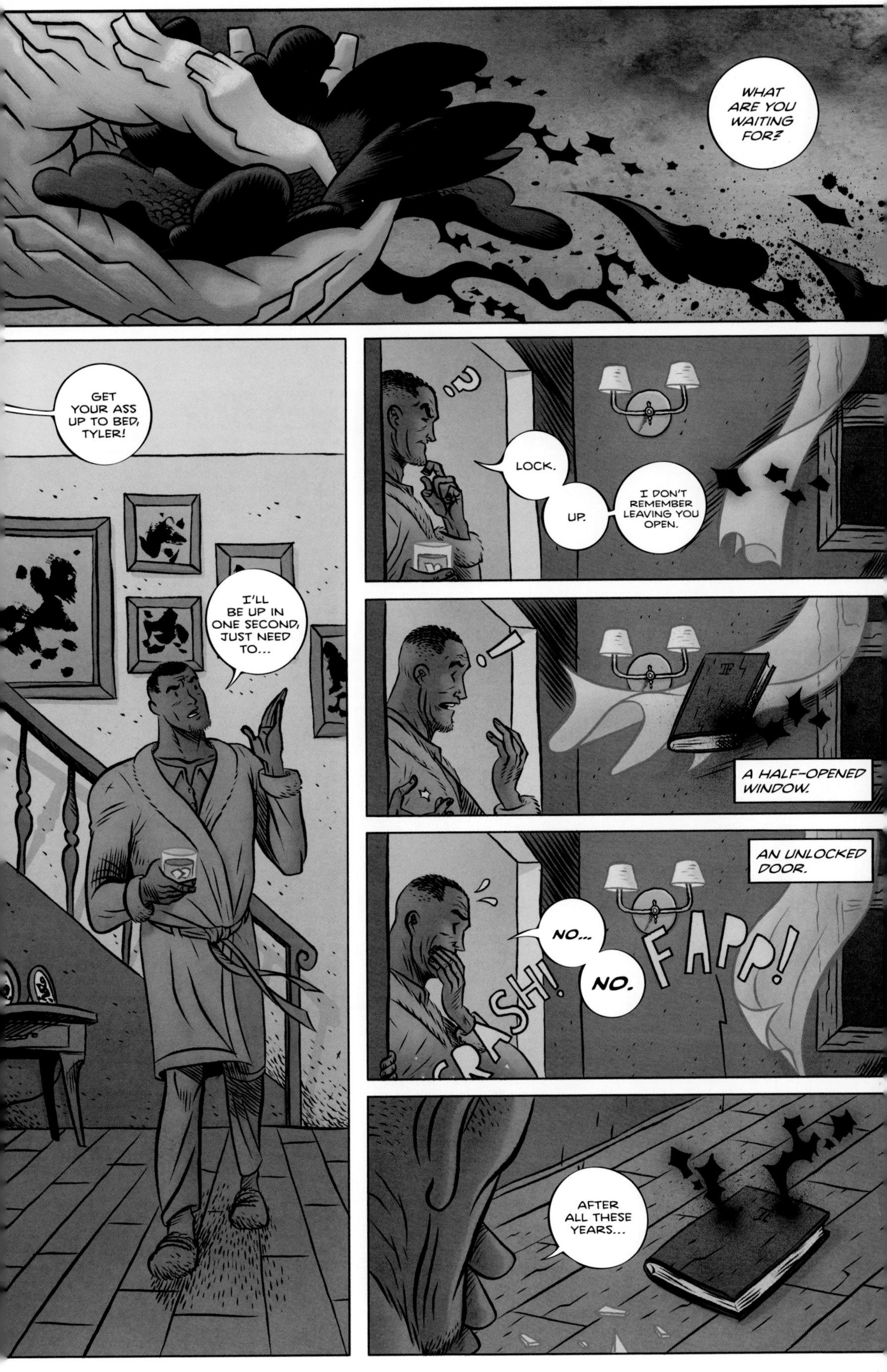
WHAT ARE YOU WAITING FOR?
GET YOUR ASS UP TO BED, TYLER!
I'LL BE UP IN ONE SECOND, JUST NEED TO...
?!
LOCK.
UP.
I DON'T REMEMBER LEAVING YOU OPEN.
!
A HALF-OPENED WINDOW.
AN UNLOCKED DOOR.
NO...
NO.
FAPP!
CRASH!
AFTER ALL THESE YEARS...

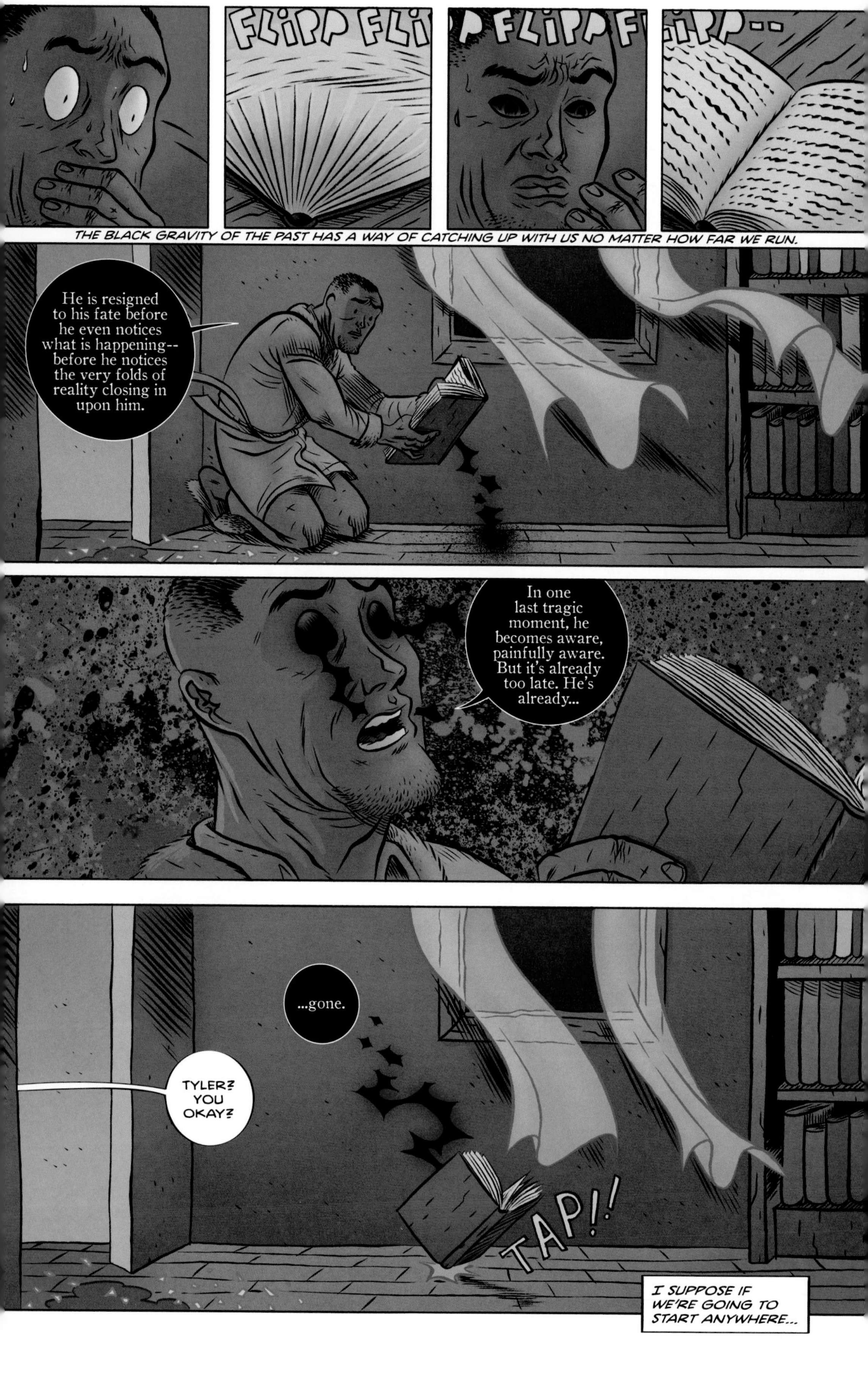
FLIPP FLIPP FLIPP FLIPP FLIPP--
THE BLACK GRAVITY OF THE PAST HAS A WAY OF CATCHING UP WITH US NO MATTER HOW FAR WE RUN.
He is resigned to his fate before he even notices what is happening--before he notices the very folds of reality closing in upon him.
In one last tragic moment, he becomes aware, painfully aware. But it's already too late. He's already...
...gone.
TYLER? YOU OKAY?
TAP!!
I SUPPOSE IF WE'RE GOING TO START ANYWHERE...

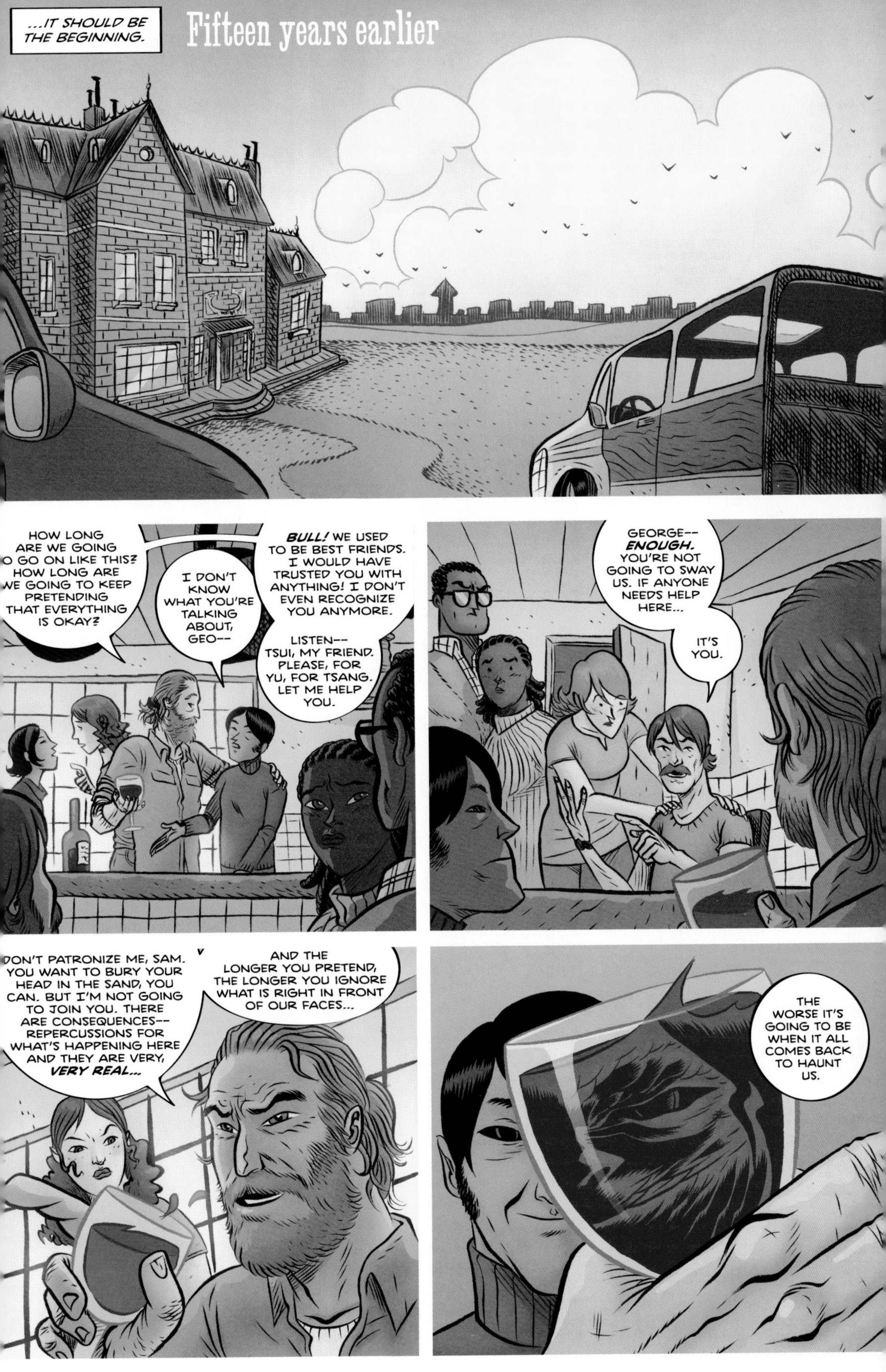
...IT SHOULD BE THE BEGINNING.
Fifteen years earlier
HOW LONG ARE WE GOING TO GO ON LIKE THIS? HOW LONG ARE WE GOING TO KEEP PRETENDING THAT EVERYTHING IS OKAY?
I DON'T KNOW WHAT YOU'RE TALKING ABOUT, GEO--
BULL! WE USED TO BE BEST FRIENDS. I WOULD HAVE TRUSTED YOU WITH ANYTHING! I DON'T EVEN RECOGNIZE YOU ANYMORE.
LISTEN-- TSUI, MY FRIEND. PLEASE, FOR YU, FOR TSANG. LET ME HELP YOU.
GEORGE-- ENOUGH. YOU'RE NOT GOING TO SWAY US. IF ANYONE NEEDS HELP HERE...
IT'S YOU.
DON'T PATRONIZE ME, SAM. YOU WANT TO BURY YOUR HEAD IN THE SAND, YOU CAN. BUT I'M NOT GOING TO JOIN YOU. THERE ARE CONSEQUENCES-- REPERCUSSIONS FOR WHAT'S HAPPENING HERE AND THEY ARE VERY, VERY REAL...
AND THE LONGER YOU PRETEND, THE LONGER YOU IGNORE WHAT IS RIGHT IN FRONT OF OUR FACES...
THE WORSE IT'S GOING TO BE WHEN IT ALL COMES BACK TO HAUNT US.

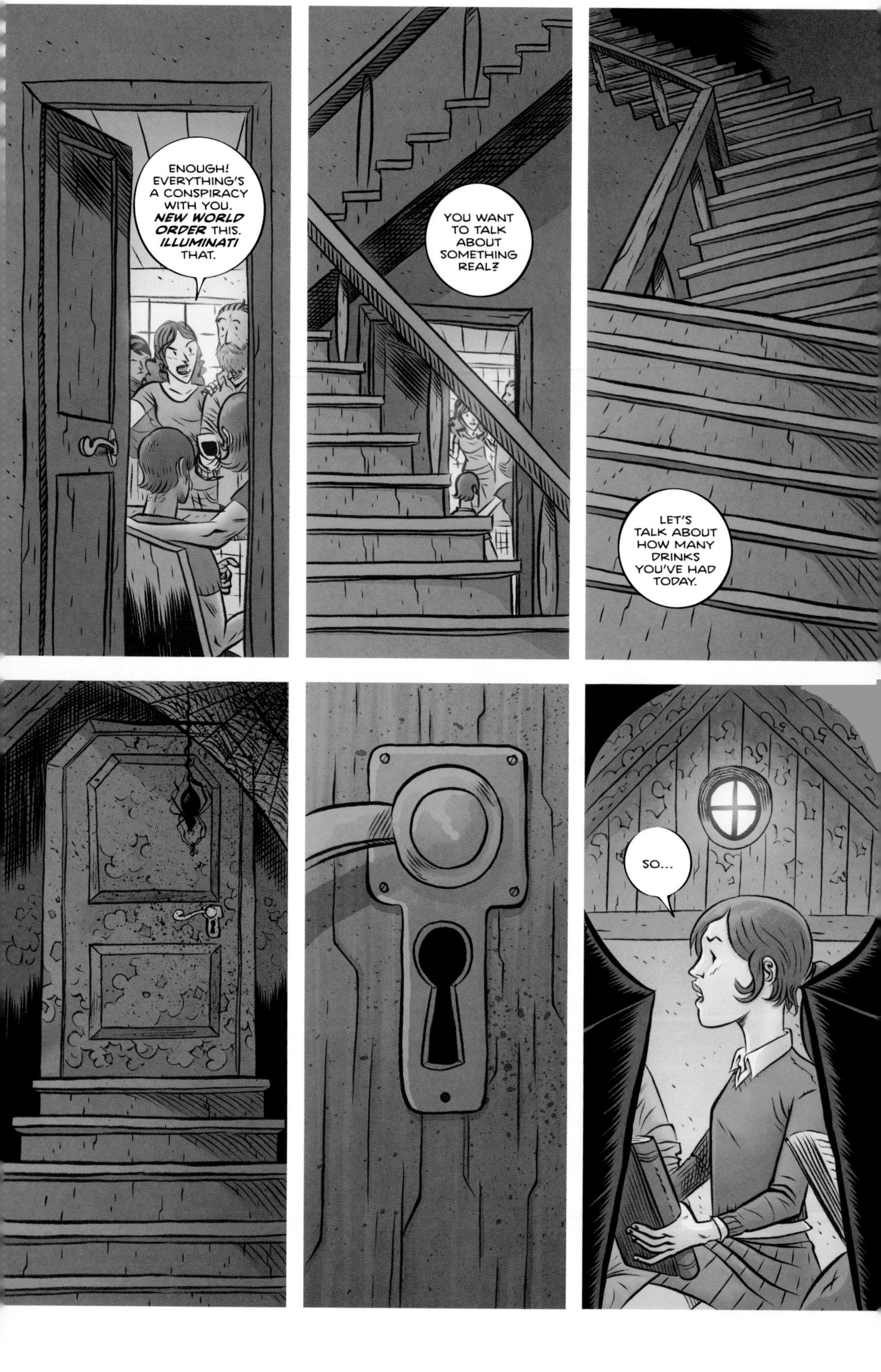
ENOUGH! EVERYTHING'S A CONSPIRACY WITH YOU. NEW WORLD ORDER THIS. ILLUMINATI THAT.
YOU WANT TO TALK ABOUT SOMETHING REAL?
LET'S TALK ABOUT HOW MANY DRINKS YOU'VE HAD TODAY.
SO...

WHAT DO YOU THINK THEY'RE TALKING ABOUT, ANYWAYS?
WHO?
THE PARENTS, OBV.
I DON'T KNOW, DO I LOOK LIKE I HAVE SUPER HEARING? DO I LOOK LIKE SUPERMAN?
Y'KNOW WHAT? DON'T ANSWER THAT.
GOOD CALL.
WOULD YOU TWO JUST GET A ROOM ALREADY?
SHUT YOUR FACE, TYLER.
MAKE ME.
YOU ALRIGHT, TSANG? YOU'VE BEEN SUPER QUIET.
ARE... ARE THINGS OKAY AT HOME?
I THINK WHAT KASSIE IS TRYING TO ASK YOU IS...
IS YOUR DAD STILL BEING A TOTAL TOOL?
SUBTLE, MAX. NICE WORK.

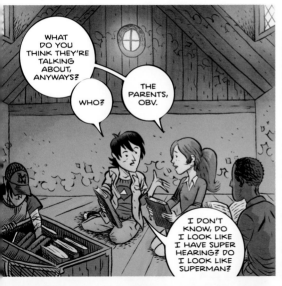

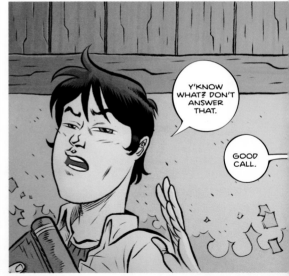

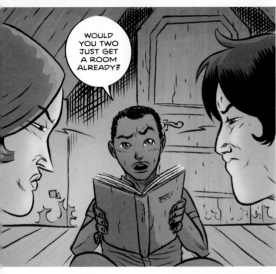

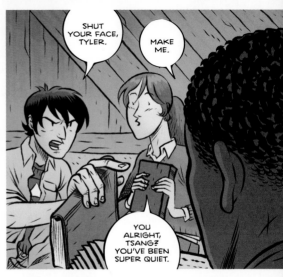

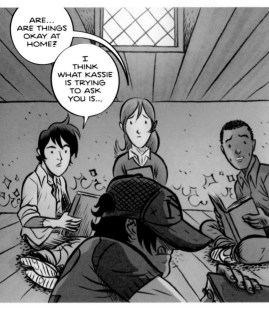

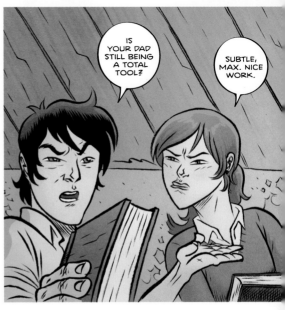

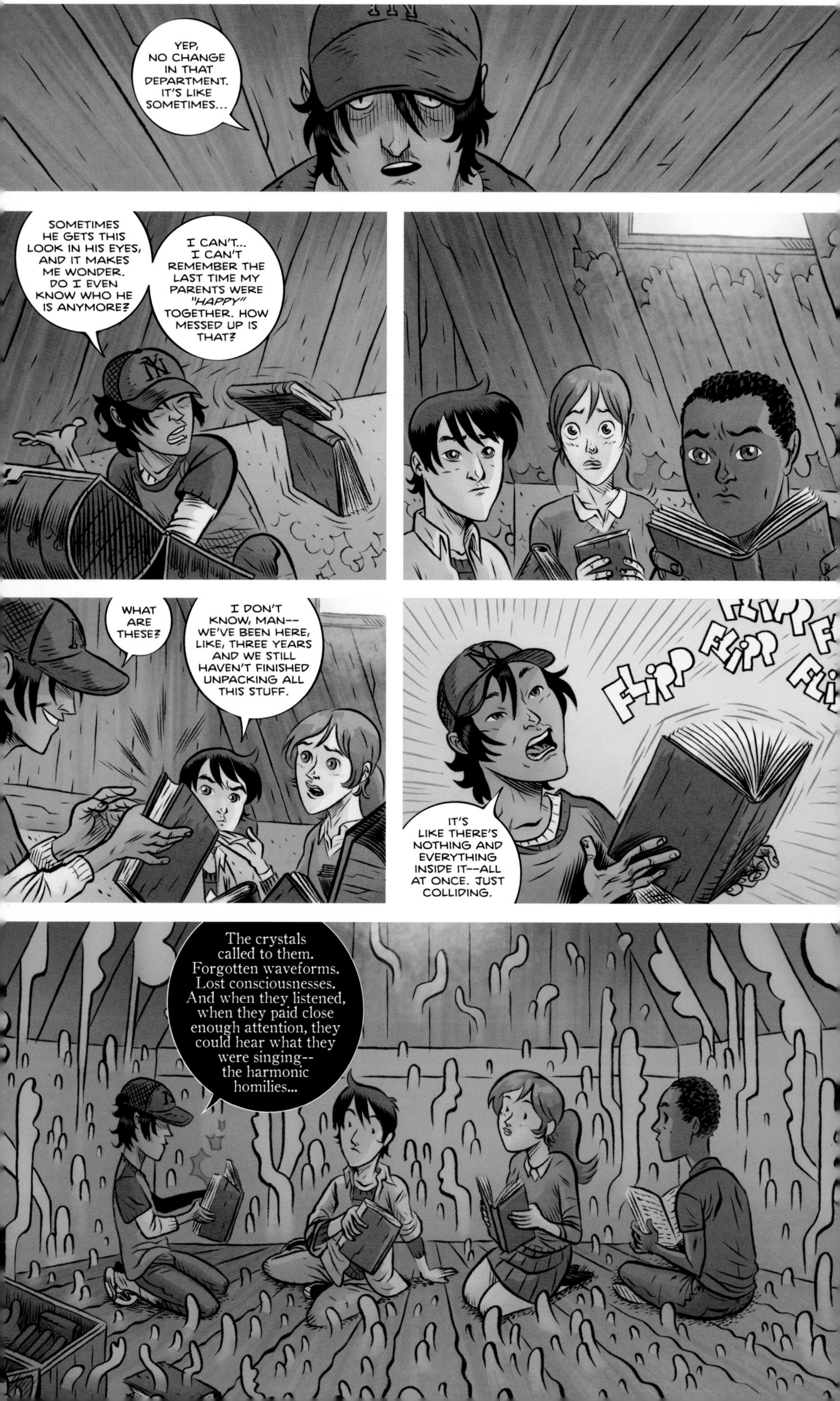

YEP, NO CHANGE IN THAT DEPARTMENT. IT'S LIKE SOMETIMES...
SOMETIMES HE GETS THIS LOOK IN HIS EYES, AND IT MAKES ME WONDER. DO I EVEN KNOW WHO HE IS ANYMORE?
I CAN'T... I CAN'T REMEMBER THE LAST TIME MY PARENTS WERE "HAPPY" TOGETHER. HOW MESSED UP IS THAT?
WHAT ARE THESE?
I DON'T KNOW, MAN--WE'VE BEEN HERE, LIKE, THREE YEARS AND WE STILL HAVEN'T FINISHED UNPACKING ALL THIS STUFF.
FLIPP FLIPP FLIPP
IT'S LIKE THERE'S NOTHING AND EVERYTHING INSIDE IT--ALL AT ONCE. JUST COLLIDING.
The crystals called to them. Forgotten waveforms. Lost consciousnesses. And when they listened, when they paid close enough attention, they could hear what they were singing-- the harmonic homilies...

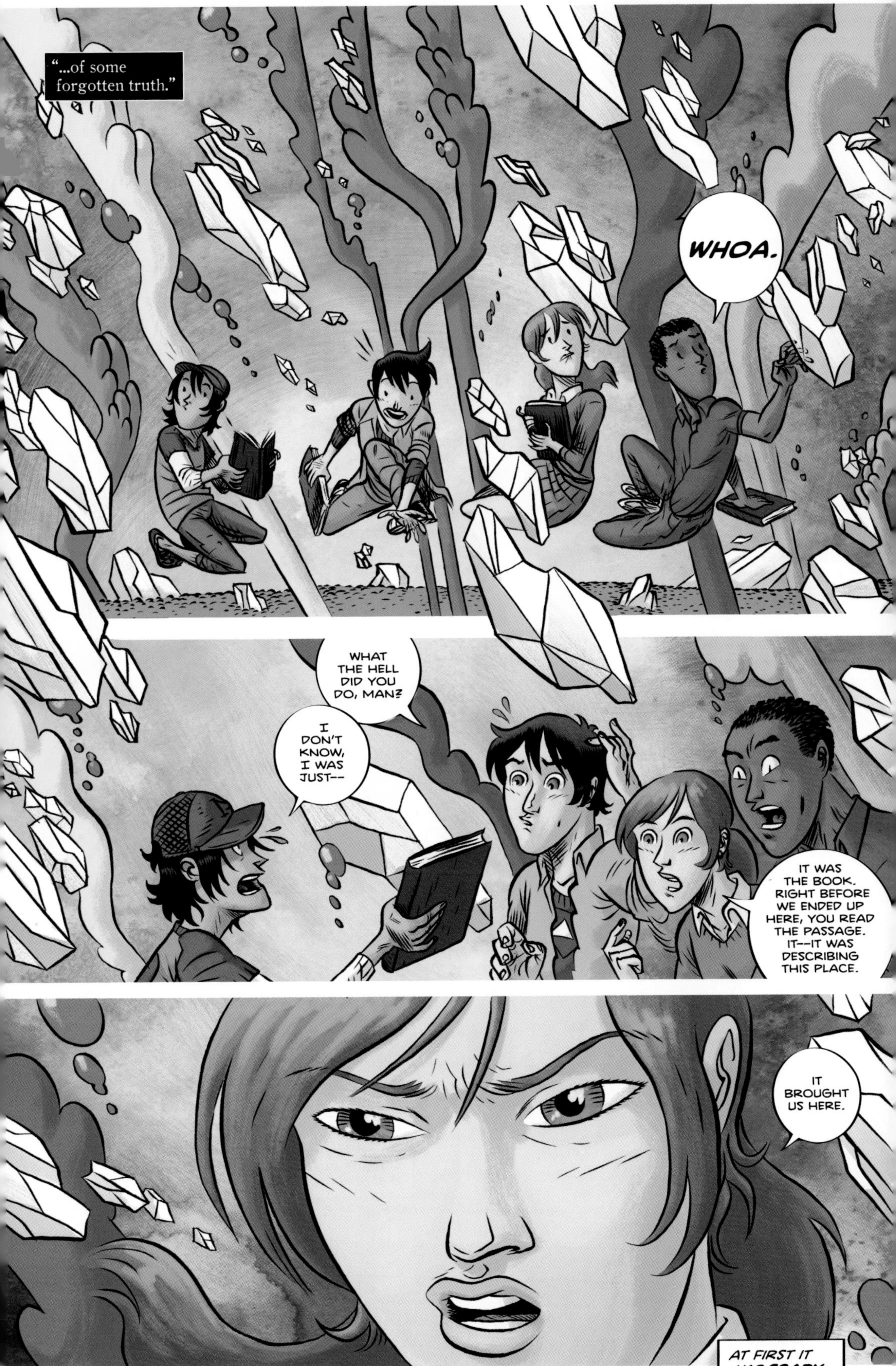
"...of some forgotten truth."
WHOA.
WHAT THE HELL DID YOU DO, MAN?
I DON'T KNOW, I WAS JUST--
IT WAS THE BOOK. RIGHT BEFORE WE ENDED UP HERE, YOU READ THE PASSAGE. IT--IT WAS DESCRIBING THIS PLACE.
IT BROUGHT US HERE.
AT FIRST IT WAS SCARY...

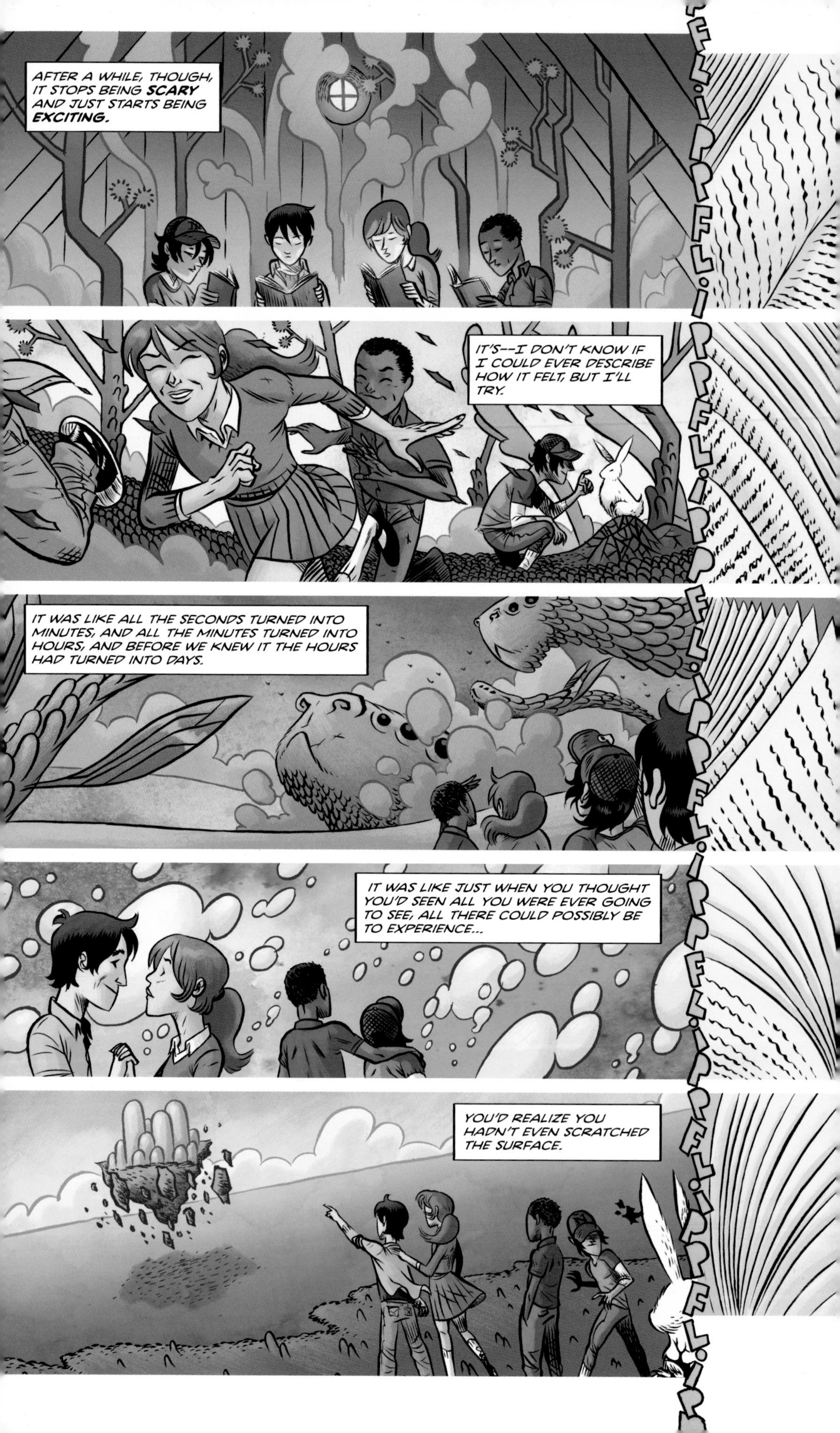
AFTER A WHILE, THOUGH, IT STOPS BEING **SCARY** AND JUST STARTS BEING **EXCITING.**
IT'S--I DON'T KNOW IF I COULD EVER DESCRIBE HOW IT FELT, BUT I'LL TRY.
IT WAS LIKE ALL THE SECONDS TURNED INTO MINUTES, AND ALL THE MINUTES TURNED INTO HOURS, AND BEFORE WE KNEW IT THE HOURS HAD TURNED INTO DAYS.
IT WAS LIKE JUST WHEN YOU THOUGHT YOU'D SEEN ALL YOU WERE EVER GOING TO SEE, ALL THERE COULD POSSIBLY BE TO EXPERIENCE...
YOU'D REALIZE YOU HADN'T EVEN SCRATCHED THE SURFACE.

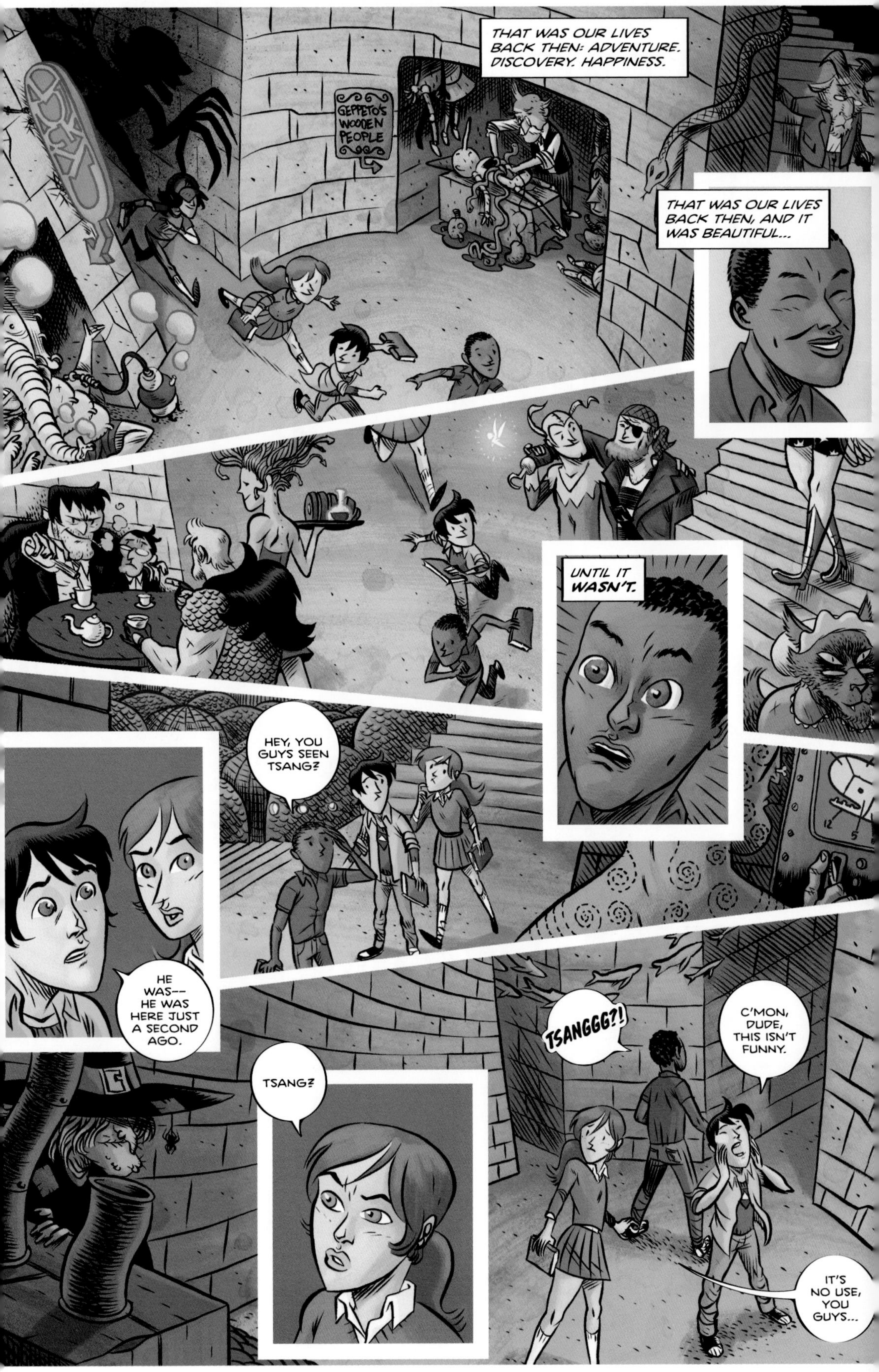
THAT WAS OUR LIVES BACK THEN: ADVENTURE. DISCOVERY. HAPPINESS.
GEPPETO'S WOODEN PEOPLE
THAT WAS OUR LIVES BACK THEN, AND IT WAS BEAUTIFUL...
UNTIL IT WASN'T.
HEY, YOU GUYS SEEN TSANG?
HE WAS-- HE WAS HERE JUST A SECOND AGO.
TSANG?
TSANGGG?!
C'MON, DUDE, THIS ISN'T FUNNY.
IT'S NO USE, YOU GUYS...

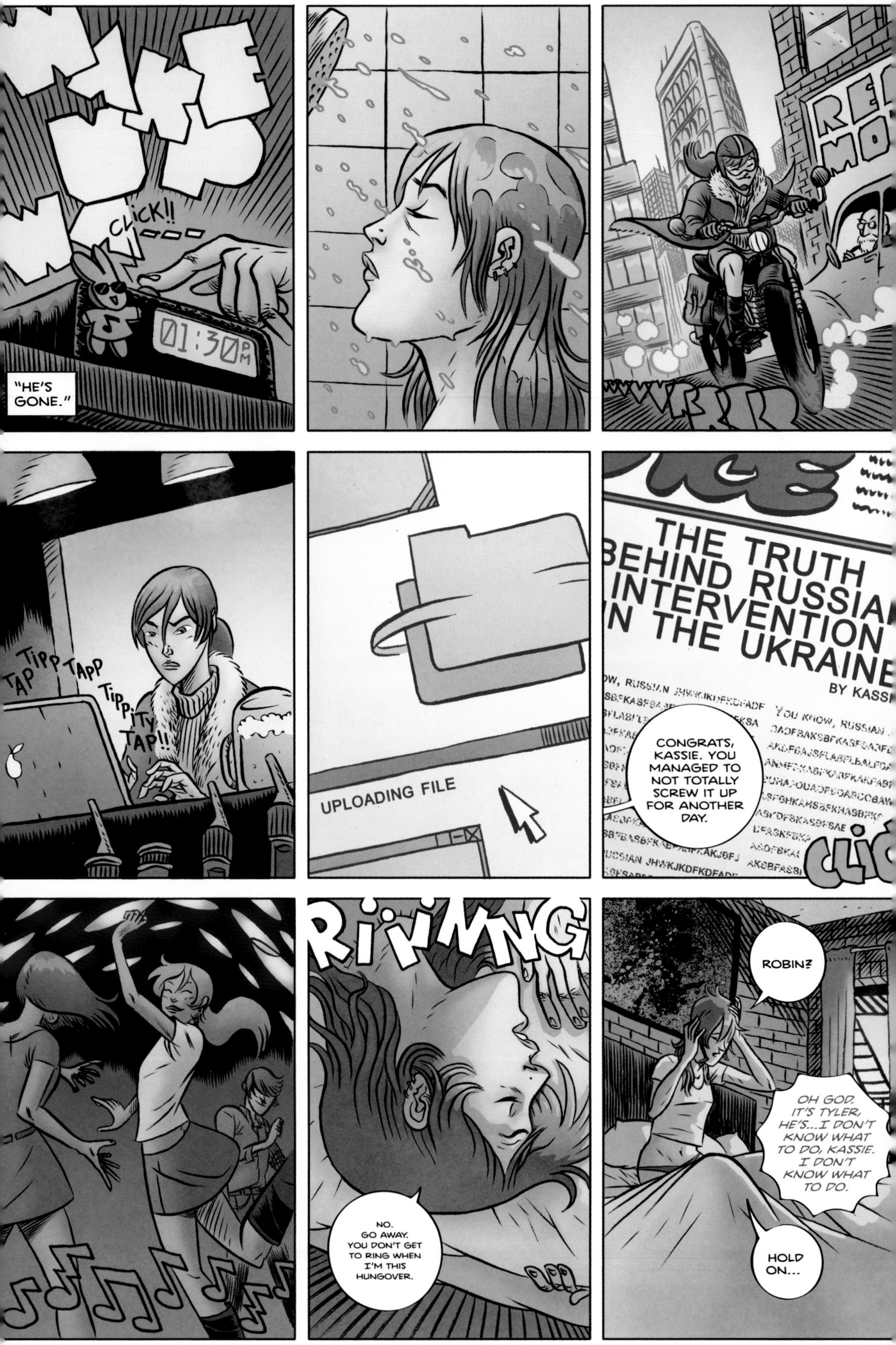
CLICK!!
01:30 PM
"HE'S GONE."
TAP TIPP TAPP TIPPITY TAP!!
UPLOADING FILE
THE TRUTH
BEHIND RUSSIA
INTERVENTION
N THE UKRAINE
BY KASS
CONGRATS, KASSIE. YOU MANAGED TO NOT TOTALLY SCREW IT UP FOR ANOTHER DAY.
CLIC
NO. GO AWAY. YOU DON'T GET TO RING WHEN I'M THIS HUNGOVER.
ROBIN?
OH GOD. IT'S TYLER, HE'S...I DON'T KNOW WHAT TO DO, KASSIE. I DON'T KNOW WHAT TO DO.
HOLD ON...

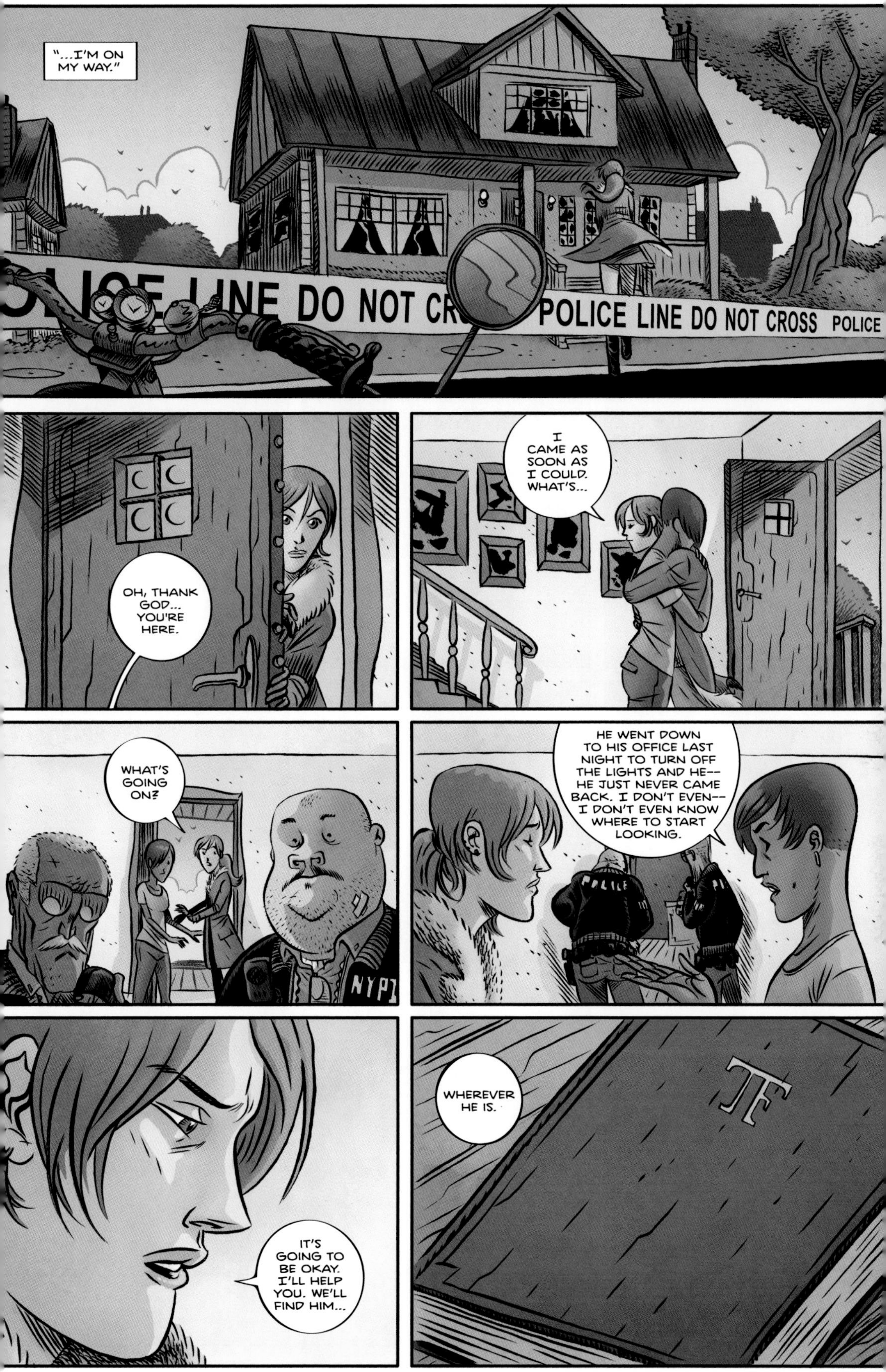
"...I'M ON MY WAY."
POLICE LINE DO NOT CROSS POLICE LINE DO NOT CROSS POLICE
OH, THANK GOD... YOU'RE HERE.
I CAME AS SOON AS I COULD. WHAT'S...
WHAT'S GOING ON?
NYPD
HE WENT DOWN TO HIS OFFICE LAST NIGHT TO TURN OFF THE LIGHTS AND HE-- HE JUST NEVER CAME BACK. I DON'T EVEN-- I DON'T EVEN KNOW WHERE TO START LOOKING.
POLICE
IT'S GOING TO BE OKAY. I'LL HELP YOU. WE'LL FIND HIM...
WHEREVER HE IS.

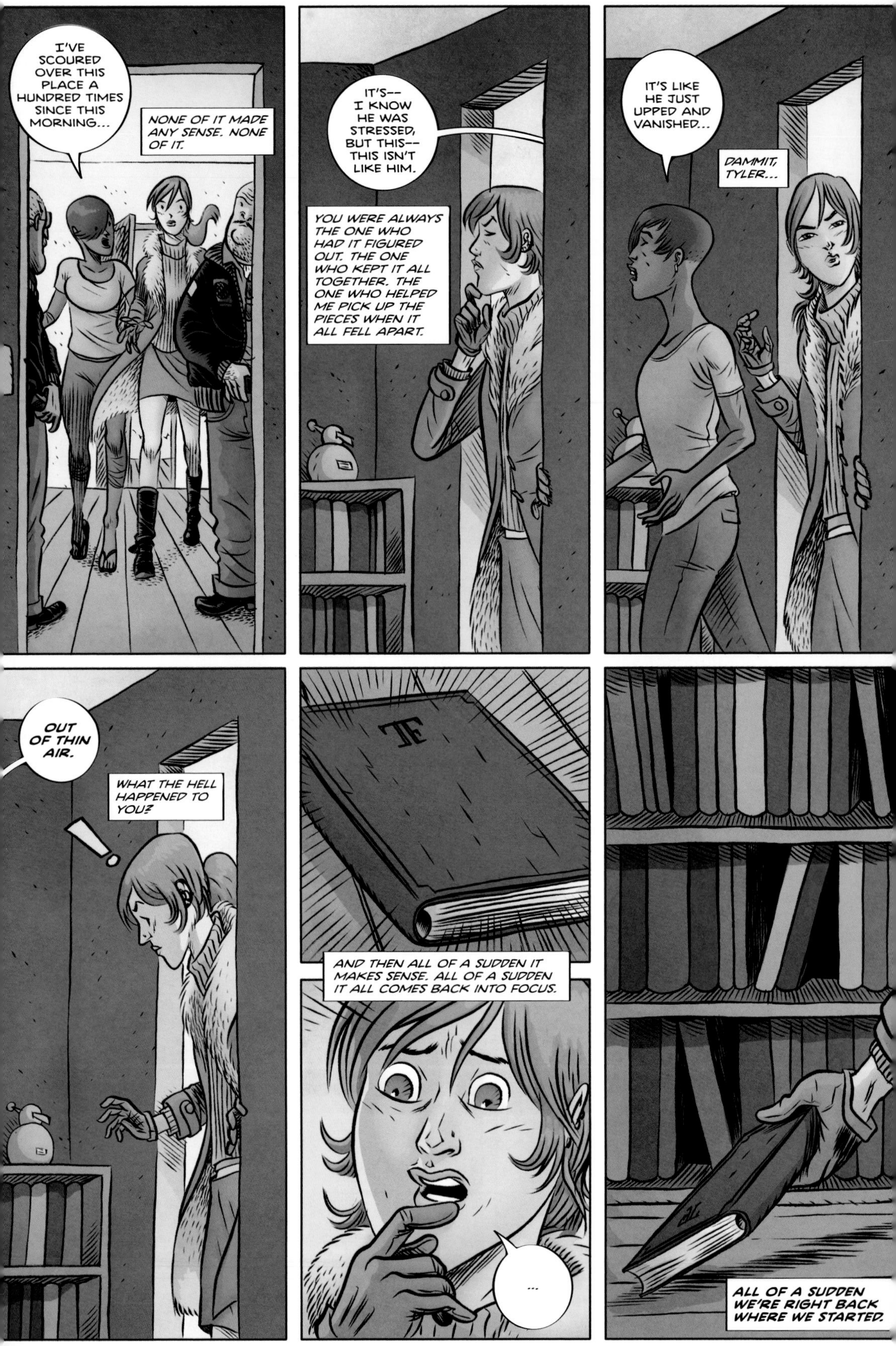
I'VE SCOURED OVER THIS PLACE A HUNDRED TIMES SINCE THIS MORNING...
NONE OF IT MADE ANY SENSE. NONE OF IT.
IT'S-- I KNOW HE WAS STRESSED, BUT THIS-- THIS ISN'T LIKE HIM.
YOU WERE ALWAYS THE ONE WHO HAD IT FIGURED OUT. THE ONE WHO KEPT IT ALL TOGETHER. THE ONE WHO HELPED ME PICK UP THE PIECES WHEN IT ALL FELL APART.
IT'S LIKE HE JUST UPPED AND VANISHED...
DAMMIT, TYLER...
OUT OF THIN AIR.
WHAT THE HELL HAPPENED TO YOU?
!
TF
AND THEN ALL OF A SUDDEN IT MAKES SENSE. ALL OF A SUDDEN IT ALL COMES BACK INTO FOCUS.
...
ALL OF A SUDDEN WE'RE RIGHT BACK WHERE WE STARTED.

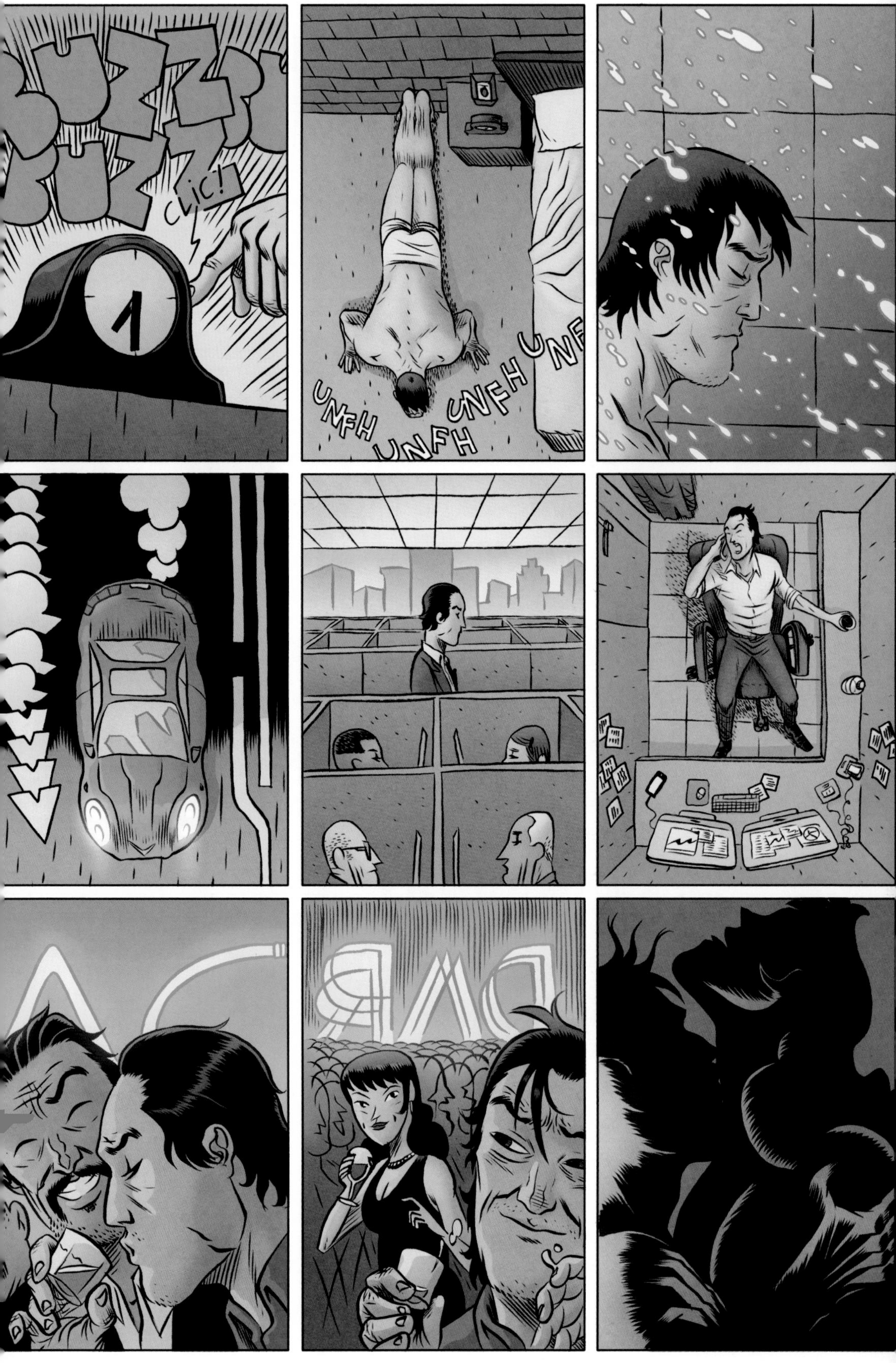
BUZZZ
CLIC!
UNFH UNFH UNFH UNFH UNF

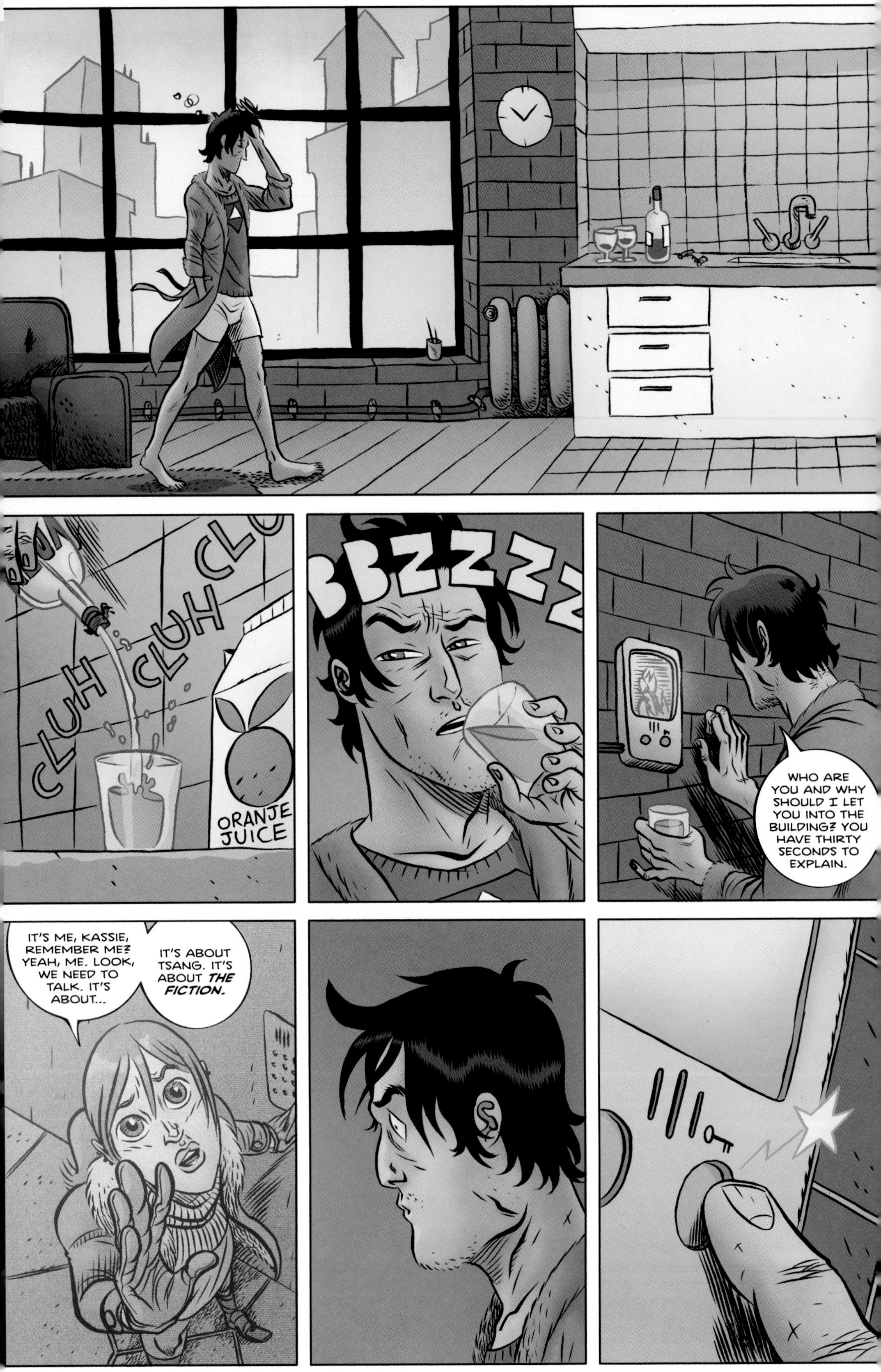
CLUH CLUH CLU
ORANJE JUICE
BBZZZZ
WHO ARE YOU AND WHY SHOULD I LET YOU INTO THE BUILDING? YOU HAVE THIRTY SECONDS TO EXPLAIN.
IT'S ME, KASSIE, REMEMBER ME? YEAH, ME. LOOK, WE NEED TO TALK. IT'S ABOUT...
IT'S ABOUT TSANG. IT'S ABOUT *THE FICTION.*

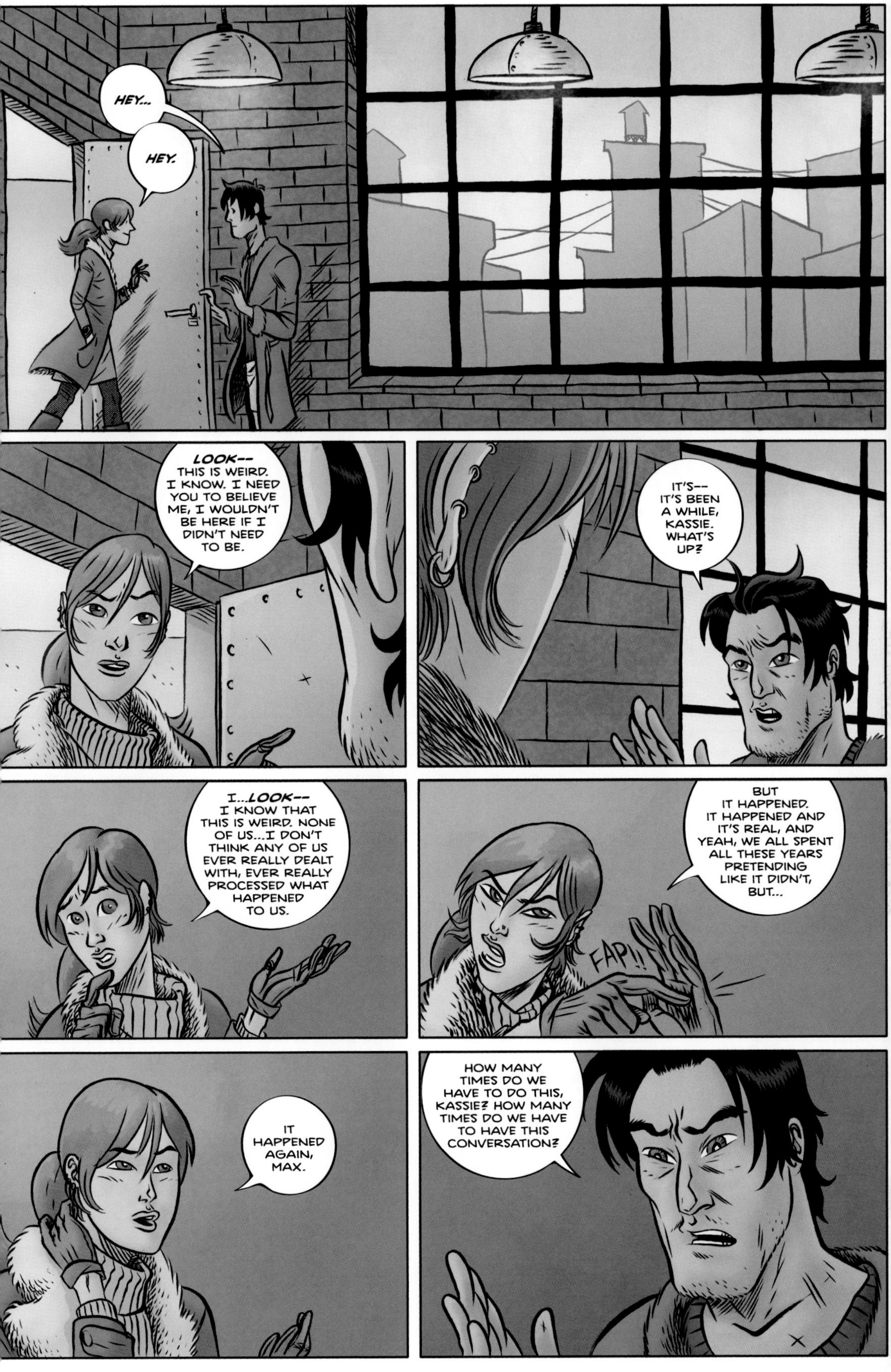
HEY...
HEY.
LOOK-- THIS IS WEIRD. I KNOW. I NEED YOU TO BELIEVE ME, I WOULDN'T BE HERE IF I DIDN'T NEED TO BE.
IT'S-- IT'S BEEN A WHILE, KASSIE. WHAT'S UP?
I...LOOK-- I KNOW THAT THIS IS WEIRD. NONE OF US...I DON'T THINK ANY OF US EVER REALLY DEALT WITH, EVER REALLY PROCESSED WHAT HAPPENED TO US.
BUT IT HAPPENED. IT HAPPENED AND IT'S REAL, AND YEAH, WE ALL SPENT ALL THESE YEARS PRETENDING LIKE IT DIDN'T, BUT...
FAP!!
IT HAPPENED AGAIN, MAX.
HOW MANY TIMES DO WE HAVE TO DO THIS, KASSIE? HOW MANY TIMES DO WE HAVE TO HAVE THIS CONVERSATION?

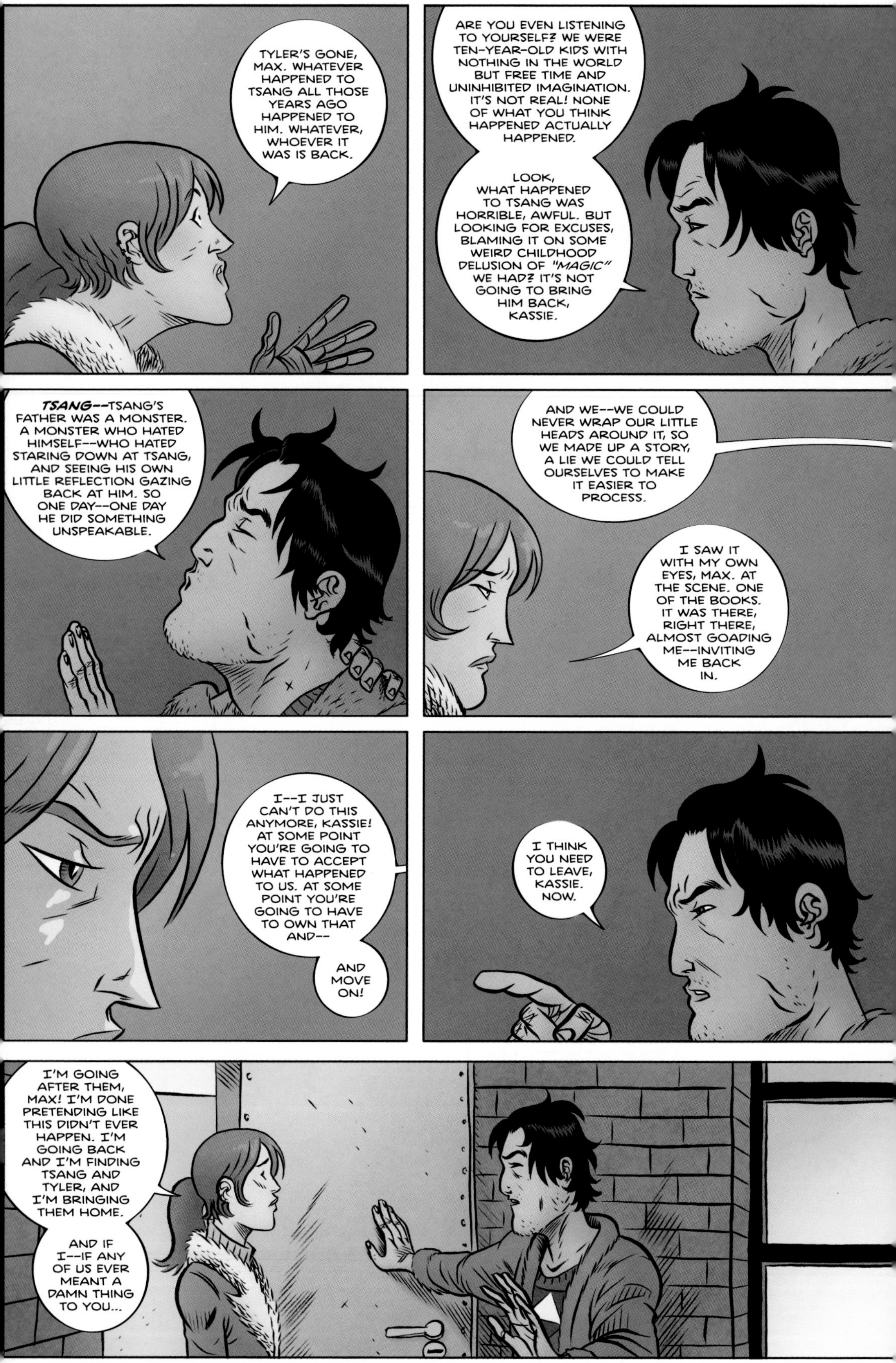
TYLER'S GONE, MAX. WHATEVER HAPPENED TO TSANG ALL THOSE YEARS AGO HAPPENED TO HIM. WHATEVER, WHOEVER IT WAS IS BACK.
ARE YOU EVEN LISTENING TO YOURSELF? WE WERE TEN-YEAR-OLD KIDS WITH NOTHING IN THE WORLD BUT FREE TIME AND UNINHIBITED IMAGINATION. IT'S NOT REAL! NONE OF WHAT YOU THINK HAPPENED ACTUALLY HAPPENED.
LOOK, WHAT HAPPENED TO TSANG WAS HORRIBLE, AWFUL. BUT LOOKING FOR EXCUSES, BLAMING IT ON SOME WEIRD CHILDHOOD DELUSION OF "MAGIC" WE HAD? IT'S NOT GOING TO BRING HIM BACK, KASSIE.
TSANG--TSANG'S FATHER WAS A MONSTER. A MONSTER WHO HATED HIMSELF--WHO HATED STARING DOWN AT TSANG, AND SEEING HIS OWN LITTLE REFLECTION GAZING BACK AT HIM. SO ONE DAY--ONE DAY HE DID SOMETHING UNSPEAKABLE.
AND WE--WE COULD NEVER WRAP OUR LITTLE HEADS AROUND IT, SO WE MADE UP A STORY, A LIE WE COULD TELL OURSELVES TO MAKE IT EASIER TO PROCESS.
I SAW IT WITH MY OWN EYES, MAX. AT THE SCENE. ONE OF THE BOOKS. IT WAS THERE, RIGHT THERE, ALMOST GOADING ME--INVITING ME BACK IN.
I--I JUST CAN'T DO THIS ANYMORE, KASSIE! AT SOME POINT YOU'RE GOING TO HAVE TO ACCEPT WHAT HAPPENED TO US. AT SOME POINT YOU'RE GOING TO HAVE TO OWN THAT AND--
AND MOVE ON!
I THINK YOU NEED TO LEAVE, KASSIE. NOW.
I'M GOING AFTER THEM, MAX! I'M DONE PRETENDING LIKE THIS DIDN'T EVER HAPPEN. I'M GOING BACK AND I'M FINDING TSANG AND TYLER, AND I'M BRINGING THEM HOME.
AND IF I--IF ANY OF US EVER MEANT A DAMN THING TO YOU...

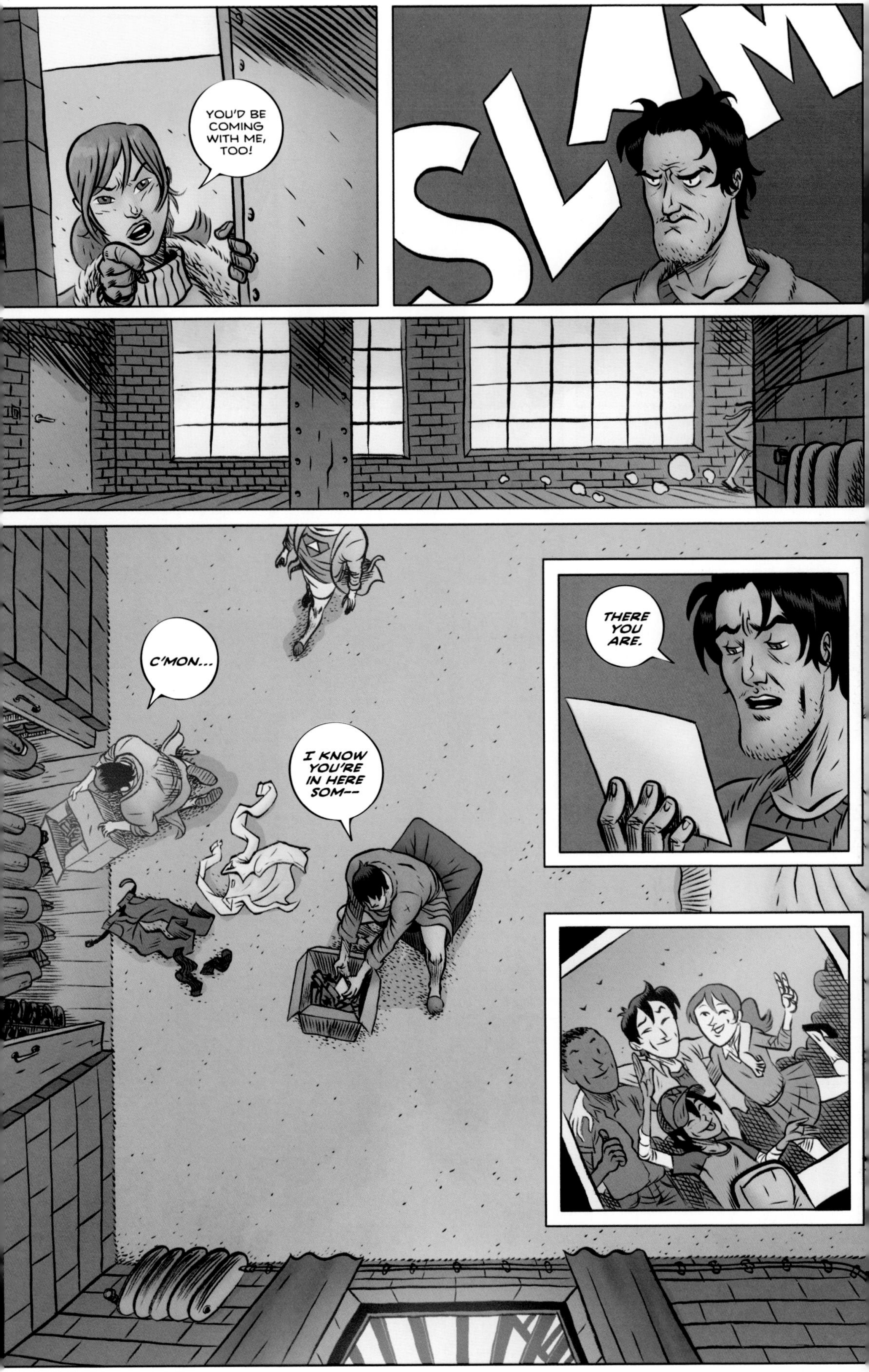
YOU'D BE COMING WITH ME, TOO!
SLAM
C'MON...
I KNOW YOU'RE IN HERE SOM--
THERE YOU ARE.

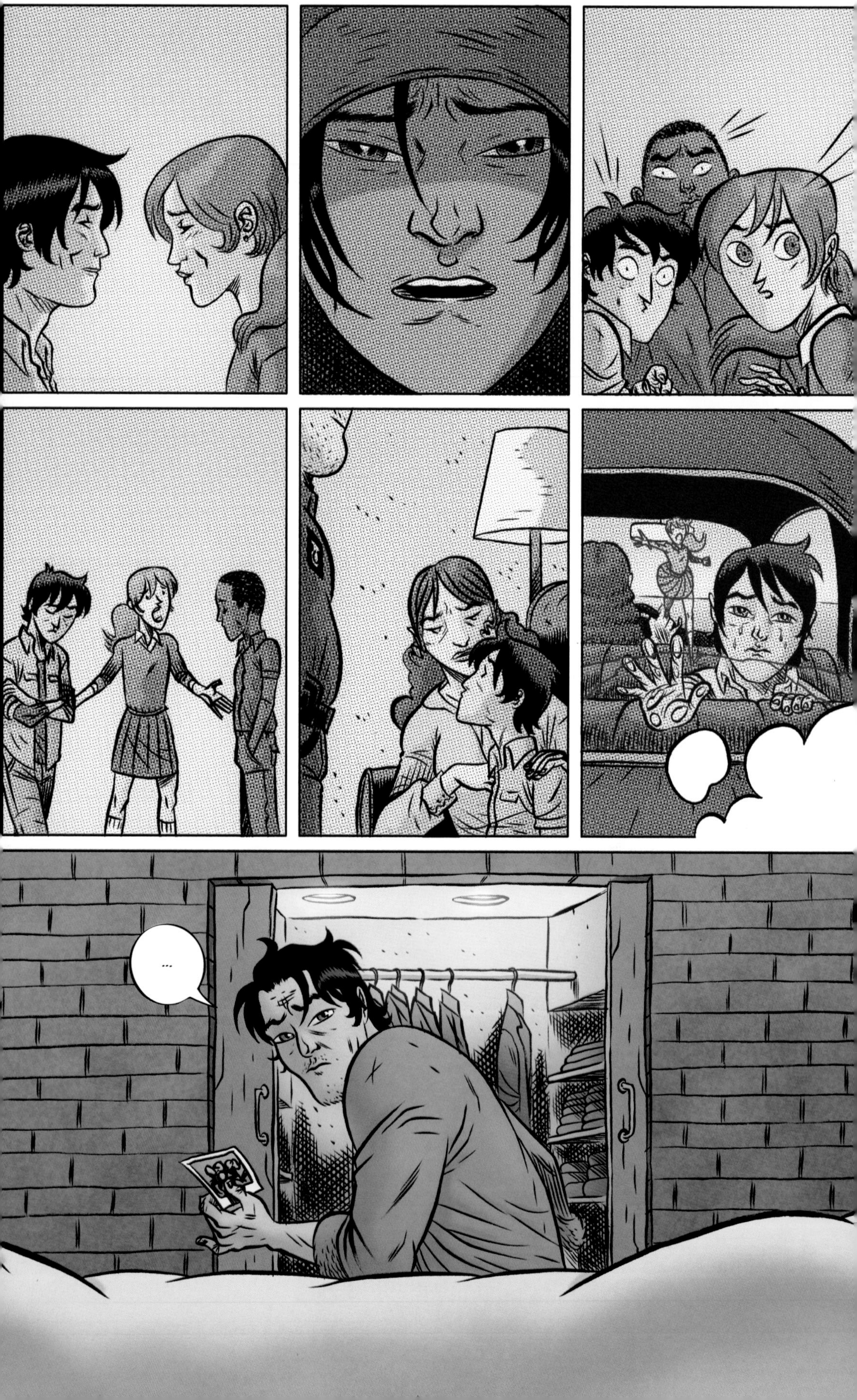
...

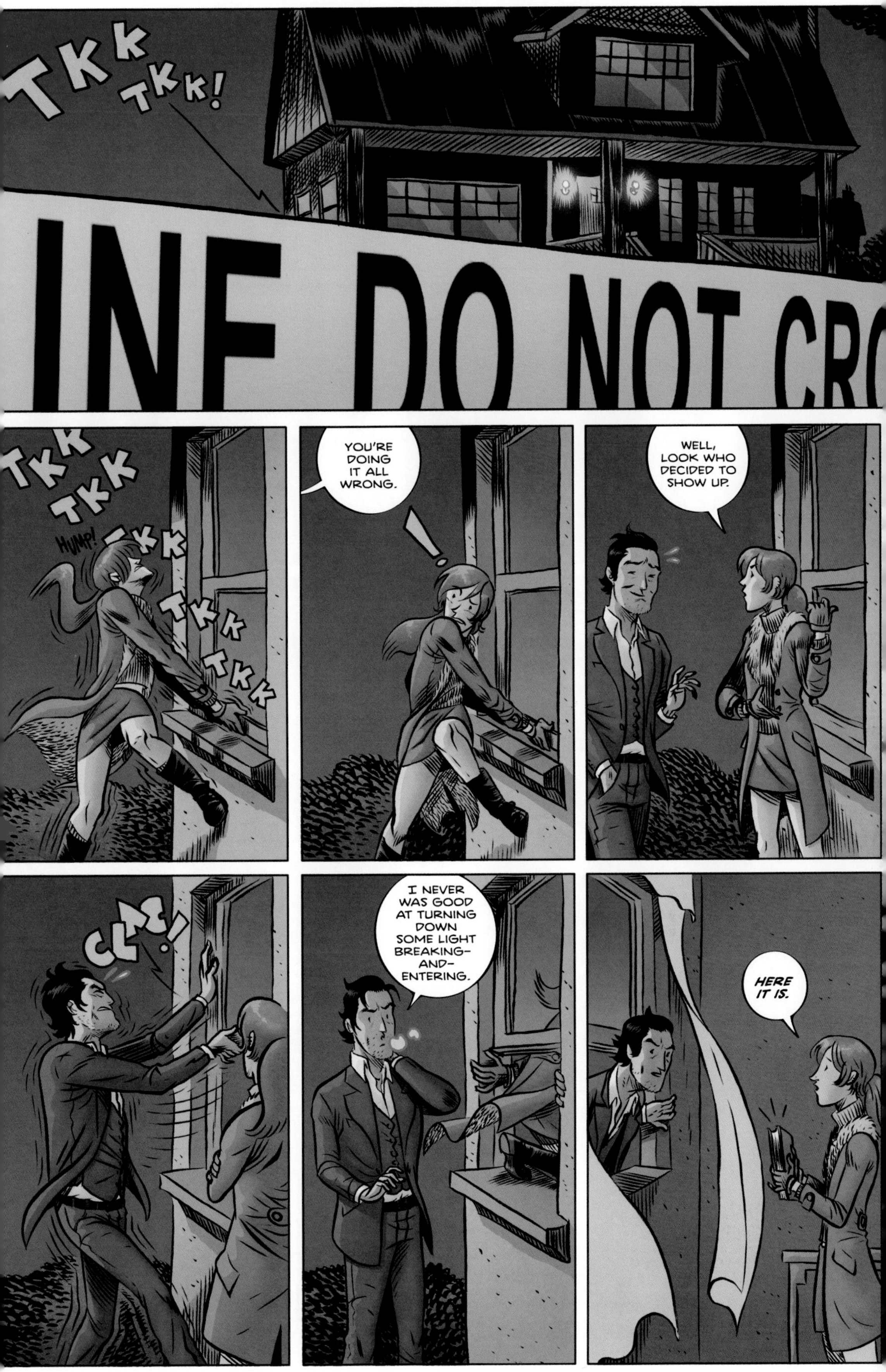
TKK TKK!
INE DO NOT CRO
TKK TKK
HUMP!
TKK
TKK
TKK
YOU'RE DOING IT ALL WRONG.
!
WELL, LOOK WHO DECIDED TO SHOW UP.
I NEVER WAS GOOD AT TURNING DOWN SOME LIGHT BREAKING-AND-ENTERING.
HERE IT IS.

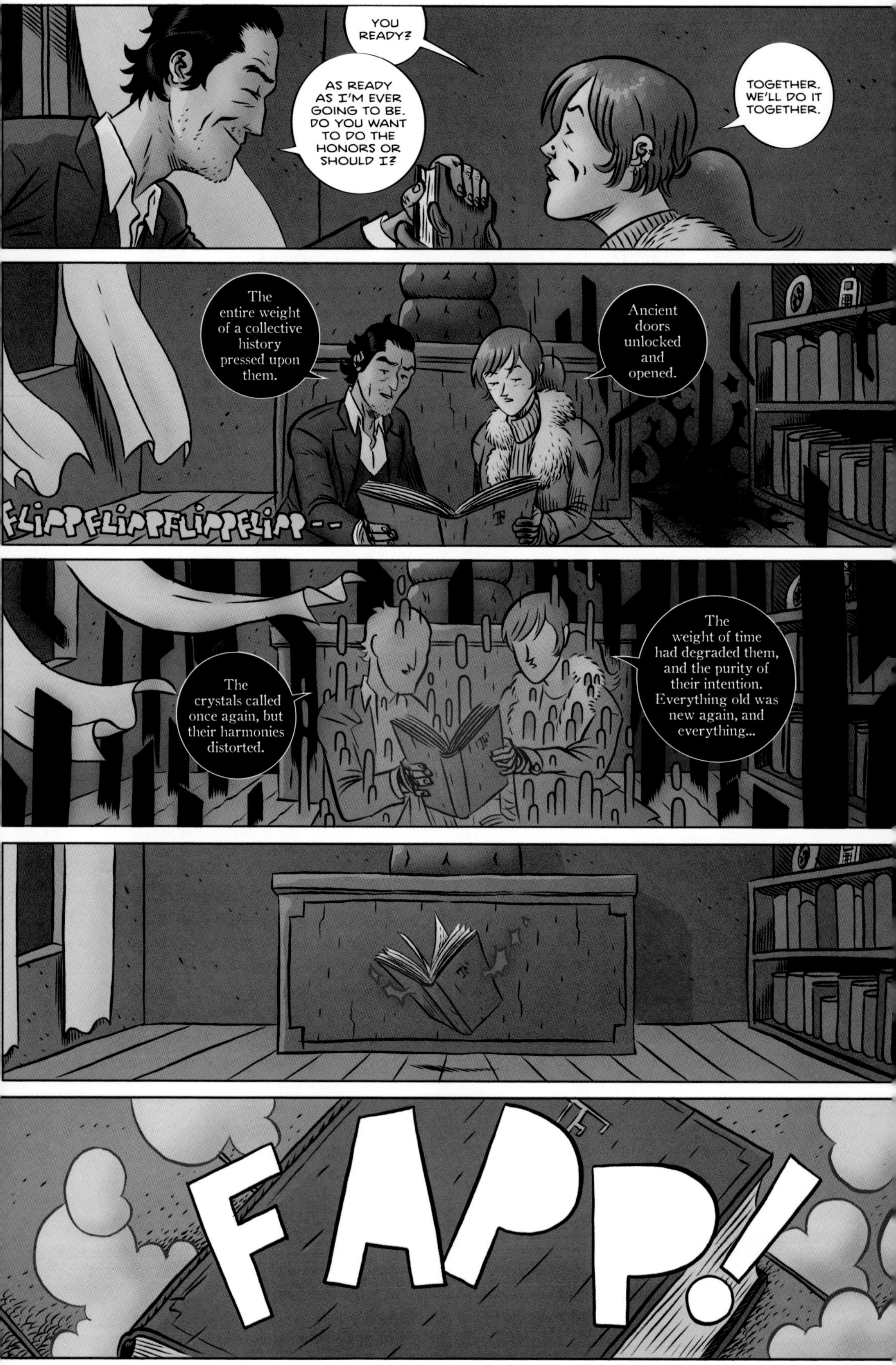
YOU READY?
AS READY AS I'M EVER GOING TO BE. DO YOU WANT TO DO THE HONORS OR SHOULD I?
TOGETHER. WE'LL DO IT TOGETHER.
The entire weight of a collective history pressed upon them.
Ancient doors unlocked and opened.
FLIPPFLIPPFLIPPFLIPP--
The crystals called once again, but their harmonies distorted.
The weight of time had degraded them, and the purity of their intention. Everything old was new again, and everything...
FAPP!

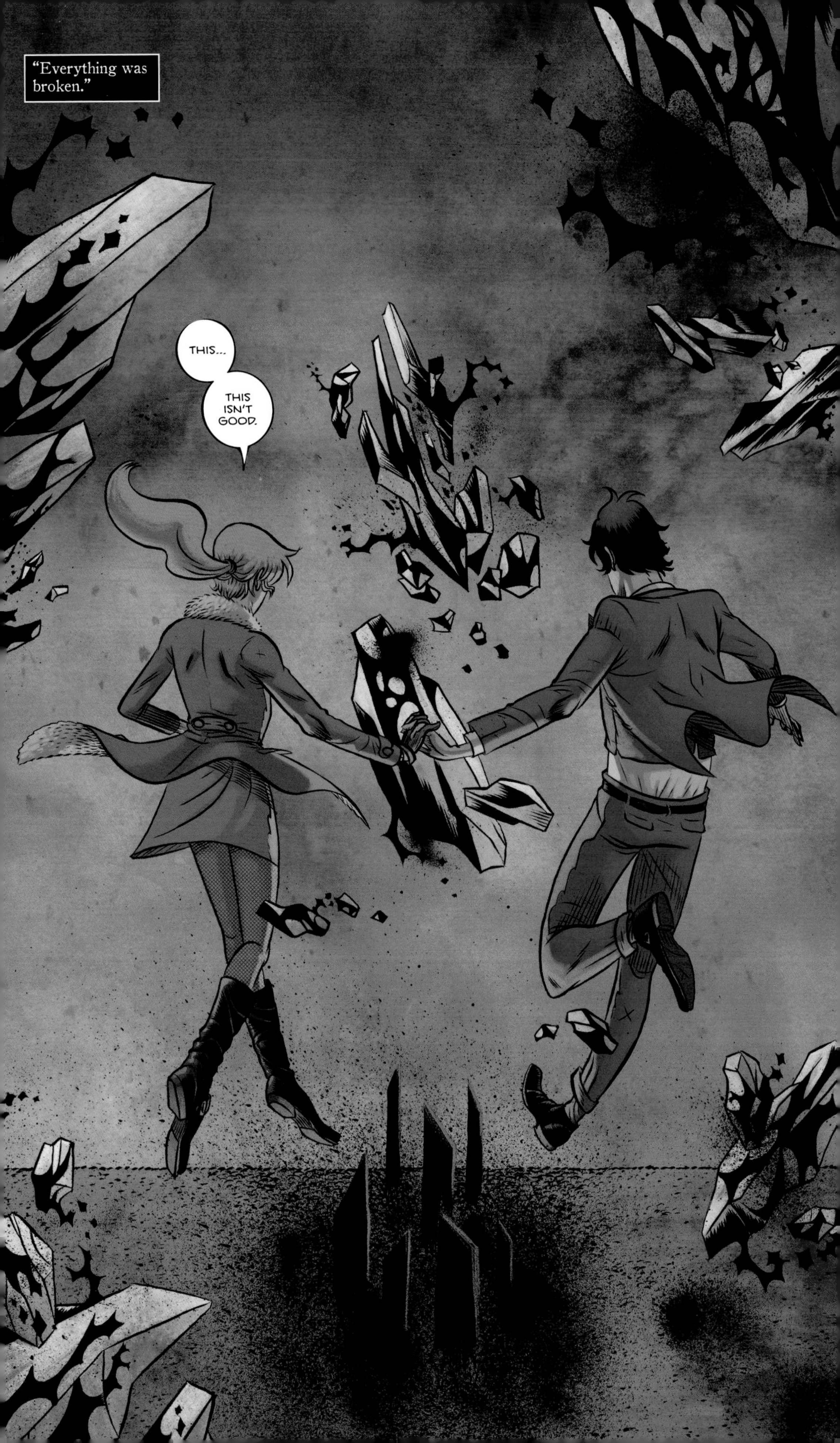
"Everything was broken."
THIS...
THIS ISN'T GOOD.

Epilogue

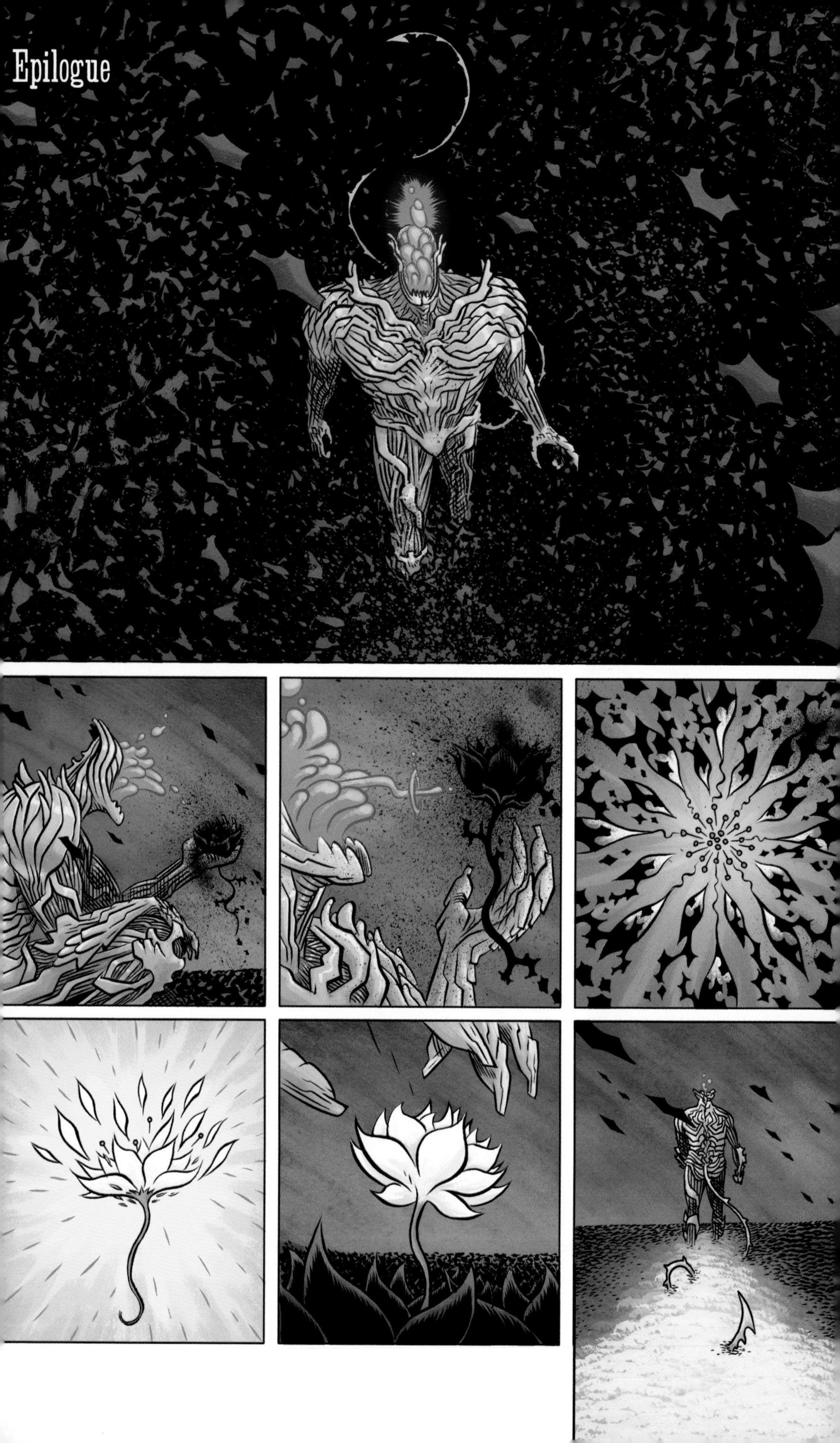

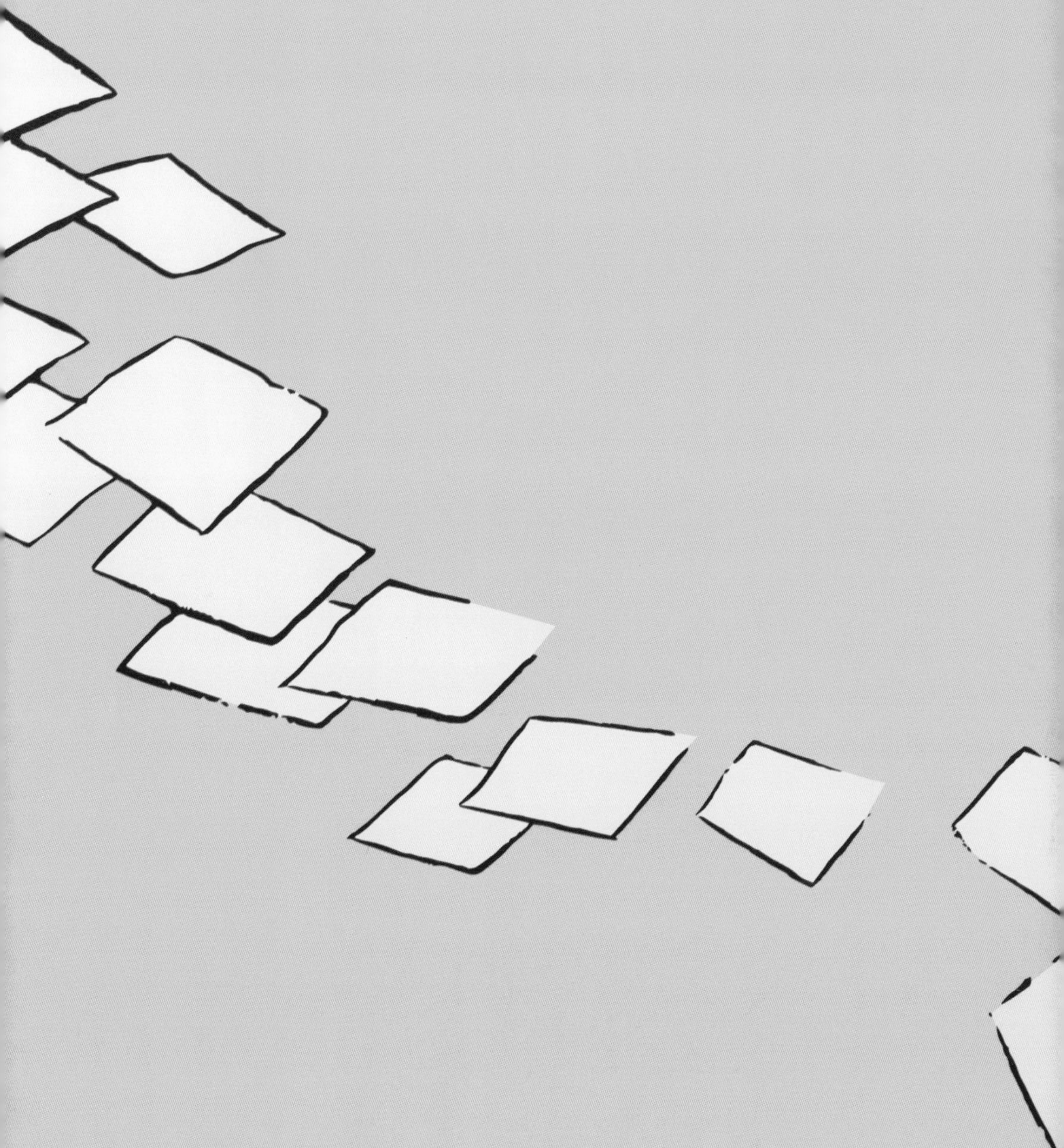

CHAPTER II
Memoria

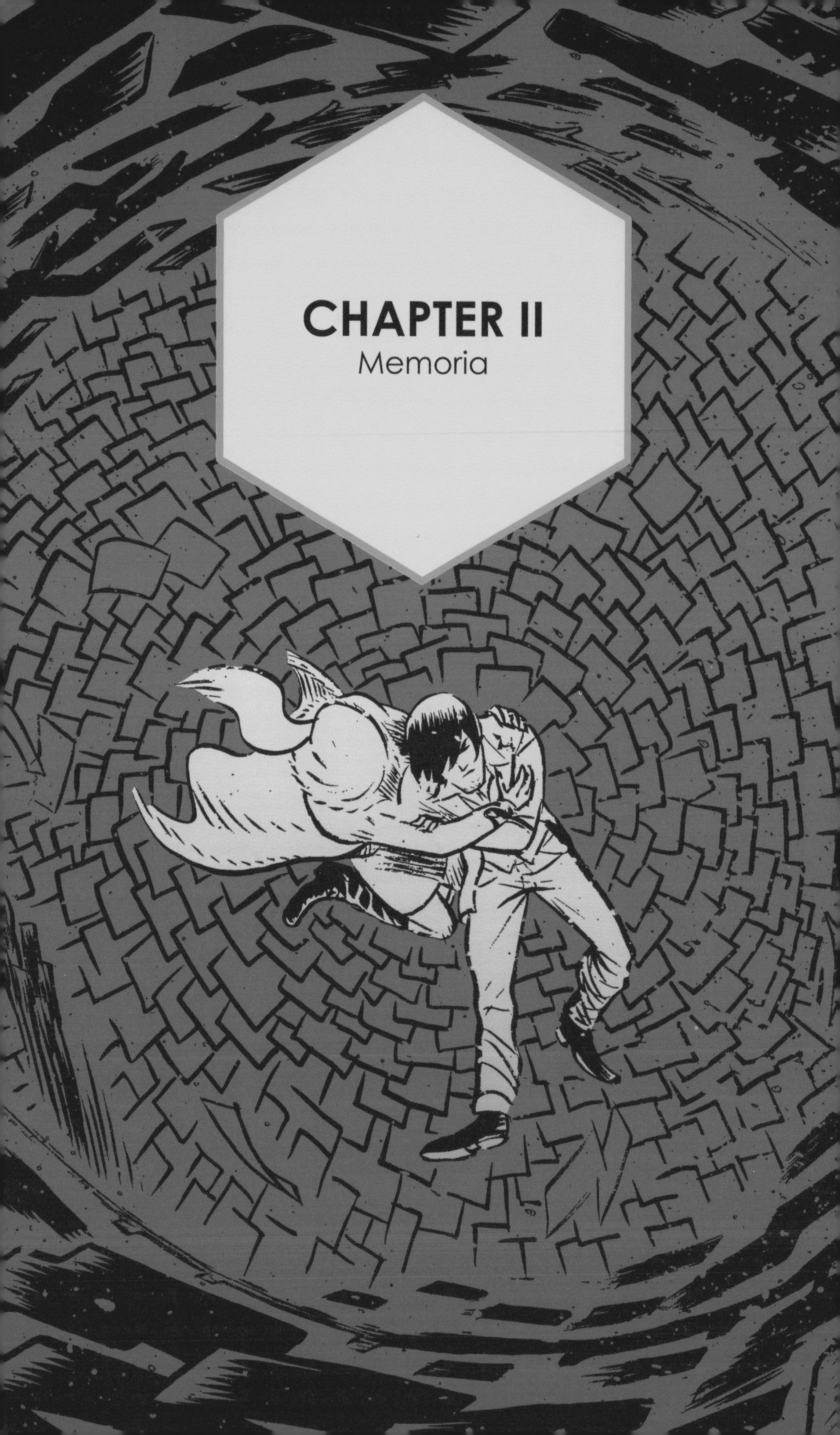

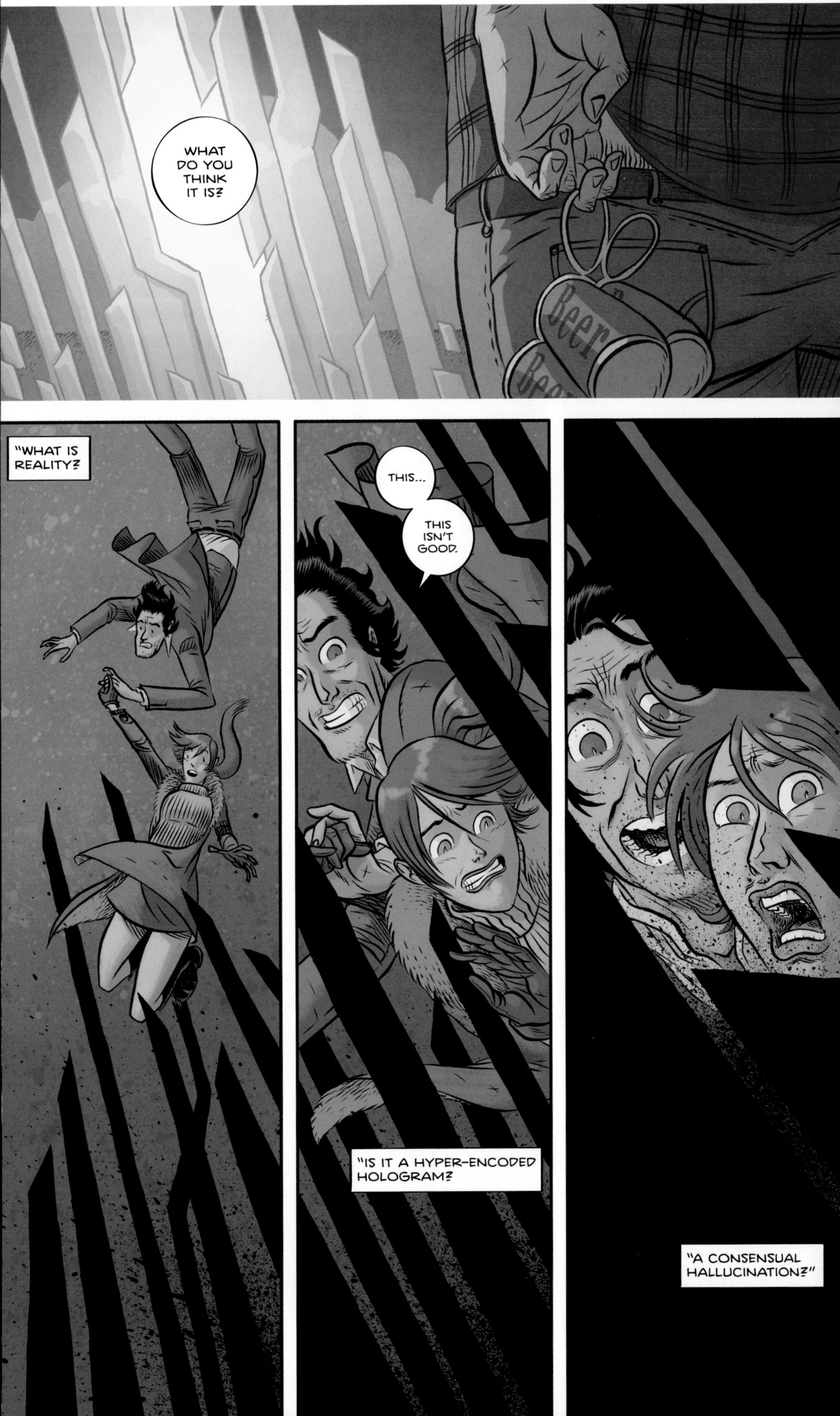
WHAT DO YOU THINK IT IS?
"WHAT IS REALITY?
THIS...
THIS ISN'T GOOD.
"IS IT A HYPER-ENCODED HOLOGRAM?
"A CONSENSUAL HALLUCINATION?"

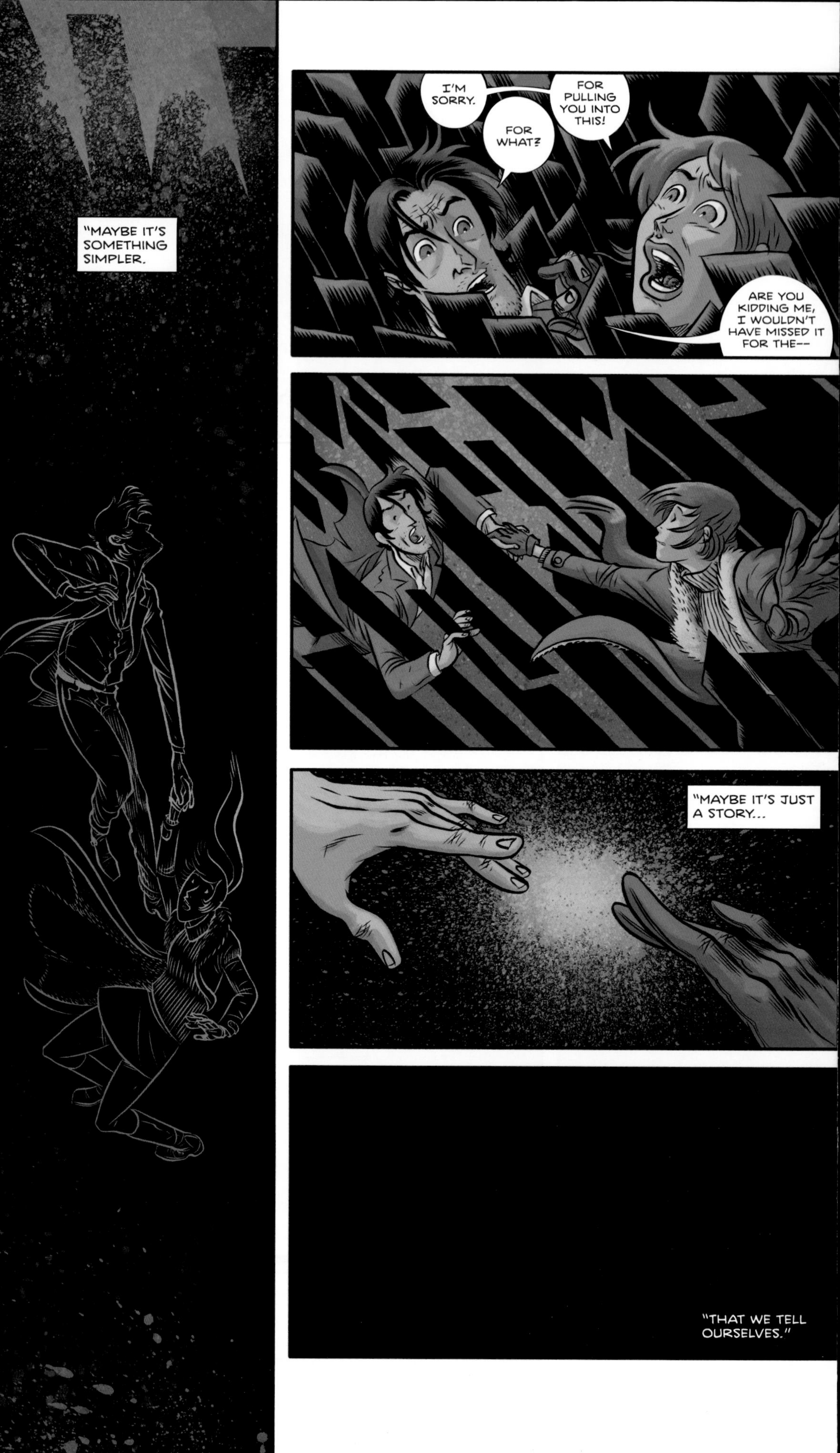
"MAYBE IT'S SOMETHING SIMPLER.
I'M SORRY.
FOR WHAT?
FOR PULLING YOU INTO THIS!
ARE YOU KIDDING ME, I WOULDN'T HAVE MISSED IT FOR THE--
"MAYBE IT'S JUST A STORY...
"THAT WE TELL OURSELVES."

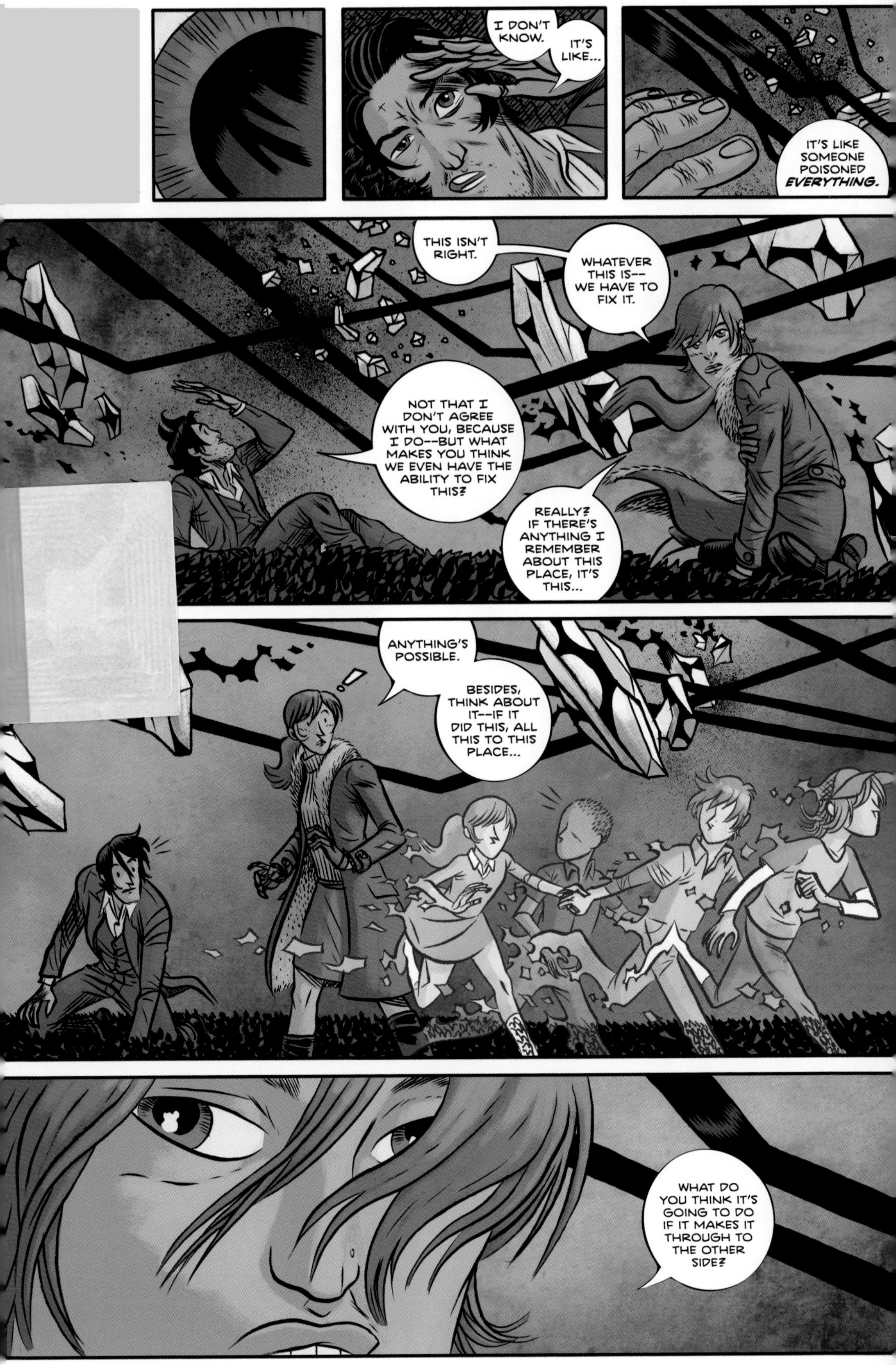
I DON'T KNOW.
IT'S LIKE...
IT'S LIKE SOMEONE POISONED EVERYTHING.
THIS ISN'T RIGHT.
WHATEVER THIS IS-- WE HAVE TO FIX IT.
NOT THAT I DON'T AGREE WITH YOU, BECAUSE I DO--BUT WHAT MAKES YOU THINK WE EVEN HAVE THE ABILITY TO FIX THIS?
REALLY? IF THERE'S ANYTHING I REMEMBER ABOUT THIS PLACE, IT'S THIS...
ANYTHING'S POSSIBLE.
!
BESIDES, THINK ABOUT IT--IF IT DID THIS, ALL THIS TO THIS PLACE...
WHAT DO YOU THINK IT'S GOING TO DO IF IT MAKES IT THROUGH TO THE OTHER SIDE?

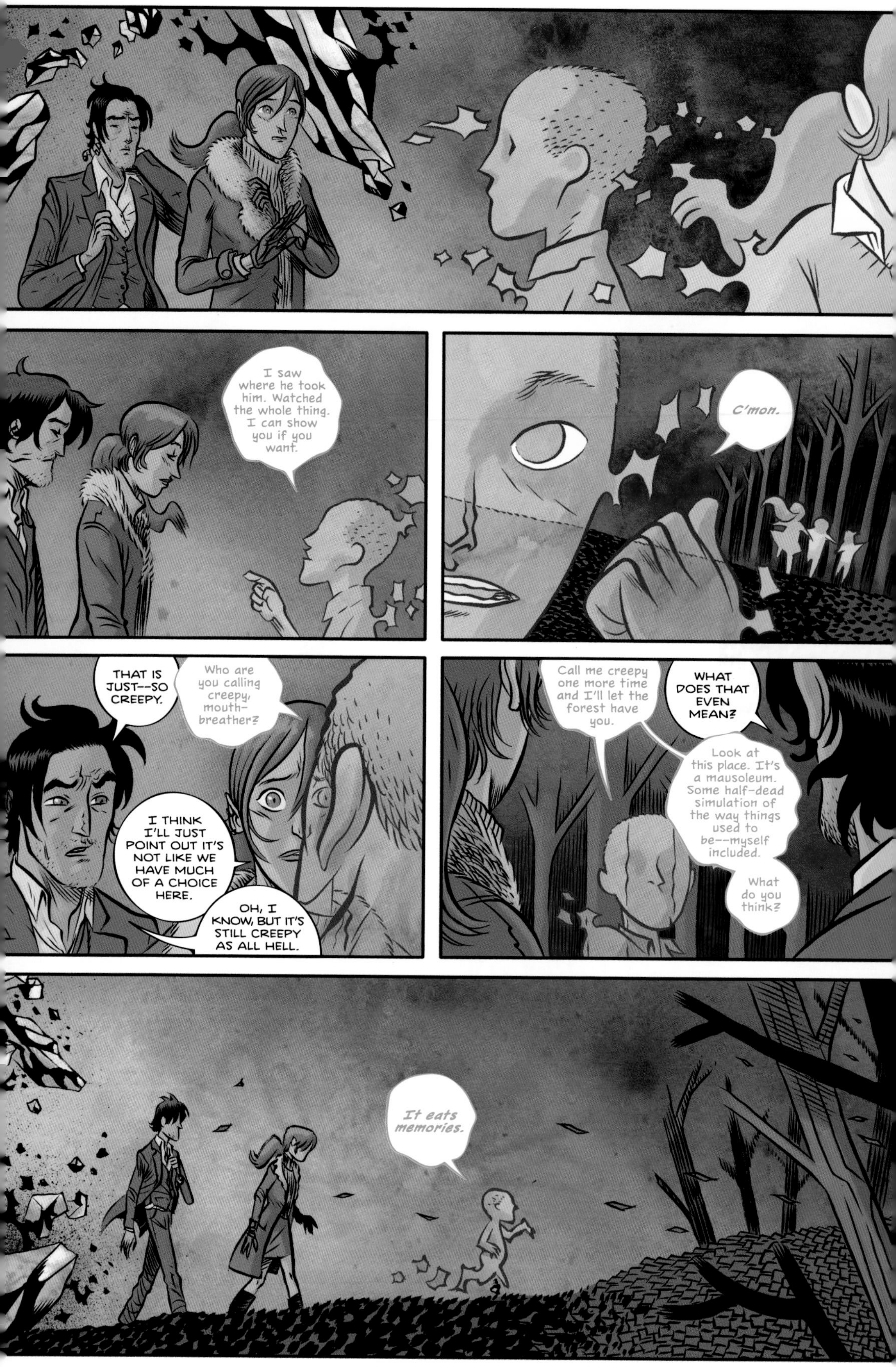

I saw where he took him. Watched the whole thing. I can show you if you want.
C'mon.
THAT IS JUST--SO CREEPY.
Who are you calling creepy, mouth-breather?
I THINK I'LL JUST POINT OUT IT'S NOT LIKE WE HAVE MUCH OF A CHOICE HERE.
OH, I KNOW, BUT IT'S STILL CREEPY AS ALL HELL.
Call me creepy one more time and I'll let the forest have you.
WHAT DOES THAT EVEN MEAN?
Look at this place. It's a mausoleum. Some half-dead simulation of the way things used to be--myself included.
What do you think?
It eats memories.

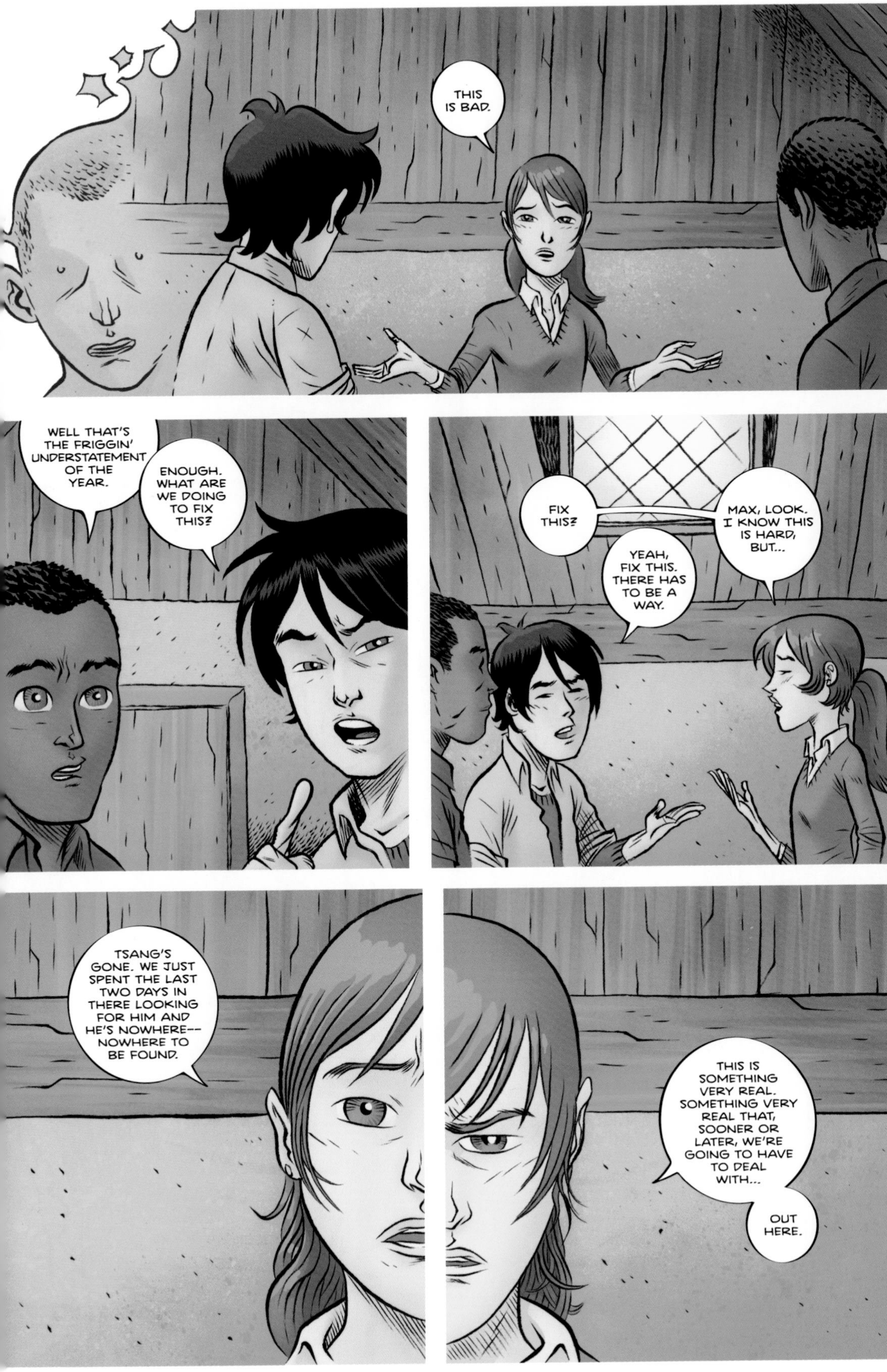
THIS IS BAD.
WELL THAT'S THE FRIGGIN' UNDERSTATEMENT OF THE YEAR.
ENOUGH. WHAT ARE WE DOING TO FIX THIS?
FIX THIS?
MAX, LOOK. I KNOW THIS IS HARD, BUT...
YEAH, FIX THIS. THERE HAS TO BE A WAY.
TSANG'S GONE. WE JUST SPENT THE LAST TWO DAYS IN THERE LOOKING FOR HIM AND HE'S NOWHERE-- NOWHERE TO BE FOUND.
THIS IS SOMETHING VERY REAL. SOMETHING VERY REAL THAT, SOONER OR LATER, WE'RE GOING TO HAVE TO DEAL WITH...
OUT HERE.

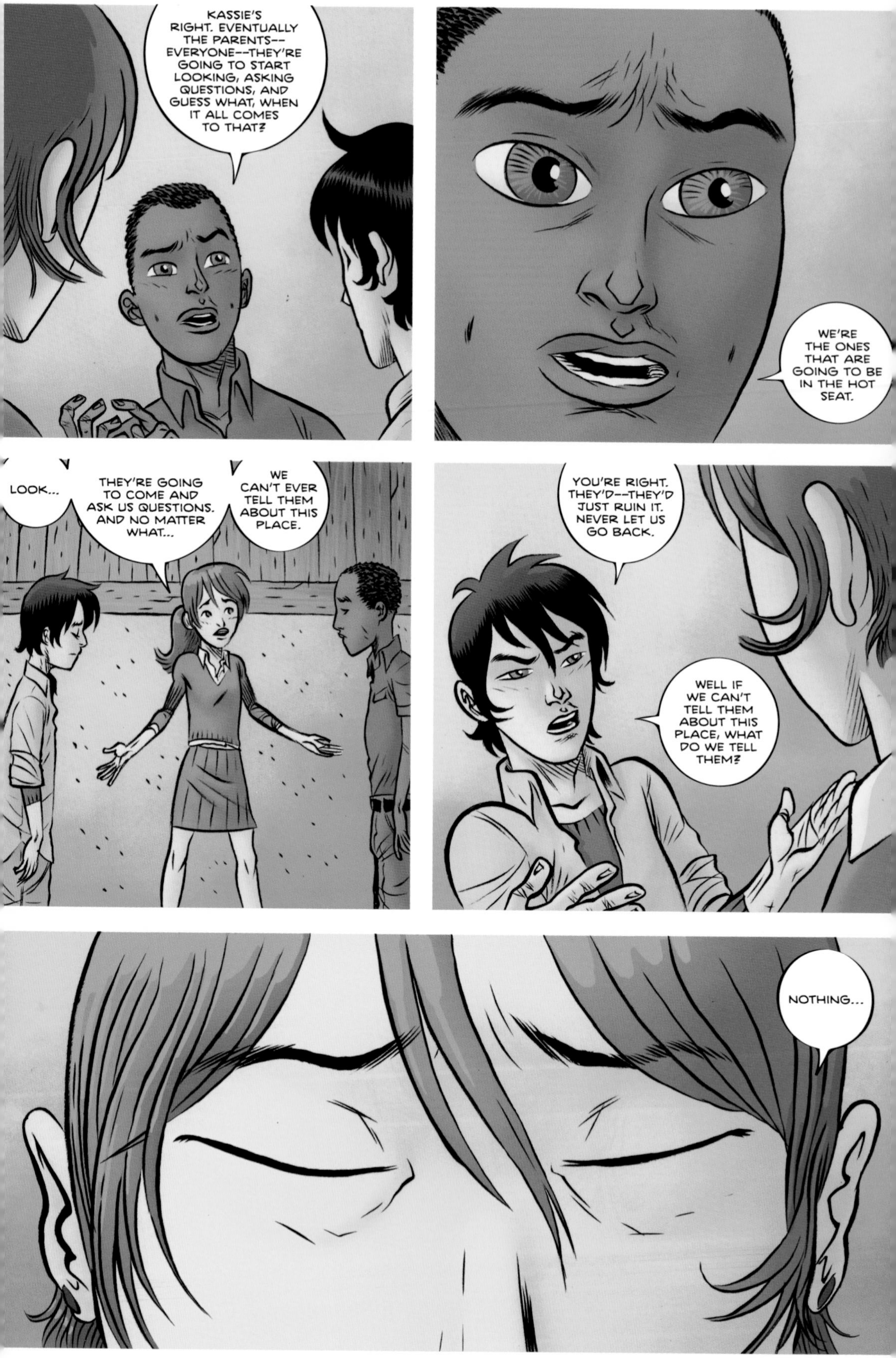
KASSIE'S RIGHT. EVENTUALLY THE PARENTS-- EVERYONE--THEY'RE GOING TO START LOOKING, ASKING QUESTIONS, AND GUESS WHAT, WHEN IT ALL COMES TO THAT?
WE'RE THE ONES THAT ARE GOING TO BE IN THE HOT SEAT.
LOOK...
THEY'RE GOING TO COME AND ASK US QUESTIONS. AND NO MATTER WHAT...
WE CAN'T EVER TELL THEM ABOUT THIS PLACE.
YOU'RE RIGHT. THEY'D--THEY'D JUST RUIN IT. NEVER LET US GO BACK.
WELL IF WE CAN'T TELL THEM ABOUT THIS PLACE, WHAT DO WE TELL THEM?
NOTHING...

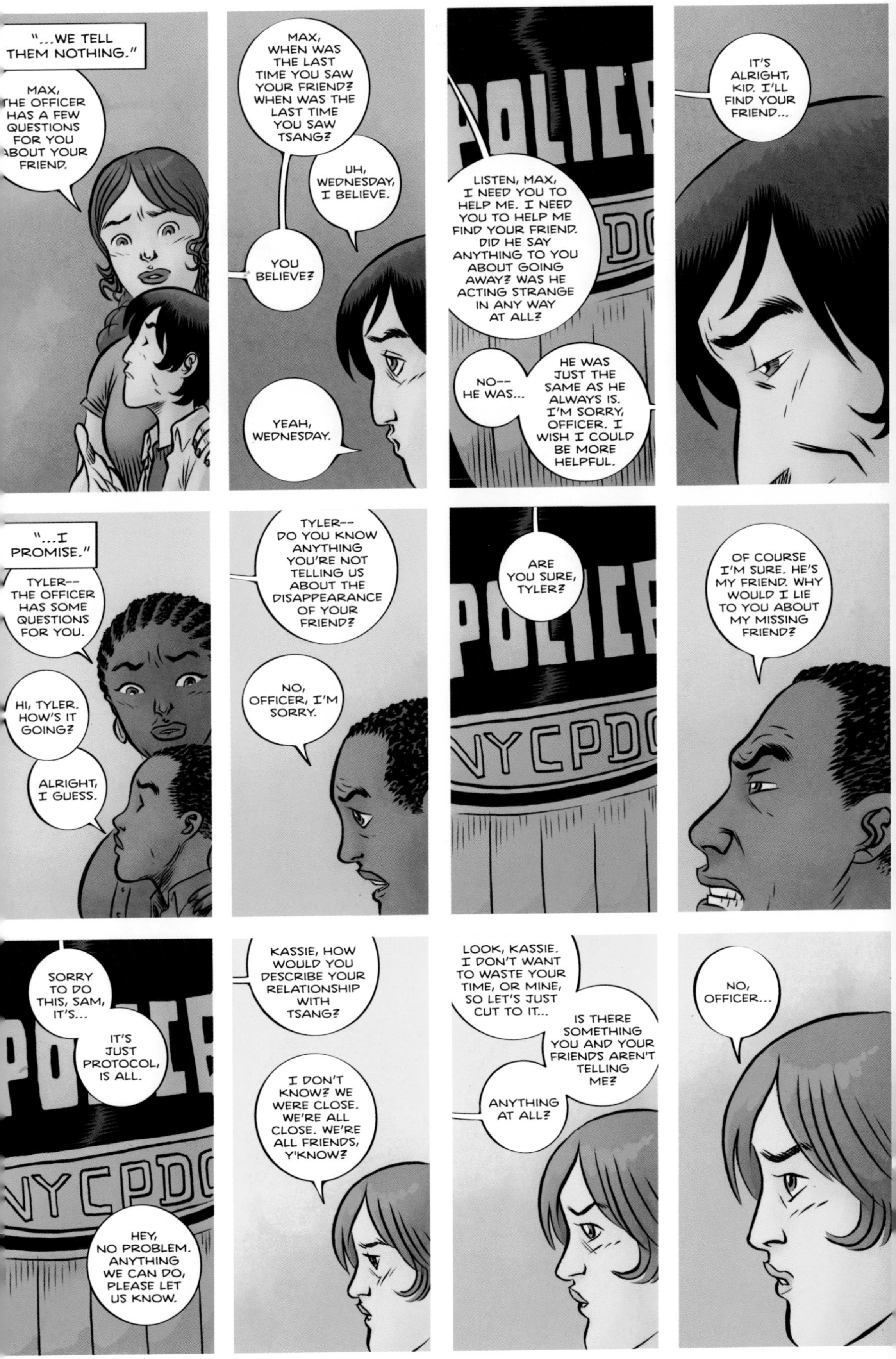
"...WE TELL THEM NOTHING."
MAX, THE OFFICER HAS A FEW QUESTIONS FOR YOU ABOUT YOUR FRIEND.
MAX, WHEN WAS THE LAST TIME YOU SAW YOUR FRIEND? WHEN WAS THE LAST TIME YOU SAW TSANG?
UH, WEDNESDAY, I BELIEVE.
YOU BELIEVE?
YEAH, WEDNESDAY.
POLICE
LISTEN, MAX, I NEED YOU TO HELP ME. I NEED YOU TO HELP ME FIND YOUR FRIEND. DID HE SAY ANYTHING TO YOU ABOUT GOING AWAY? WAS HE ACTING STRANGE IN ANY WAY AT ALL?
NO-- HE WAS...
HE WAS JUST THE SAME AS HE ALWAYS IS. I'M SORRY, OFFICER. I WISH I COULD BE MORE HELPFUL.
IT'S ALRIGHT, KID. I'LL FIND YOUR FRIEND...
"...I PROMISE."
TYLER-- THE OFFICER HAS SOME QUESTIONS FOR YOU.
HI, TYLER. HOW'S IT GOING?
ALRIGHT, I GUESS.
TYLER-- DO YOU KNOW ANYTHING YOU'RE NOT TELLING US ABOUT THE DISAPPEARANCE OF YOUR FRIEND?
NO, OFFICER, I'M SORRY.
ARE YOU SURE, TYLER?
POLICE
NYCPD
OF COURSE I'M SURE. HE'S MY FRIEND. WHY WOULD I LIE TO YOU ABOUT MY MISSING FRIEND?
SORRY TO DO THIS, SAM, IT'S...
IT'S JUST PROTOCOL, IS ALL.
POLICE
NYCPD
HEY, NO PROBLEM. ANYTHING WE CAN DO, PLEASE LET US KNOW.
KASSIE, HOW WOULD YOU DESCRIBE YOUR RELATIONSHIP WITH TSANG?
I DON'T KNOW? WE WERE CLOSE. WE'RE ALL CLOSE. WE'RE ALL FRIENDS, Y'KNOW?
LOOK, KASSIE. I DON'T WANT TO WASTE YOUR TIME, OR MINE, SO LET'S JUST CUT TO IT...
IS THERE SOMETHING YOU AND YOUR FRIENDS AREN'T TELLING ME?
ANYTHING AT ALL?
NO, OFFICER...

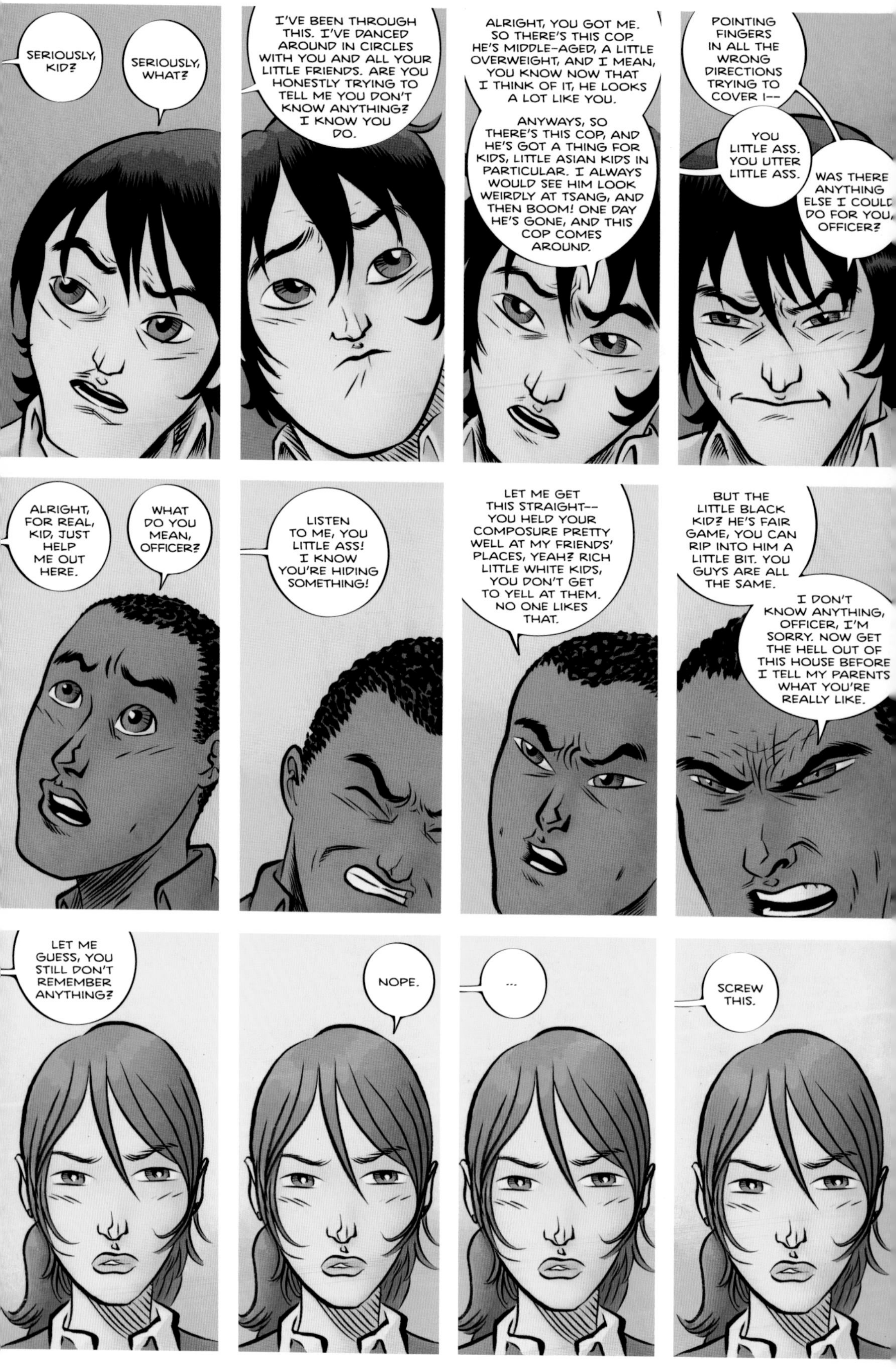
SERIOUSLY, KID?
SERIOUSLY, WHAT?
I'VE BEEN THROUGH THIS. I'VE DANCED AROUND IN CIRCLES WITH YOU AND ALL YOUR LITTLE FRIENDS. ARE YOU HONESTLY TRYING TO TELL ME YOU DON'T KNOW ANYTHING? I KNOW YOU DO.
ALRIGHT, YOU GOT ME. SO THERE'S THIS COP. HE'S MIDDLE-AGED, A LITTLE OVERWEIGHT, AND I MEAN, YOU KNOW NOW THAT I THINK OF IT, HE LOOKS A LOT LIKE YOU.
ANYWAYS, SO THERE'S THIS COP, AND HE'S GOT A THING FOR KIDS, LITTLE ASIAN KIDS IN PARTICULAR. I ALWAYS WOULD SEE HIM LOOK WEIRDLY AT TSANG, AND THEN BOOM! ONE DAY HE'S GONE, AND THIS COP COMES AROUND.
POINTING FINGERS IN ALL THE WRONG DIRECTIONS TRYING TO COVER I--
YOU LITTLE ASS. YOU UTTER LITTLE ASS.
WAS THERE ANYTHING ELSE I COULD DO FOR YOU, OFFICER?
ALRIGHT, FOR REAL, KID, JUST HELP ME OUT HERE.
WHAT DO YOU MEAN, OFFICER?
LISTEN TO ME, YOU LITTLE ASS! I KNOW YOU'RE HIDING SOMETHING!
LET ME GET THIS STRAIGHT-- YOU HELD YOUR COMPOSURE PRETTY WELL AT MY FRIENDS' PLACES, YEAH? RICH LITTLE WHITE KIDS, YOU DON'T GET TO YELL AT THEM. NO ONE LIKES THAT.
BUT THE LITTLE BLACK KID? HE'S FAIR GAME, YOU CAN RIP INTO HIM A LITTLE BIT. YOU GUYS ARE ALL THE SAME.
I DON'T KNOW ANYTHING, OFFICER, I'M SORRY. NOW GET THE HELL OUT OF THIS HOUSE BEFORE I TELL MY PARENTS WHAT YOU'RE REALLY LIKE.
LET ME GUESS, YOU STILL DON'T REMEMBER ANYTHING?
NOPE.
...
SCREW THIS.

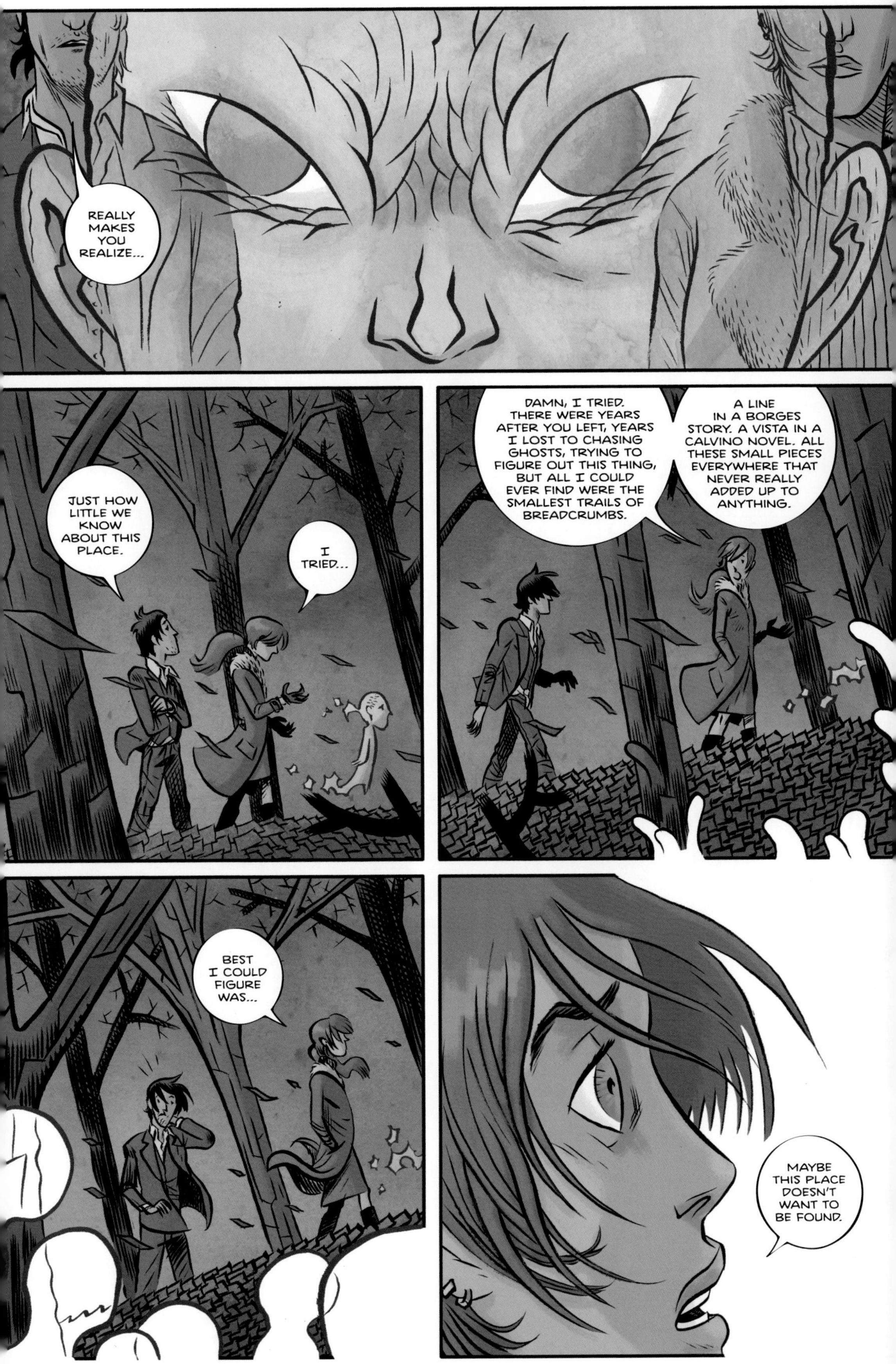
REALLY MAKES YOU REALIZE...
JUST HOW LITTLE WE KNOW ABOUT THIS PLACE.
I TRIED...
DAMN, I TRIED. THERE WERE YEARS AFTER YOU LEFT, YEARS I LOST TO CHASING GHOSTS, TRYING TO FIGURE OUT THIS THING, BUT ALL I COULD EVER FIND WERE THE SMALLEST TRAILS OF BREADCRUMBS.
A LINE IN A BORGES STORY. A VISTA IN A CALVINO NOVEL. ALL THESE SMALL PIECES EVERYWHERE THAT NEVER REALLY ADDED UP TO ANYTHING.
BEST I COULD FIGURE WAS...
MAYBE THIS PLACE DOESN'T WANT TO BE FOUND.

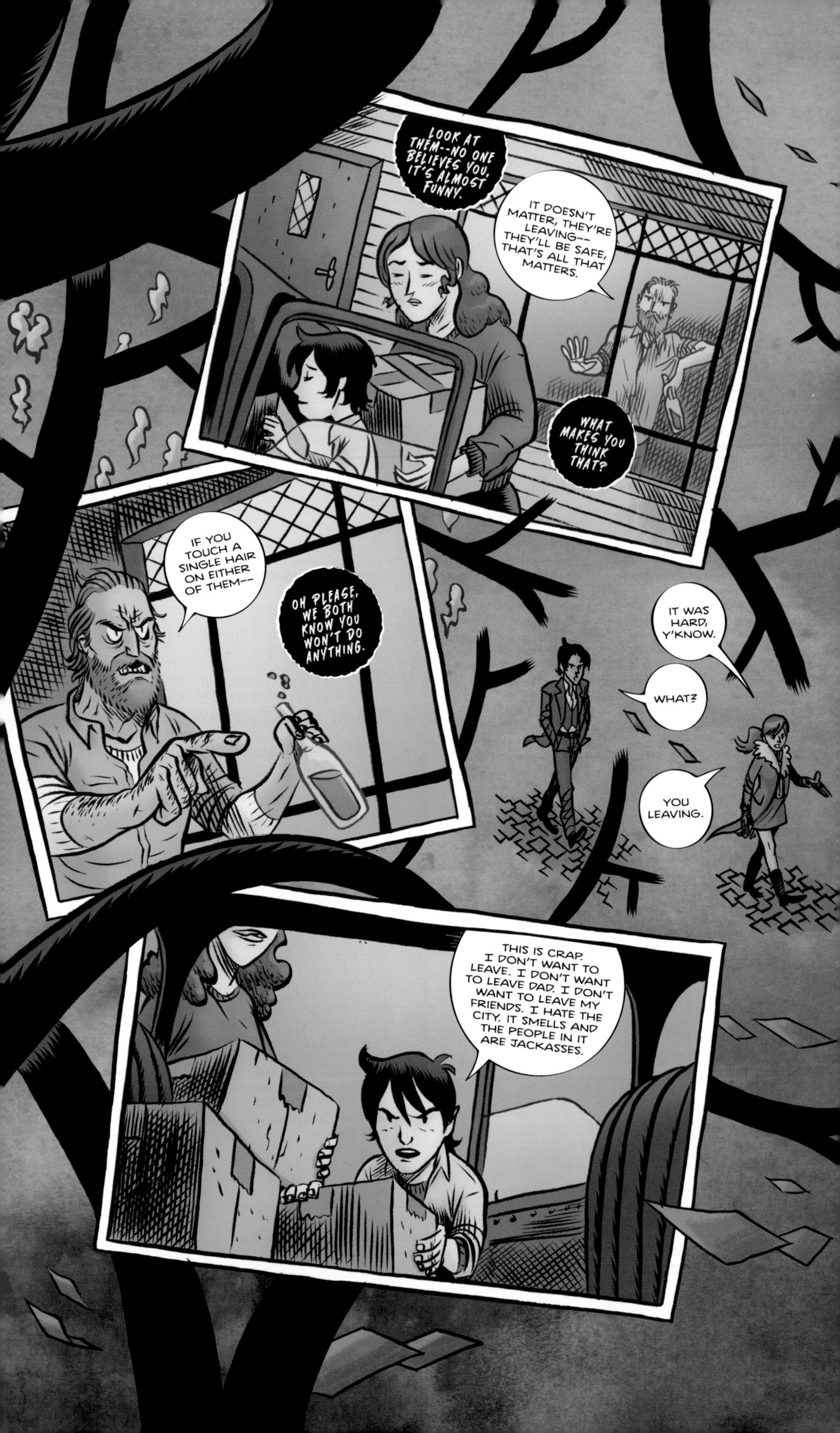
LOOK AT THEM--NO ONE BELIEVES YOU. IT'S ALMOST FUNNY.
IT DOESN'T MATTER, THEY'RE LEAVING-- THEY'LL BE SAFE, THAT'S ALL THAT MATTERS.
WHAT MAKES YOU THINK THAT?
IF YOU TOUCH A SINGLE HAIR ON EITHER OF THEM--
OH PLEASE, WE BOTH KNOW YOU WON'T DO ANYTHING.
IT WAS HARD, Y'KNOW.
WHAT?
YOU LEAVING.
THIS IS CRAP. I DON'T WANT TO LEAVE. I DON'T WANT TO LEAVE DAD. I DON'T WANT TO LEAVE MY FRIENDS. I HATE THE CITY. IT SMELLS AND THE PEOPLE IN IT ARE JACKASSES.

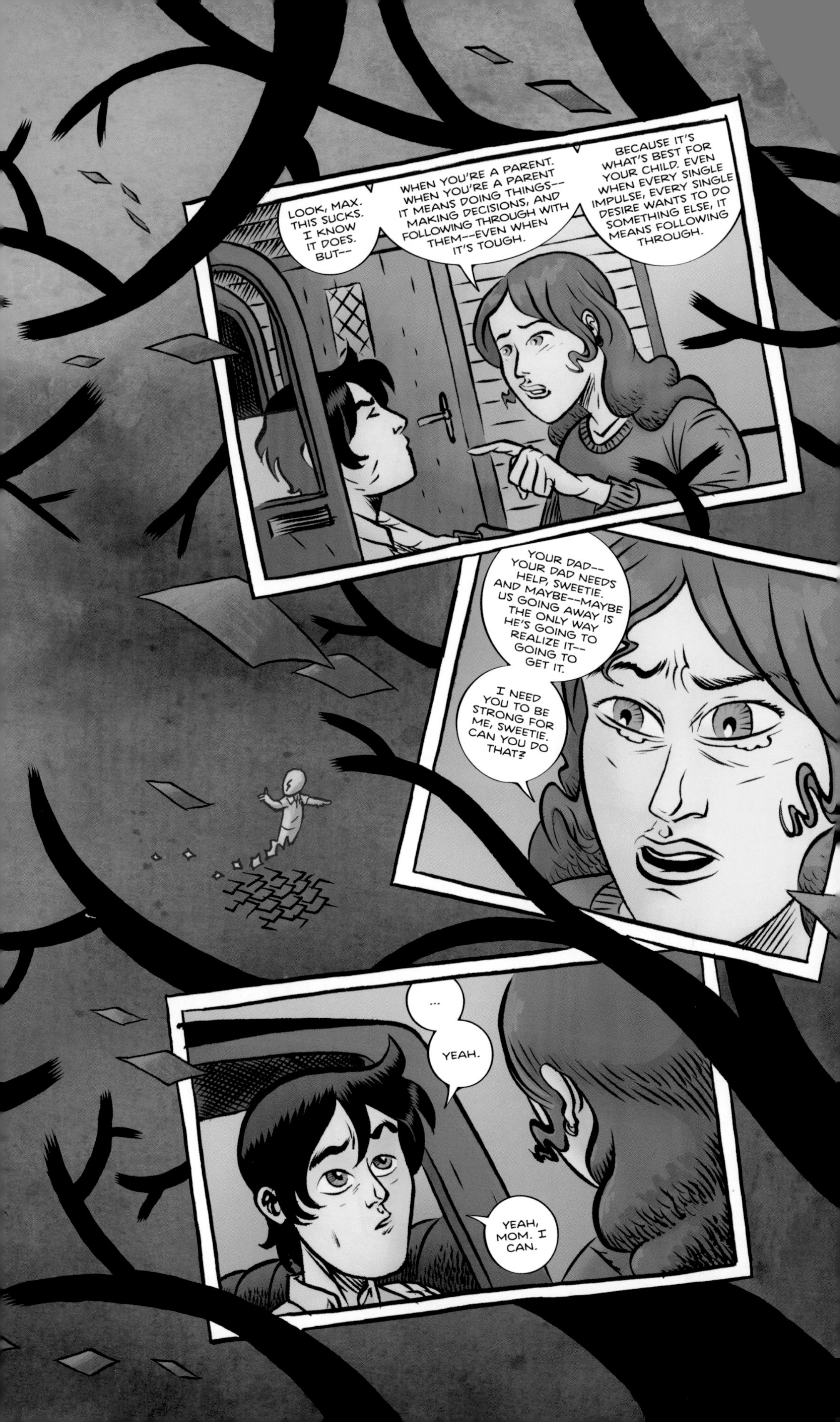
LOOK, MAX. THIS SUCKS. I KNOW IT DOES. BUT--
WHEN YOU'RE A PARENT. WHEN YOU'RE A PARENT IT MEANS DOING THINGS-- MAKING DECISIONS, AND FOLLOWING THROUGH WITH THEM--EVEN WHEN IT'S TOUGH.
BECAUSE IT'S WHAT'S BEST FOR YOUR CHILD. EVEN WHEN EVERY SINGLE IMPULSE, EVERY SINGLE DESIRE WANTS TO DO SOMETHING ELSE, IT MEANS FOLLOWING THROUGH.
YOUR DAD-- YOUR DAD NEEDS HELP, SWEETIE. AND MAYBE--MAYBE US GOING AWAY IS THE ONLY WAY HE'S GOING TO REALIZE IT-- GOING TO GET IT.
I NEED YOU TO BE STRONG FOR ME, SWEETIE. CAN YOU DO THAT?
...
YEAH.
YEAH, MOM. I CAN.

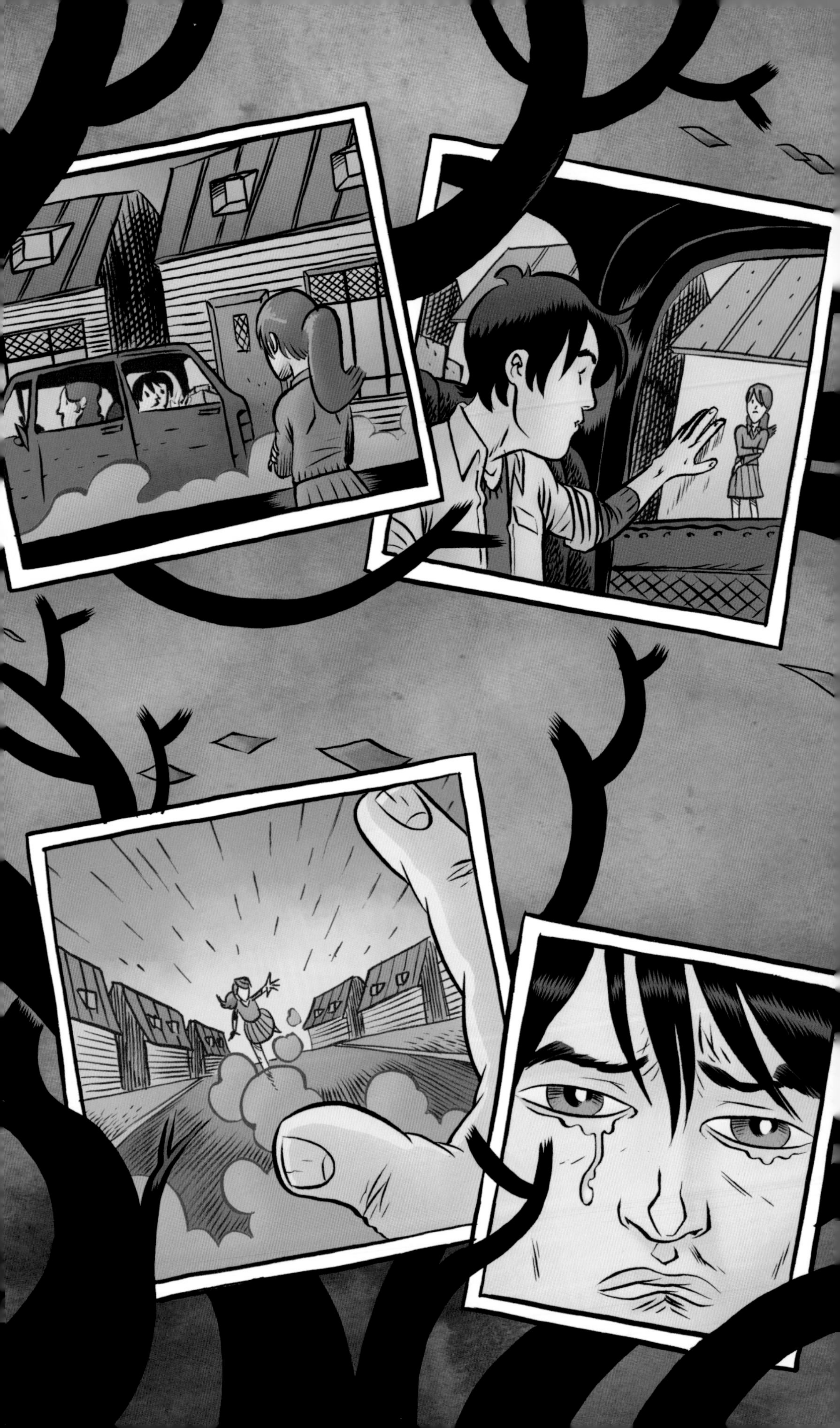

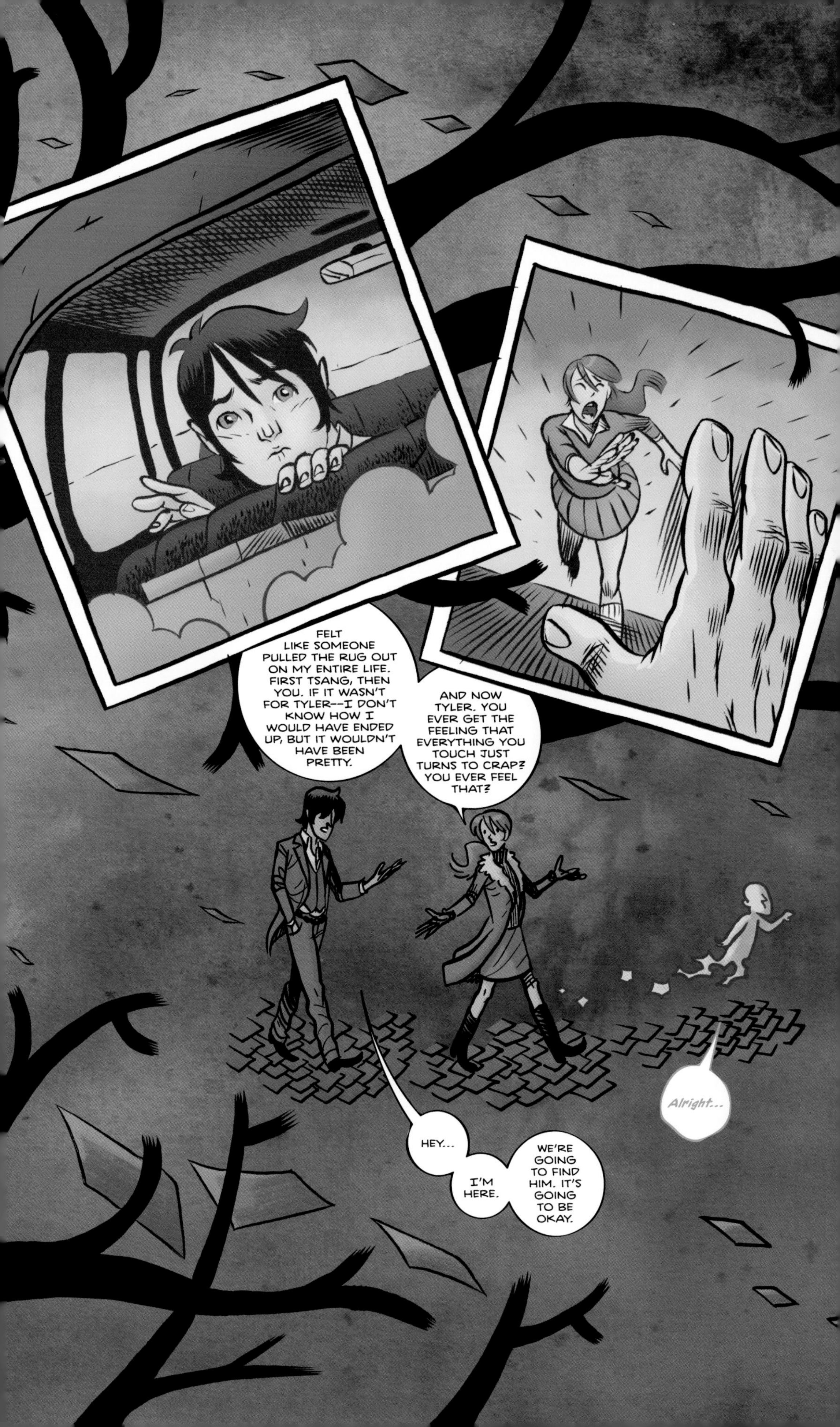
FELT LIKE SOMEONE PULLED THE RUG OUT ON MY ENTIRE LIFE. FIRST TSANG, THEN YOU. IF IT WASN'T FOR TYLER--I DON'T KNOW HOW I WOULD HAVE ENDED UP, BUT IT WOULDN'T HAVE BEEN PRETTY.
AND NOW TYLER. YOU EVER GET THE FEELING THAT EVERYTHING YOU TOUCH JUST TURNS TO CRAP? YOU EVER FEEL THAT?
Alright...
HEY...
I'M HERE.
WE'RE GOING TO FIND HIM. IT'S GOING TO BE OKAY.

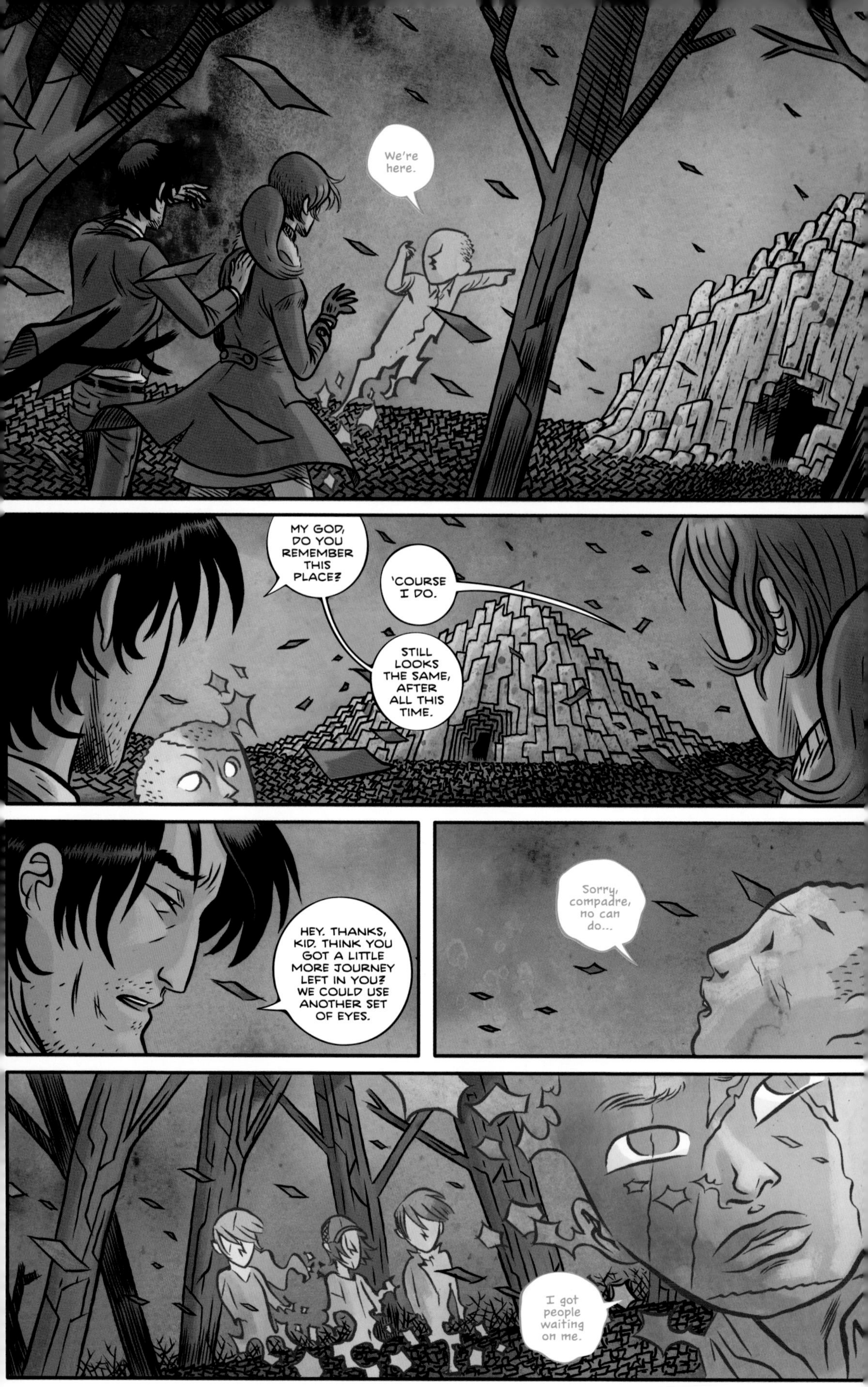

We're here.
MY GOD, DO YOU REMEMBER THIS PLACE?
'COURSE I DO.
STILL LOOKS THE SAME, AFTER ALL THIS TIME.
HEY. THANKS, KID. THINK YOU GOT A LITTLE MORE JOURNEY LEFT IN YOU? WE COULD USE ANOTHER SET OF EYES.
Sorry, compadre, no can do...
I got people waiting on me.

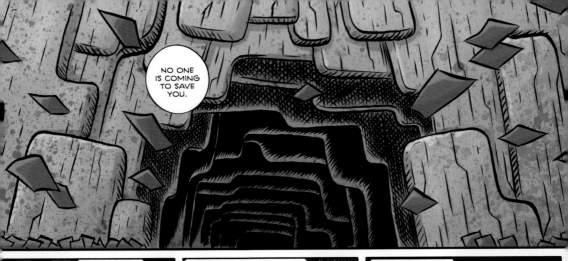

NO ONE IS COMING TO SAVE YOU.

WHO...WHO ARE YOU? WHAT DO YOU--WHY'D YOU BRING ME BACK HERE?

OH, TYLER. YOU KNOW WHO I AM. AND AS FOR BRINGING YOU HERE, WELL, YOU DID MOST OF THE WORK YOURSELF, I MERELY LEFT THE FRONT DOOR OPEN.

NO, IT'S-- IT'S BEEN YEARS. WE NEVER EVEN TOLD--IT CAN'T BE.

OH, DOES THIS FACE NOT WORK FOR YOU? HOLD ON A SEC. LET ME PUT ON ANOTHER ONE.

RRRIIIPP

SSLLUC

GGEERRTT

HHHH--

HOW'S THIS?

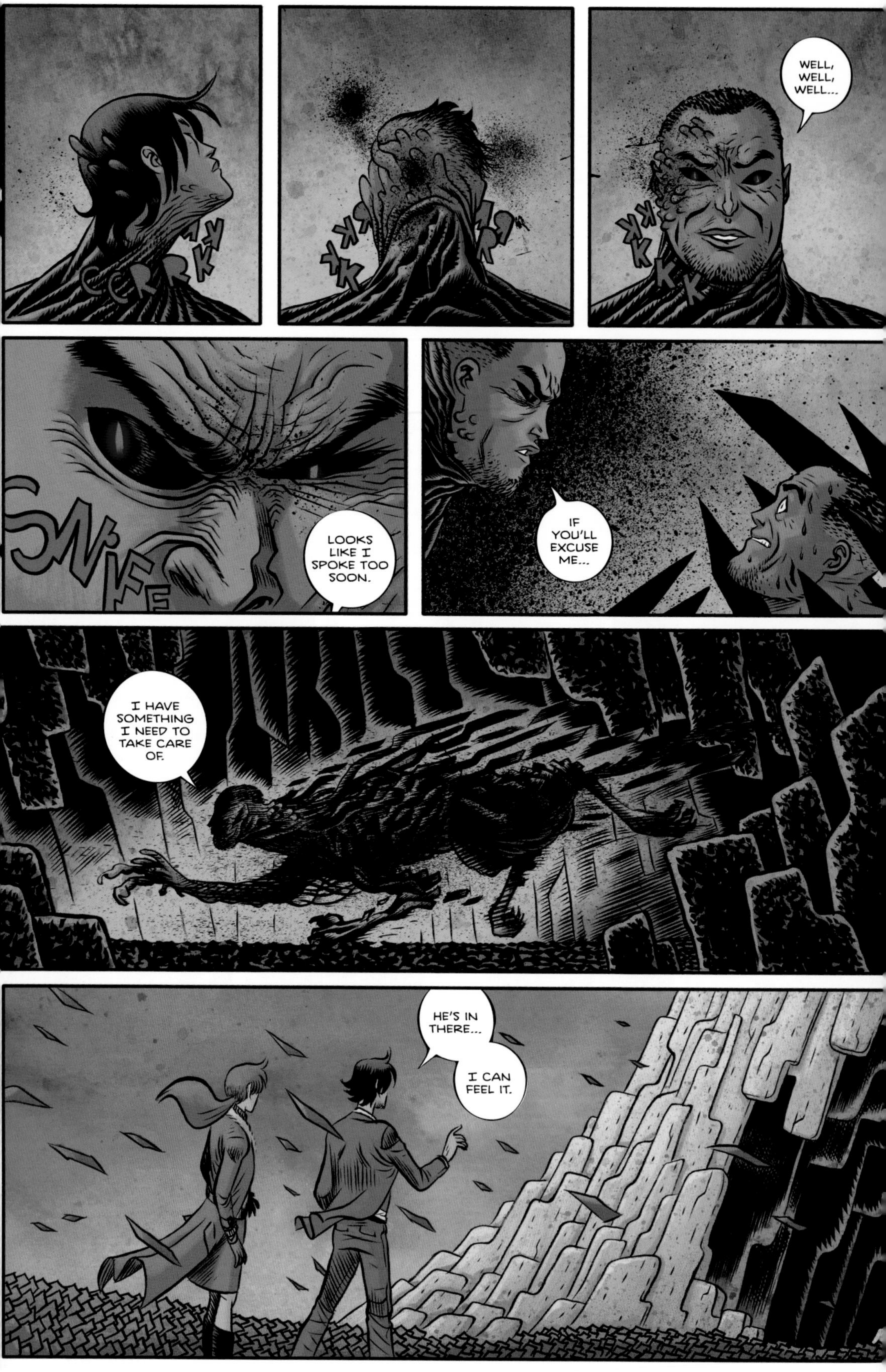
CERRKKKK
KKKKRR
WELL, WELL, WELL...
KKKKK
SNIFF
LOOKS LIKE I SPOKE TOO SOON.
IF YOU'LL EXCUSE ME...
I HAVE SOMETHING I NEED TO TAKE CARE OF.
HE'S IN THERE...
I CAN FEEL IT.

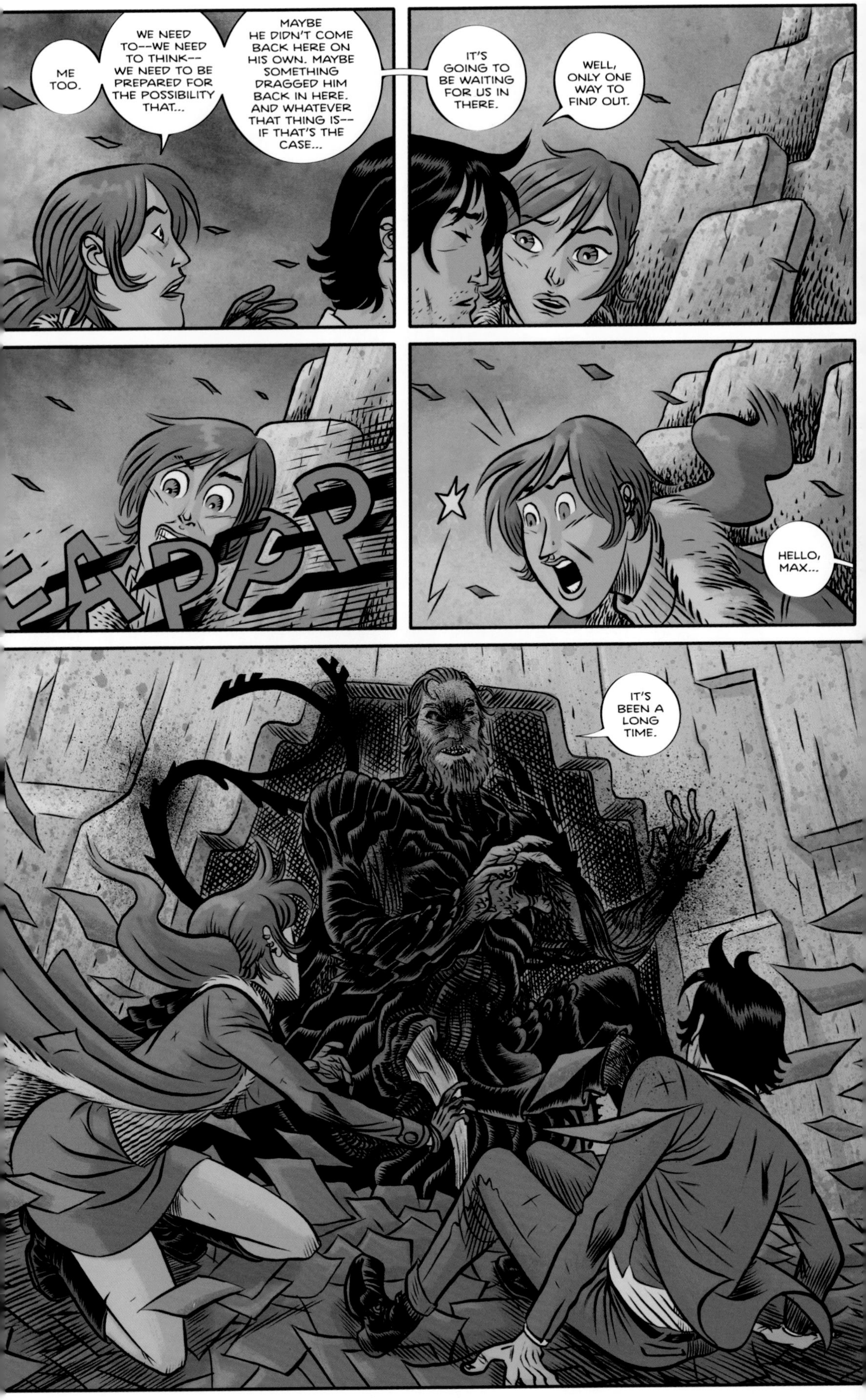
ME TOO.
WE NEED TO--WE NEED TO THINK-- WE NEED TO BE PREPARED FOR THE POSSIBILITY THAT...
MAYBE HE DIDN'T COME BACK HERE ON HIS OWN. MAYBE SOMETHING DRAGGED HIM BACK IN HERE. AND WHATEVER THAT THING IS-- IF THAT'S THE CASE...
IT'S GOING TO BE WAITING FOR US IN THERE.
WELL, ONLY ONE WAY TO FIND OUT.
HELLO, MAX...
IT'S BEEN A LONG TIME.

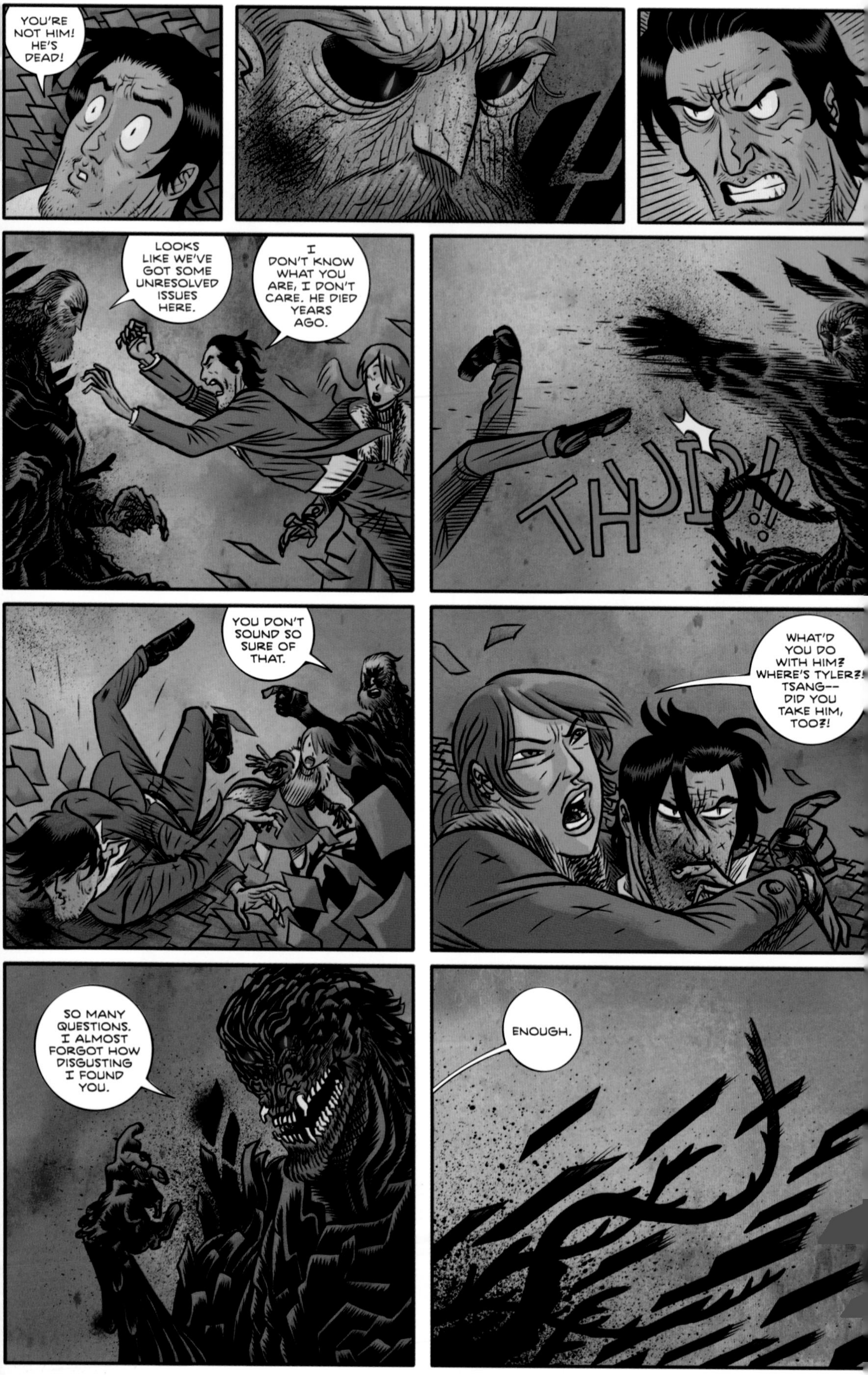
YOU'RE NOT HIM! HE'S DEAD!
LOOKS LIKE WE'VE GOT SOME UNRESOLVED ISSUES HERE.
I DON'T KNOW WHAT YOU ARE, I DON'T CARE. HE DIED YEARS AGO.
THUD!!
YOU DON'T SOUND SO SURE OF THAT.
WHAT'D YOU DO WITH HIM? WHERE'S TYLER?! TSANG-- DID YOU TAKE HIM, TOO?!
SO MANY QUESTIONS. I ALMOST FORGOT HOW DISGUSTING I FOUND YOU.
ENOUGH.

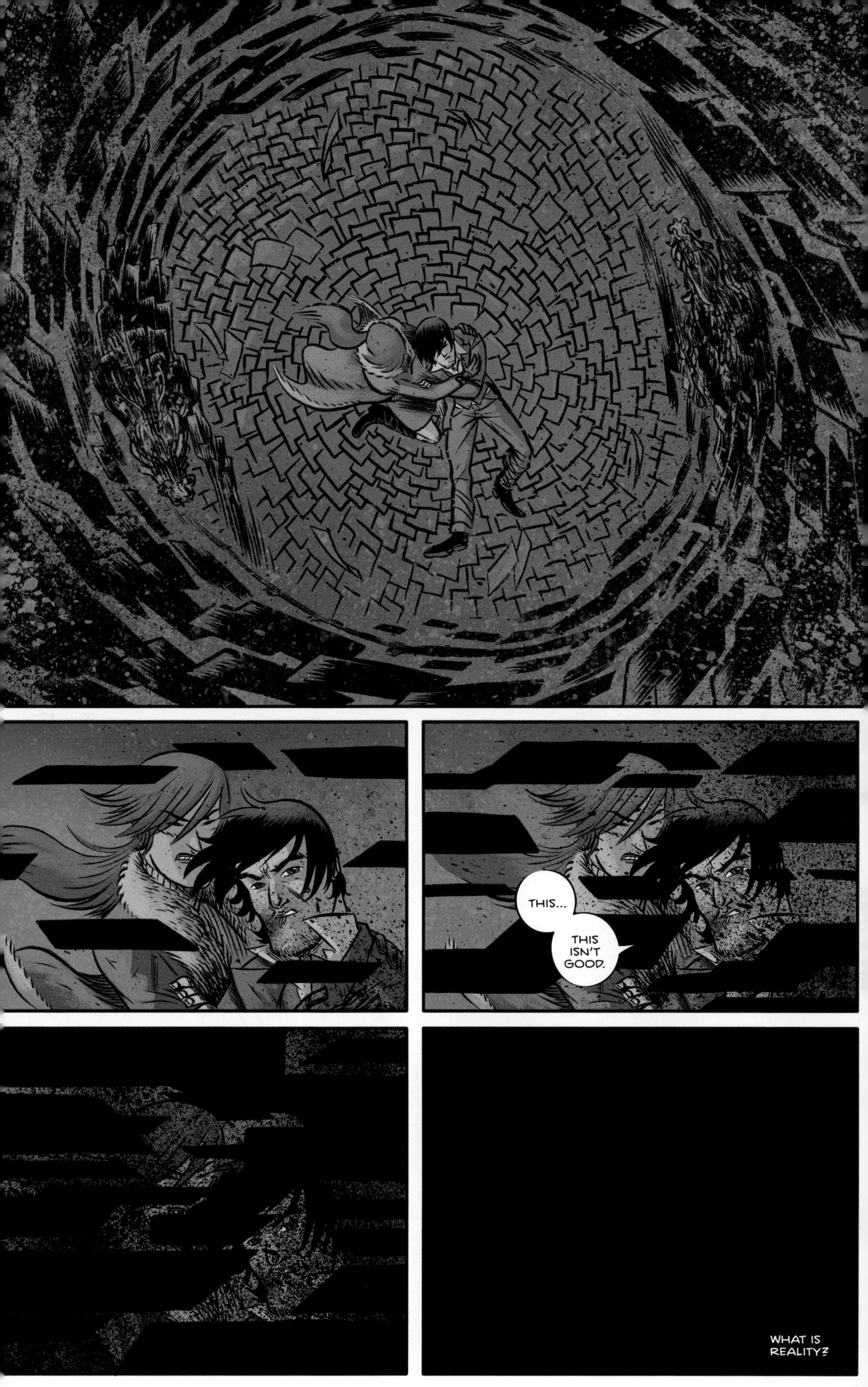
THIS...
THIS ISN'T GOOD.
WHAT IS REALITY?

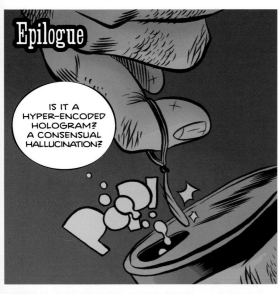

Epilogue

IS IT A HYPER-ENCODED HOLOGRAM? A CONSENSUAL HALLUCINATION?

MAYBE IT'S SOMETHING SIMPLER.

MAYBE IT'S JUST A STORY THAT WE TELL OURSELVES.

DO YOU ALWAYS GET LIKE THIS WHEN YOU GET HIGH?

THAT'S MY SECRET, SAM, I'M ALWAYS--

FUSSHH

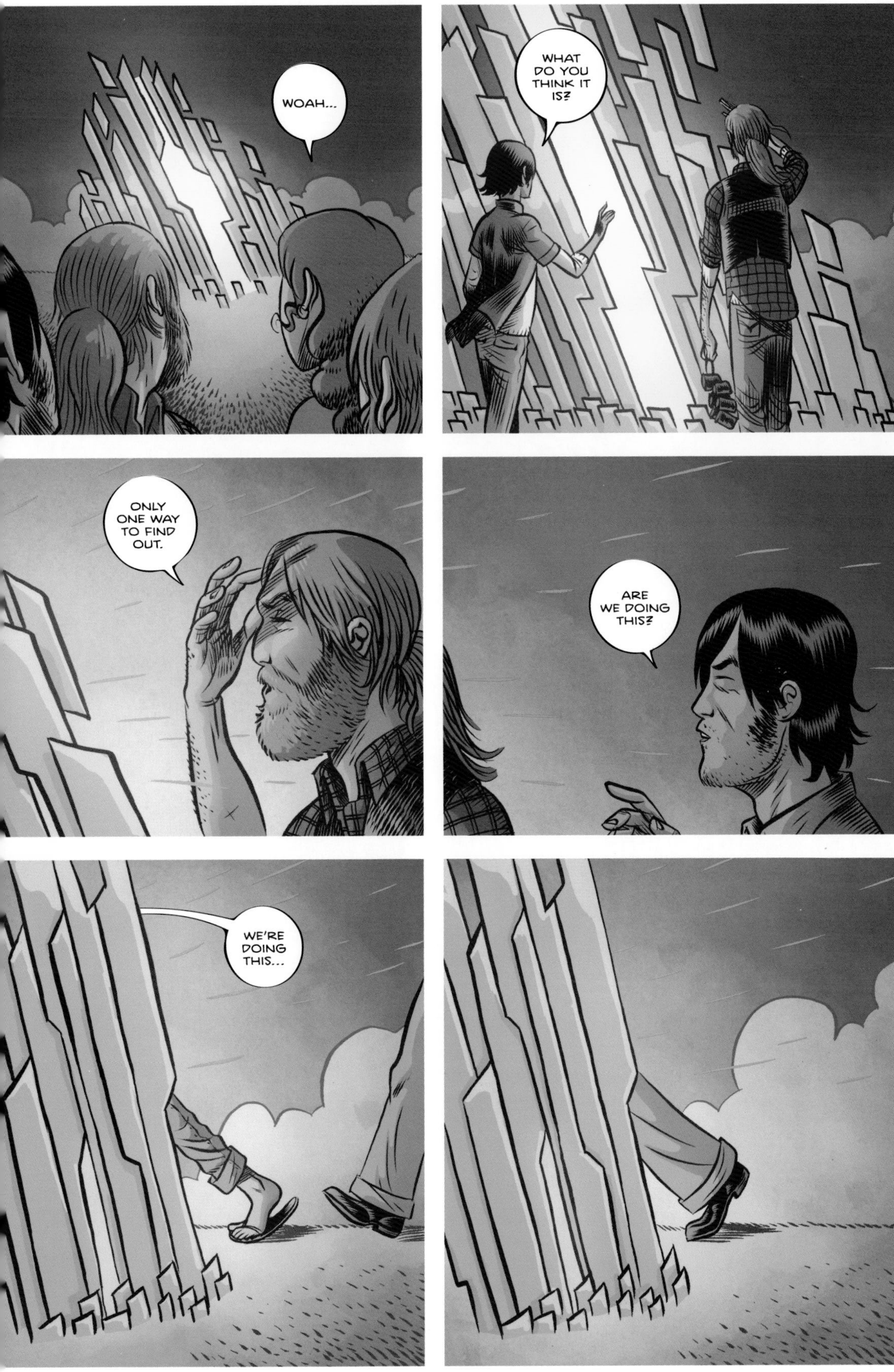
WOAH...
WHAT DO YOU THINK IT IS?
ONLY ONE WAY TO FIND OUT.
ARE WE DOING THIS?
WE'RE DOING THIS...

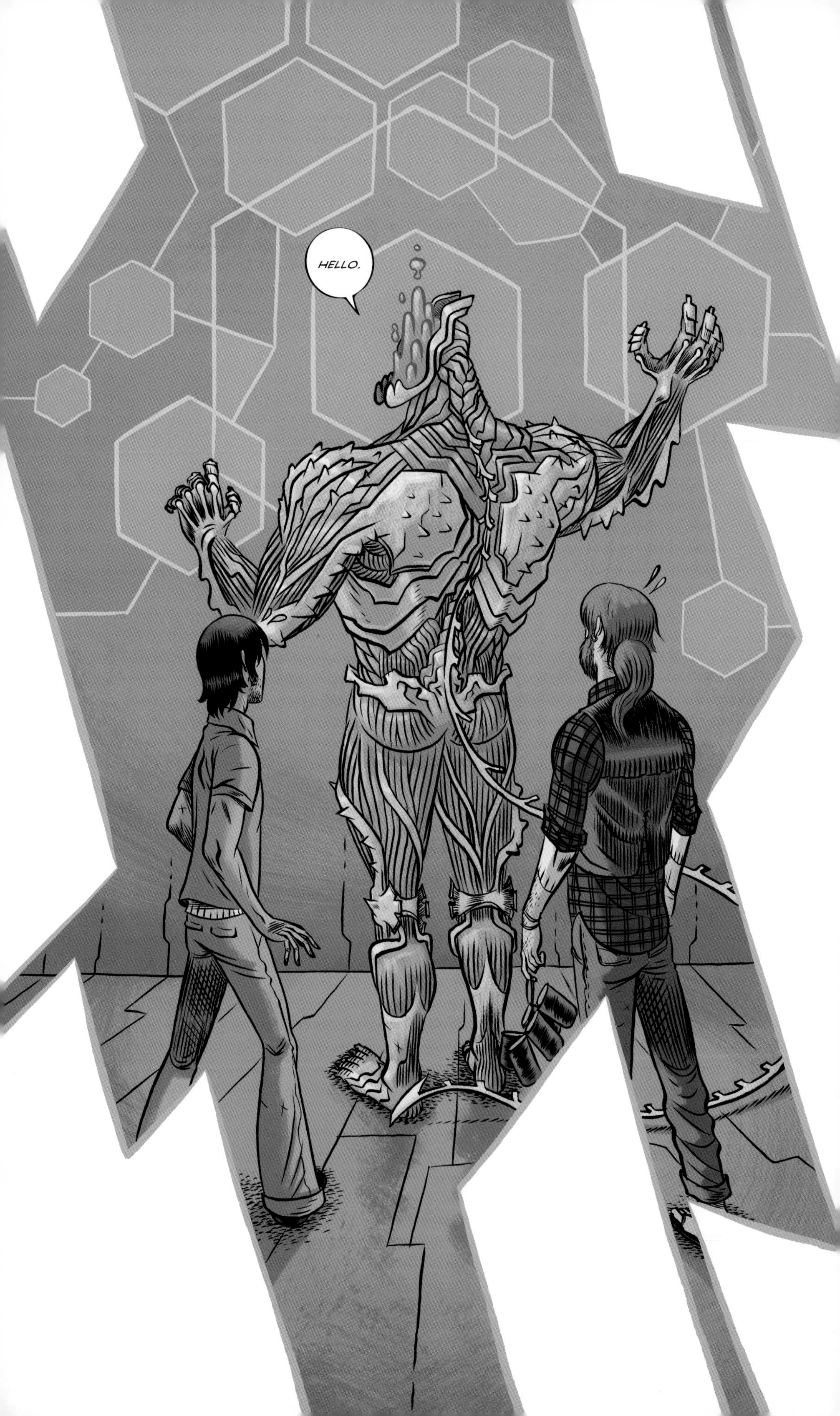
HELLO.

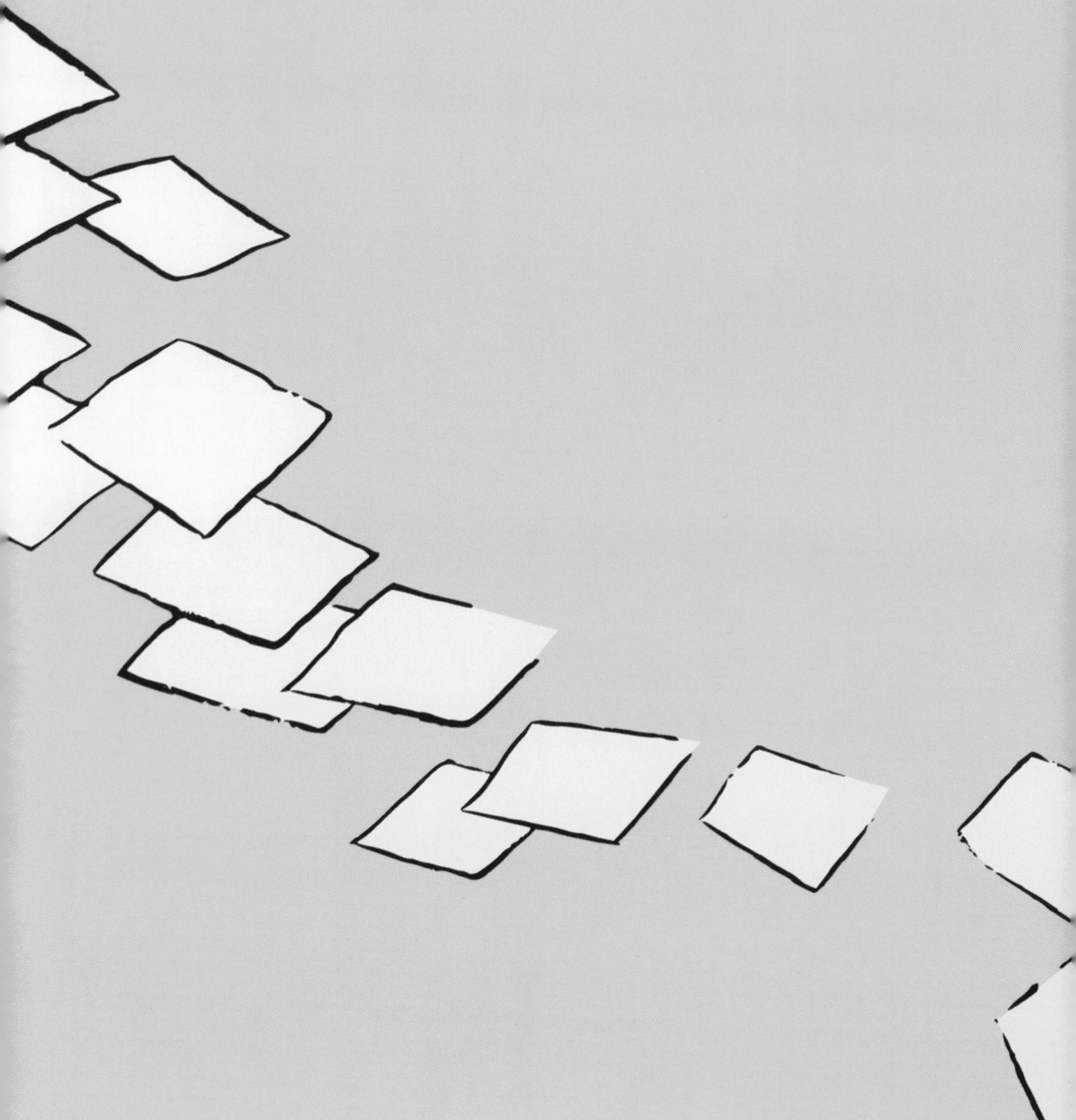

CHAPTER III
Where the Sky Hangs
or
Four Years Gone

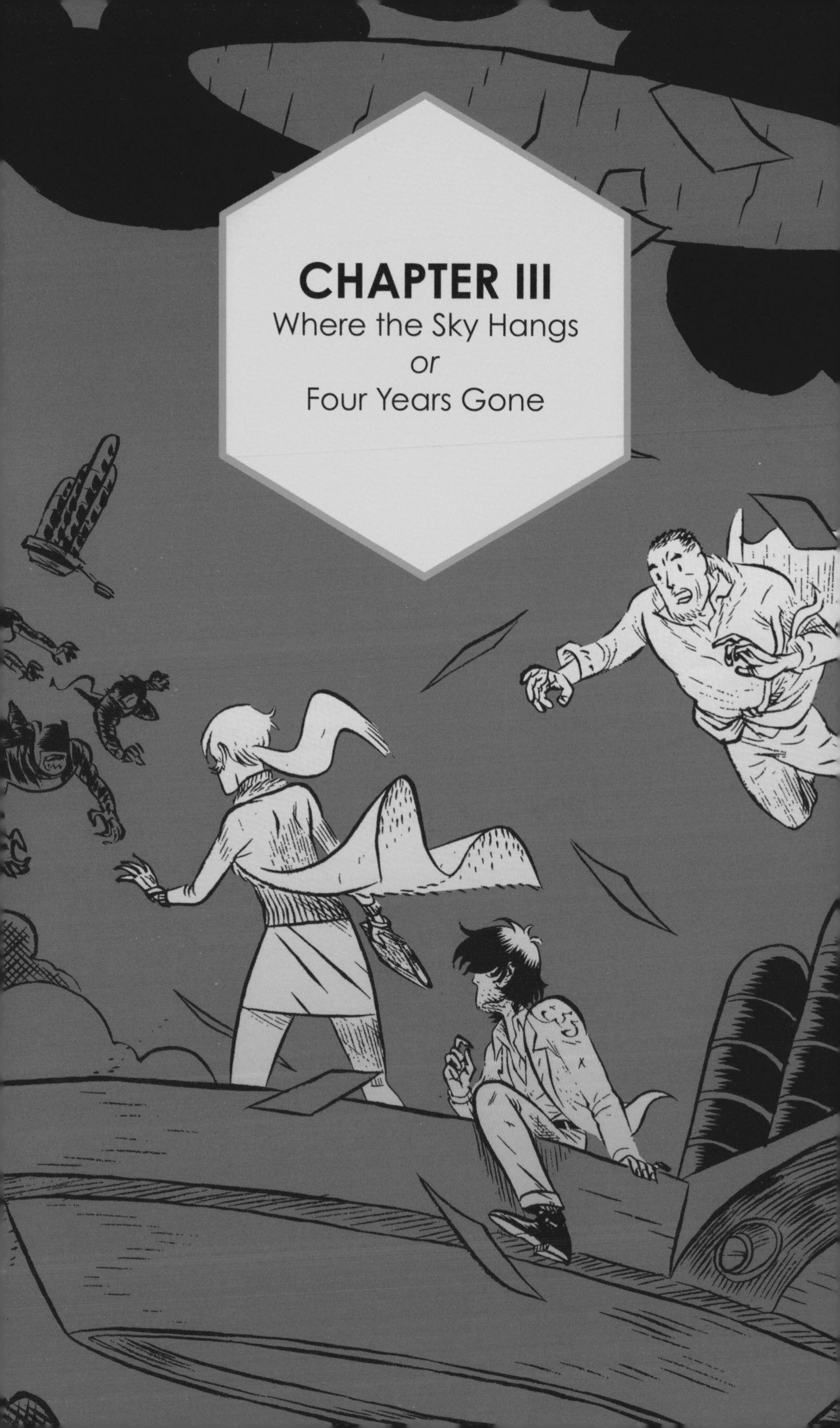

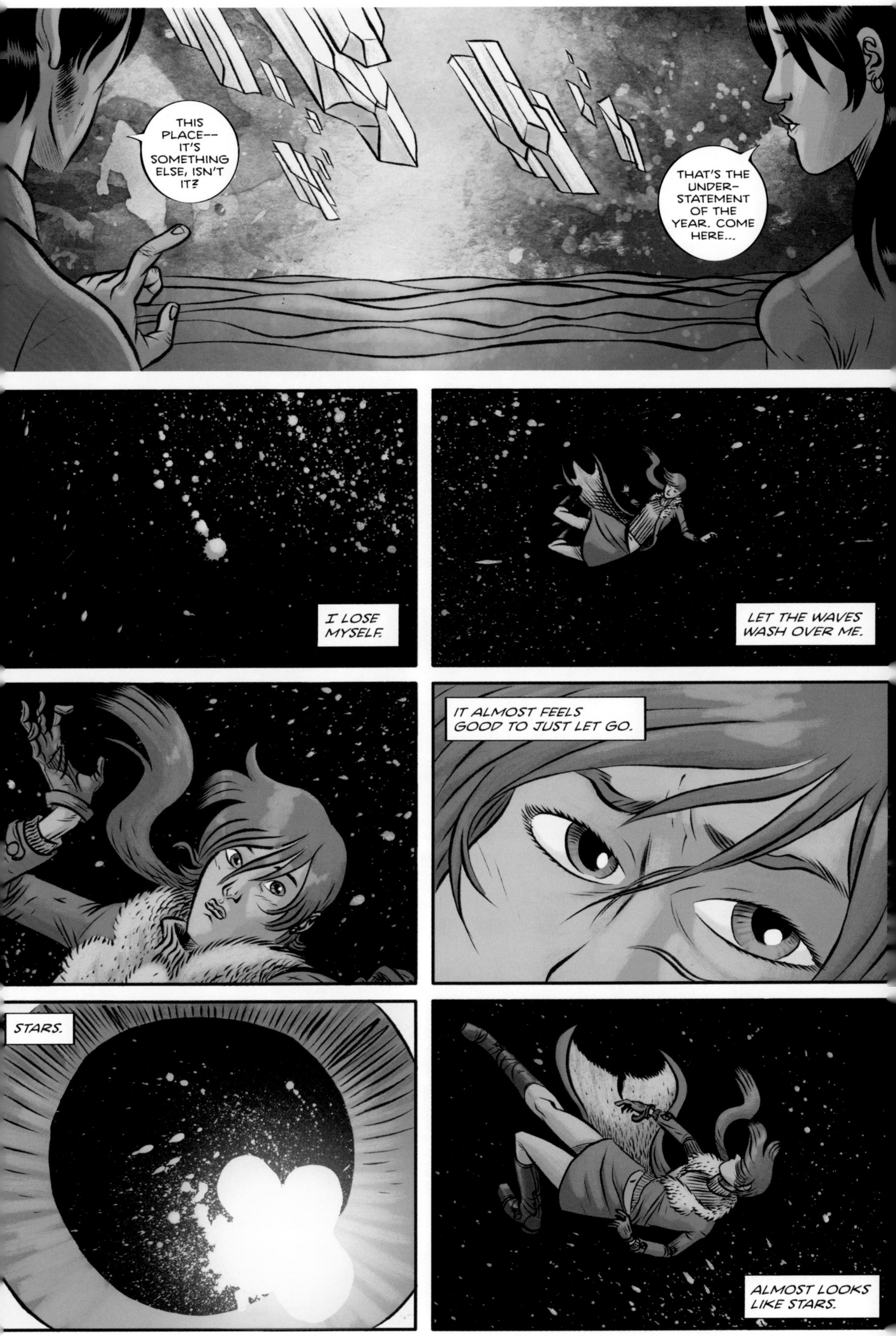

THIS PLACE-- IT'S SOMETHING ELSE, ISN'T IT?
THAT'S THE UNDER-STATEMENT OF THE YEAR. COME HERE...
I LOSE MYSELF.
LET THE WAVES WASH OVER ME.
IT ALMOST FEELS GOOD TO JUST LET GO.
STARS.
ALMOST LOOKS LIKE STARS.

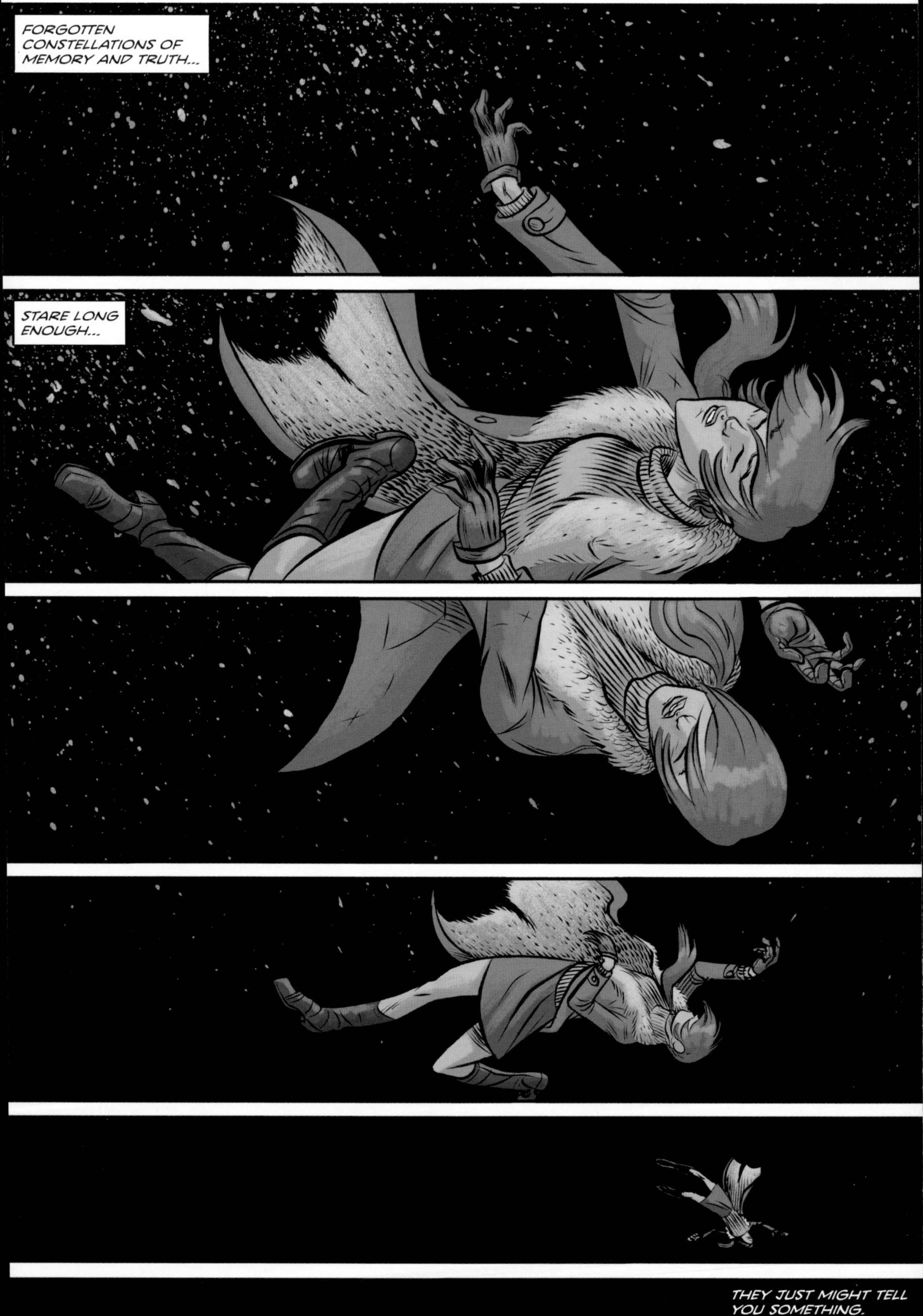
FORGOTTEN CONSTELLATIONS OF MEMORY AND TRUTH...
STARE LONG ENOUGH...
THEY JUST MIGHT TELL YOU SOMETHING.

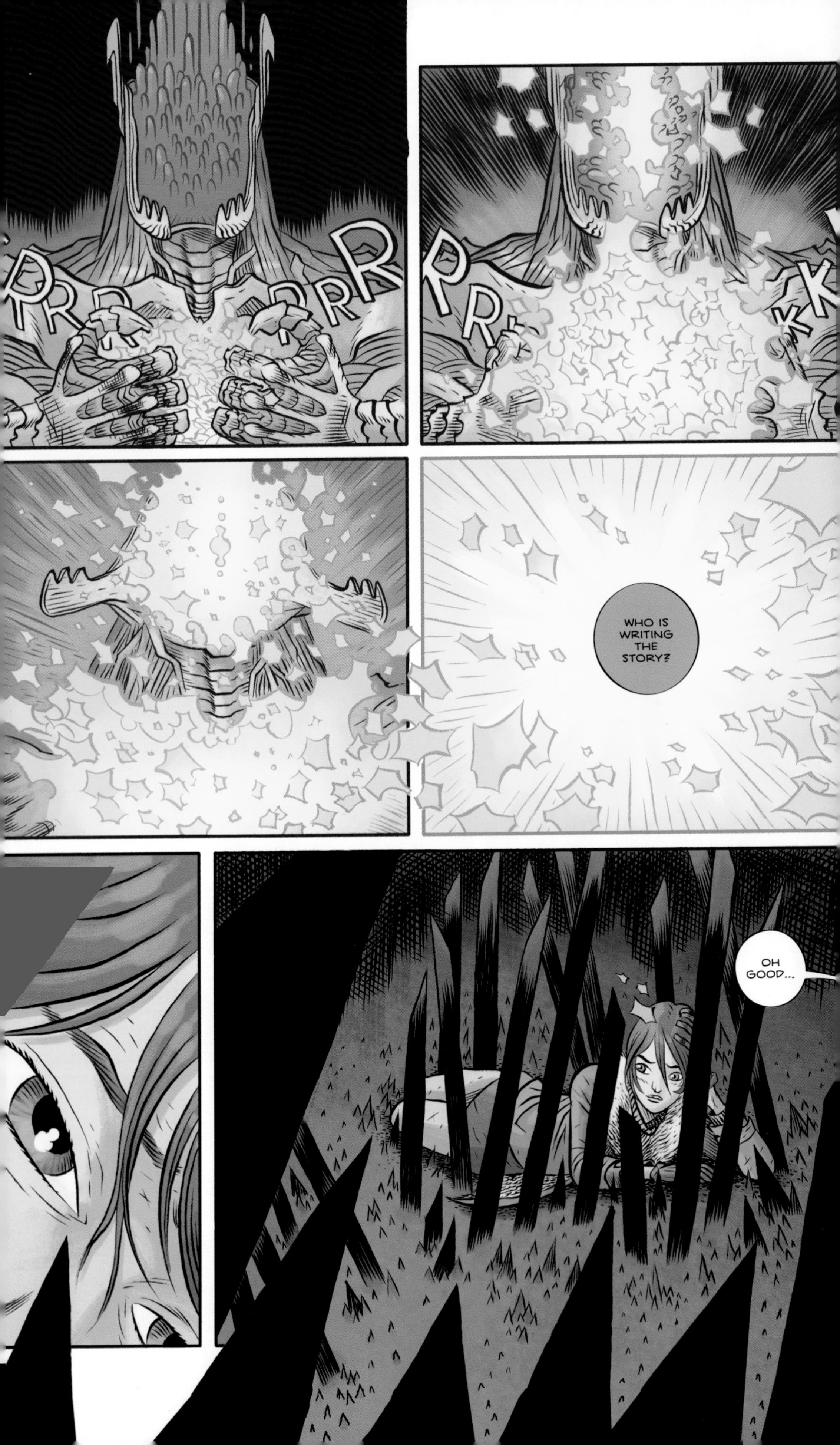
RRRRRRR
RRKKK
WHO IS WRITING THE STORY?
OH GOOD...

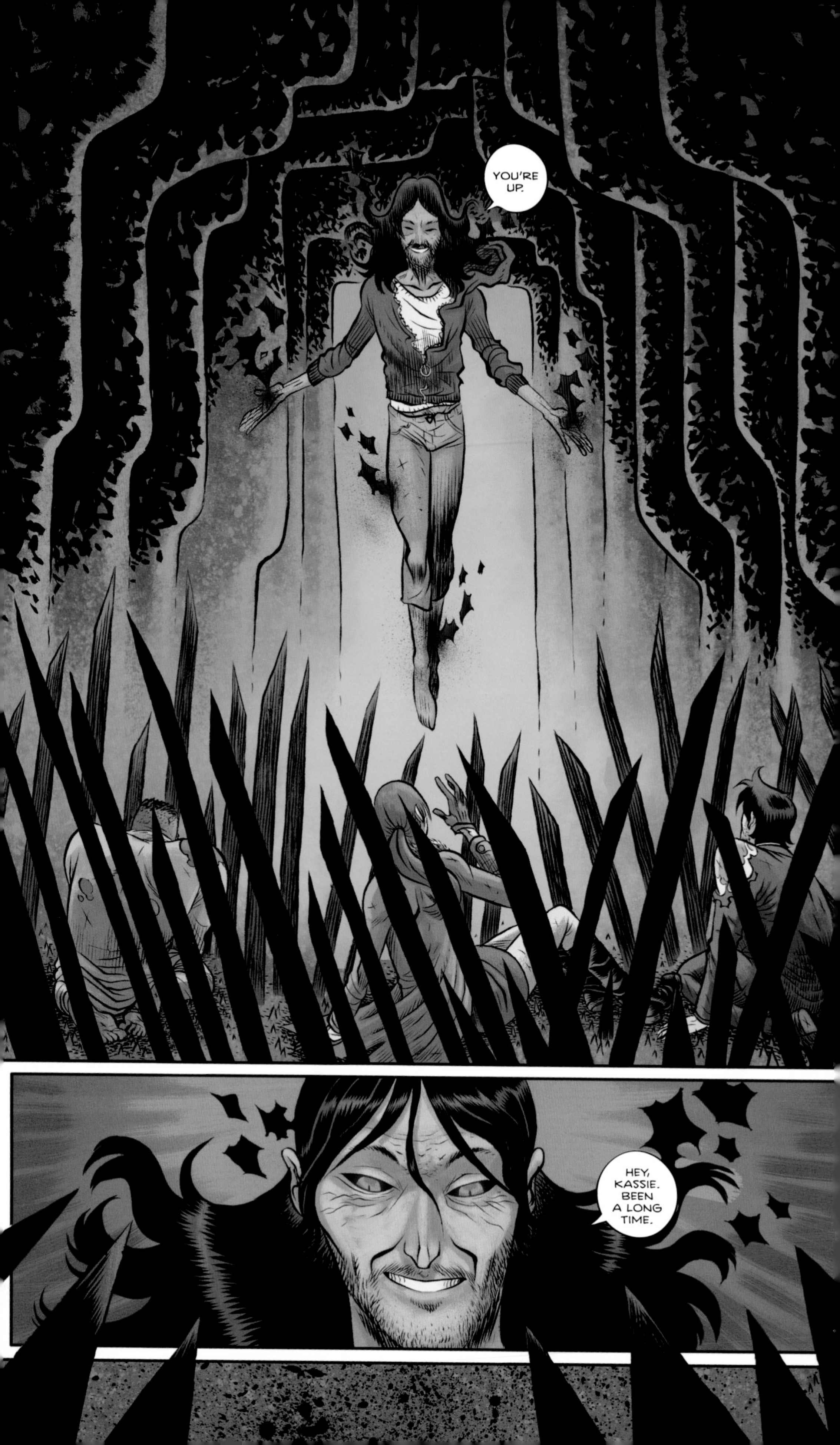
YOU'RE UP.
HEY, KASSIE. BEEN A LONG TIME.

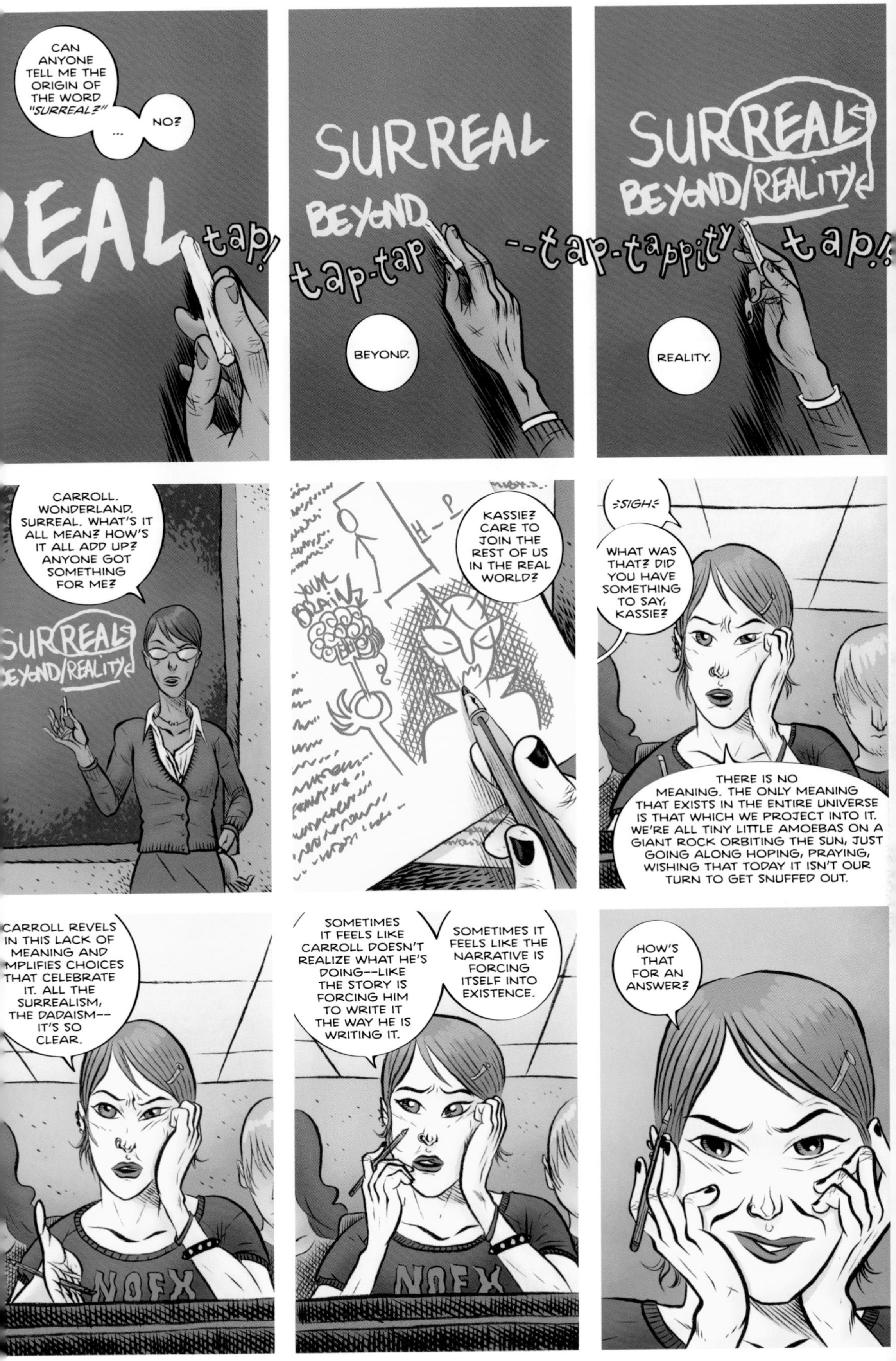
CAN ANYONE TELL ME THE ORIGIN OF THE WORD "SURREAL?"
...
NO?
REAL
tap!
SURREAL
BEYOND
tap-tap
BEYOND.
--tap-tappity
SURREAL
BEYOND/REALITY
tap!
REALITY.
CARROLL. WONDERLAND. SURREAL. WHAT'S IT ALL MEAN? HOW'S IT ALL ADD UP? ANYONE GOT SOMETHING FOR ME?
SURREAL BEYOND/REALITY
KASSIE? CARE TO JOIN THE REST OF US IN THE REAL WORLD?
YOUR BRAINZ
SIGH
WHAT WAS THAT? DID YOU HAVE SOMETHING TO SAY, KASSIE?
THERE IS NO MEANING. THE ONLY MEANING THAT EXISTS IN THE ENTIRE UNIVERSE IS THAT WHICH WE PROJECT INTO IT. WE'RE ALL TINY LITTLE AMOEBAS ON A GIANT ROCK ORBITING THE SUN, JUST GOING ALONG HOPING, PRAYING, WISHING THAT TODAY IT ISN'T OUR TURN TO GET SNUFFED OUT.
CARROLL REVELS IN THIS LACK OF MEANING AND MPLIFIES CHOICES THAT CELEBRATE IT. ALL THE SURREALISM, THE DADAISM-- IT'S SO CLEAR.
NOFX
SOMETIMES IT FEELS LIKE CARROLL DOESN'T REALIZE WHAT HE'S DOING--LIKE THE STORY IS FORCING HIM TO WRITE IT THE WAY HE IS WRITING IT.
SOMETIMES IT FEELS LIKE THE NARRATIVE IS FORCING ITSELF INTO EXISTENCE.
NOFX
HOW'S THAT FOR AN ANSWER?

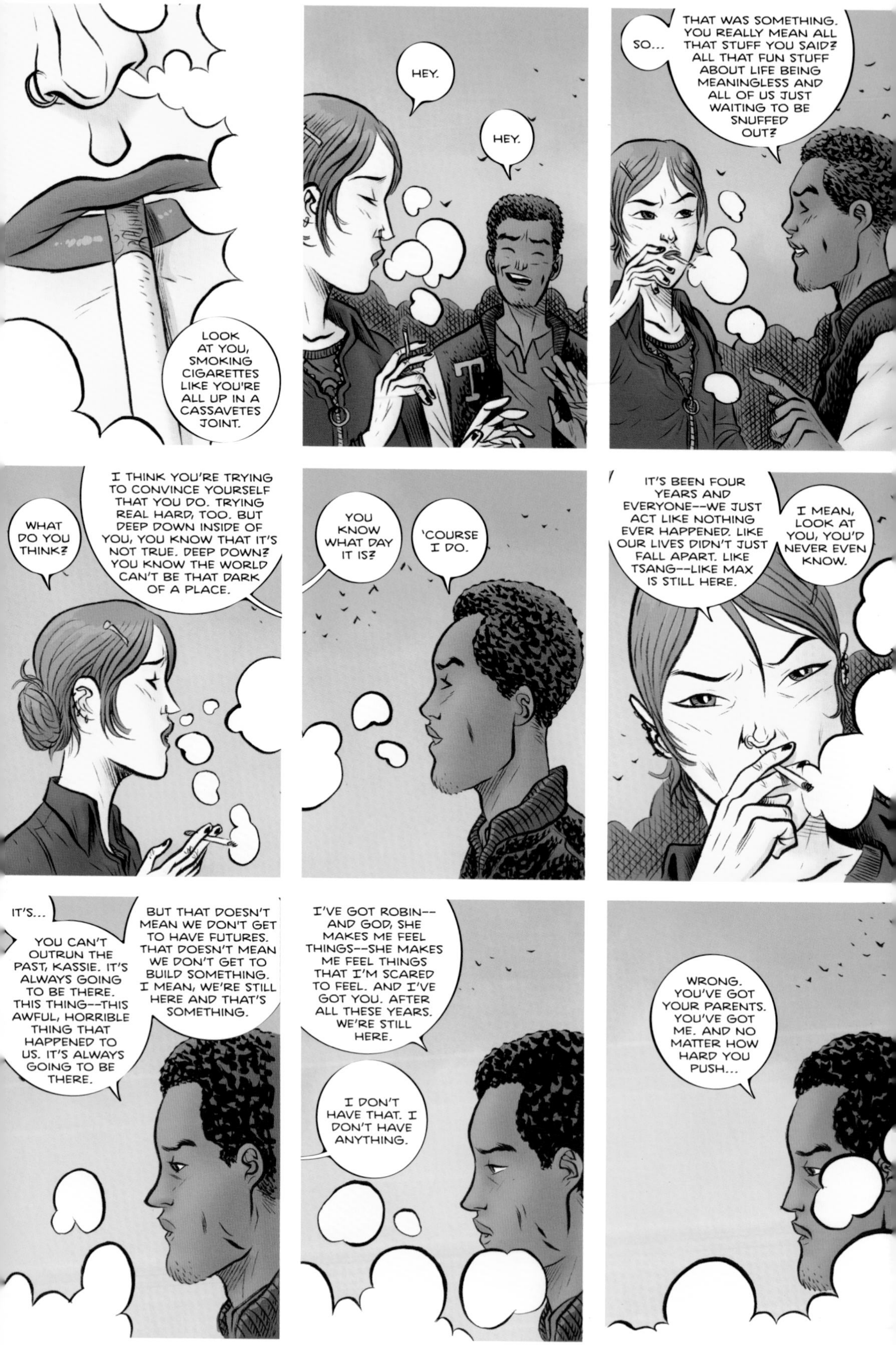
LOOK AT YOU, SMOKING CIGARETTES LIKE YOU'RE ALL UP IN A CASSAVETES JOINT.
HEY.
HEY.
SO...
THAT WAS SOMETHING. YOU REALLY MEAN ALL THAT STUFF YOU SAID? ALL THAT FUN STUFF ABOUT LIFE BEING MEANINGLESS AND ALL OF US JUST WAITING TO BE SNUFFED OUT?
WHAT DO YOU THINK?
I THINK YOU'RE TRYING TO CONVINCE YOURSELF THAT YOU DO. TRYING REAL HARD, TOO. BUT DEEP DOWN INSIDE OF YOU, YOU KNOW THAT IT'S NOT TRUE. DEEP DOWN? YOU KNOW THE WORLD CAN'T BE THAT DARK OF A PLACE.
YOU KNOW WHAT DAY IT IS?
'COURSE I DO.
IT'S BEEN FOUR YEARS AND EVERYONE--WE JUST ACT LIKE NOTHING EVER HAPPENED. LIKE OUR LIVES DIDN'T JUST FALL APART. LIKE TSANG--LIKE MAX IS STILL HERE.
I MEAN, LOOK AT YOU, YOU'D NEVER EVEN KNOW.
IT'S...
YOU CAN'T OUTRUN THE PAST, KASSIE. IT'S ALWAYS GOING TO BE THERE. THIS THING--THIS AWFUL, HORRIBLE THING THAT HAPPENED TO US. IT'S ALWAYS GOING TO BE THERE.
BUT THAT DOESN'T MEAN WE DON'T GET TO HAVE FUTURES. THAT DOESN'T MEAN WE DON'T GET TO BUILD SOMETHING. I MEAN, WE'RE STILL HERE AND THAT'S SOMETHING.
I'VE GOT ROBIN-- AND GOD, SHE MAKES ME FEEL THINGS--SHE MAKES ME FEEL THINGS THAT I'M SCARED TO FEEL. AND I'VE GOT YOU. AFTER ALL THESE YEARS. WE'RE STILL HERE.
I DON'T HAVE THAT. I DON'T HAVE ANYTHING.
WRONG. YOU'VE GOT YOUR PARENTS. YOU'VE GOT ME. AND NO MATTER HOW HARD YOU PUSH...

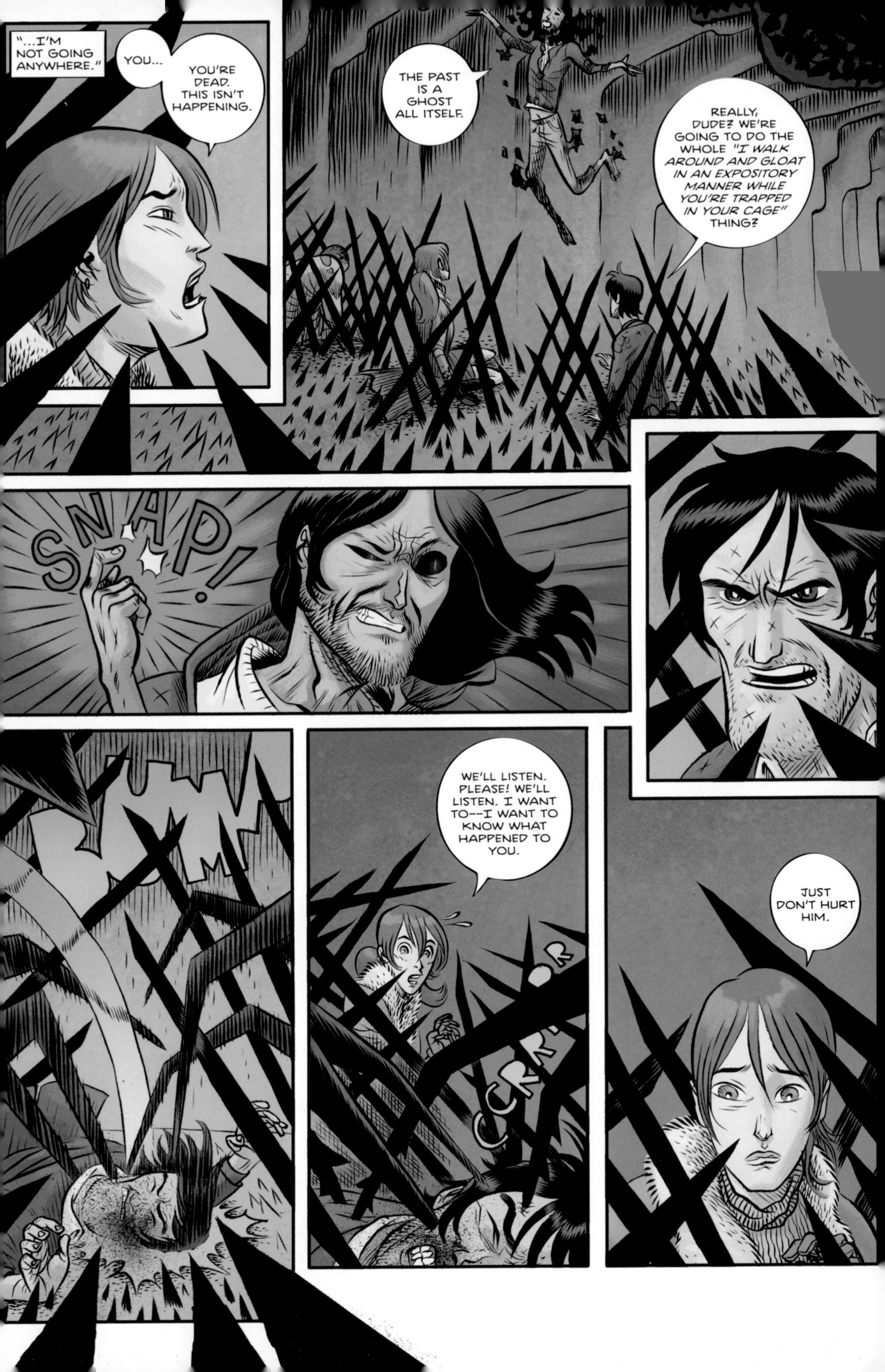
"...I'M NOT GOING ANYWHERE."
YOU...
YOU'RE DEAD. THIS ISN'T HAPPENING.
THE PAST IS A GHOST ALL ITSELF.
REALLY, DUDE? WE'RE GOING TO DO THE WHOLE "I WALK AROUND AND GLOAT IN AN EXPOSITORY MANNER WHILE YOU'RE TRAPPED IN YOUR CAGE" THING?
SNAP!
WE'LL LISTEN. PLEASE! WE'LL LISTEN. I WANT TO--I WANT TO KNOW WHAT HAPPENED TO YOU.
CRR
JUST DON'T HURT HIM.

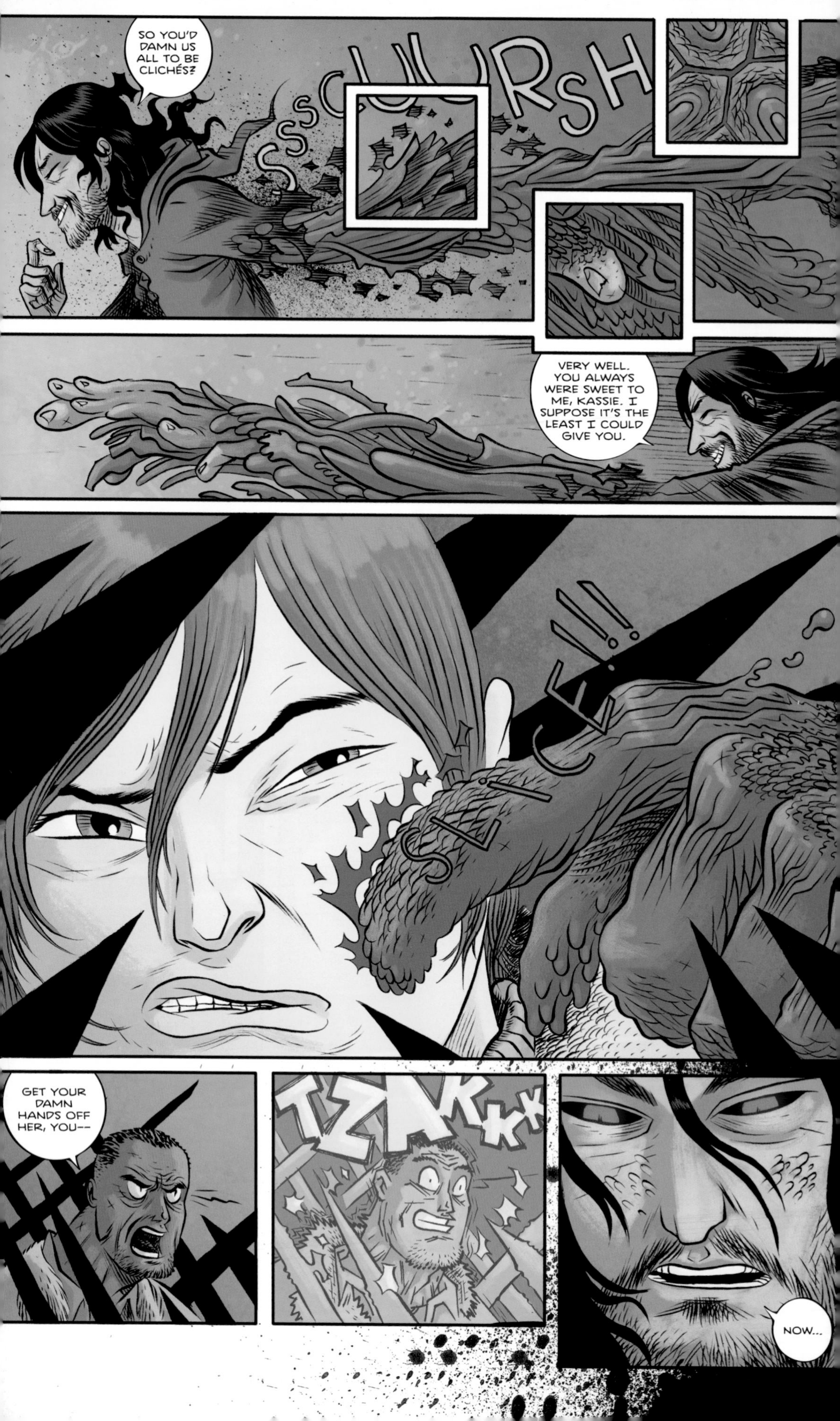
SO YOU'D DAMN US ALL TO BE CLICHÉS?
SSSCUURSH
VERY WELL. YOU ALWAYS WERE SWEET TO ME, KASSIE. I SUPPOSE IT'S THE LEAST I COULD GIVE YOU.
SLICE!!!
GET YOUR DAMN HANDS OFF HER, YOU--
TZAKKK
NOW...

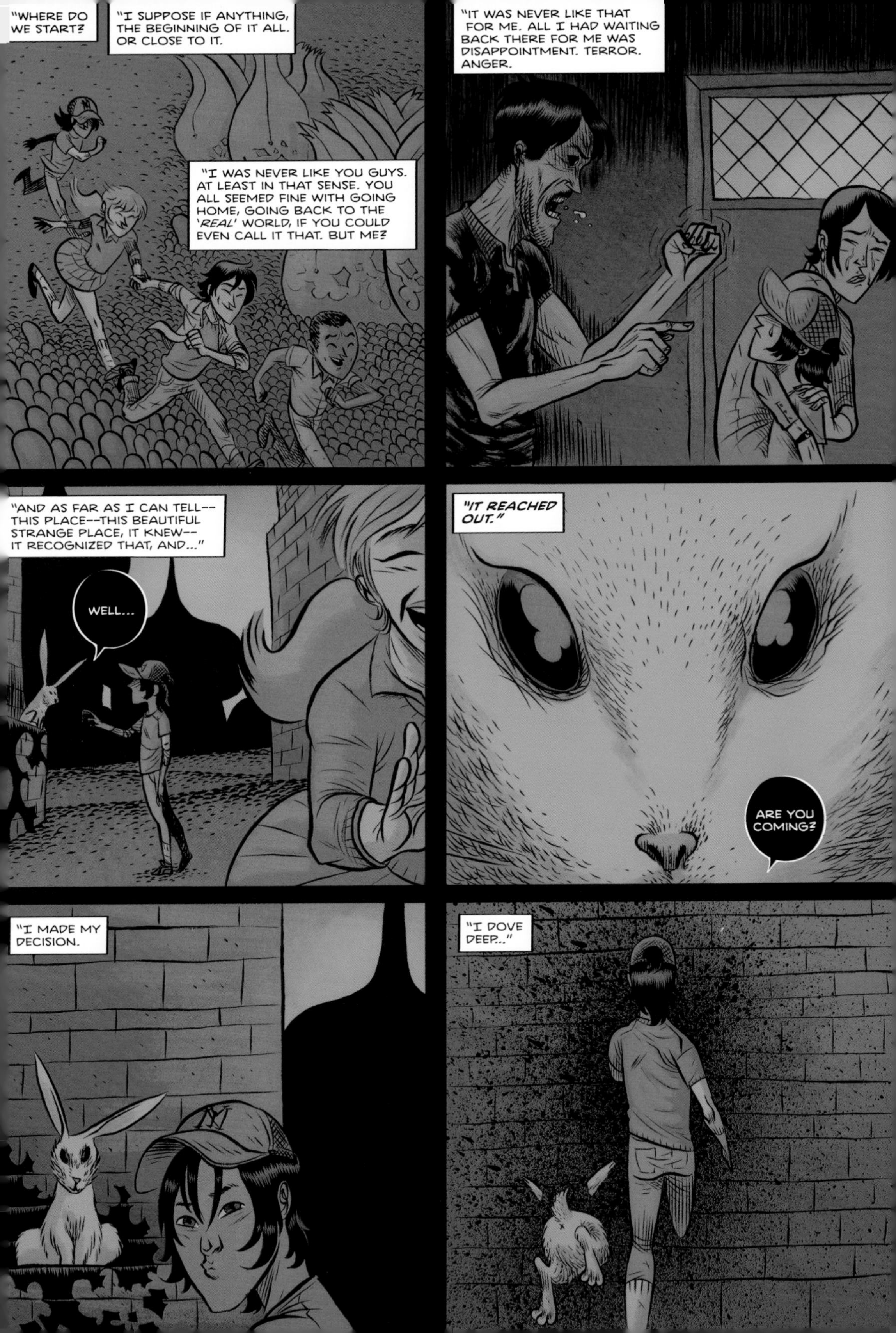
"WHERE DO WE START?
"I SUPPOSE IF ANYTHING, THE BEGINNING OF IT ALL. OR CLOSE TO IT.
"I WAS NEVER LIKE YOU GUYS. AT LEAST IN THAT SENSE. YOU ALL SEEMED FINE WITH GOING HOME, GOING BACK TO THE 'REAL' WORLD, IF YOU COULD EVEN CALL IT THAT. BUT ME?
"IT WAS NEVER LIKE THAT FOR ME. ALL I HAD WAITING BACK THERE FOR ME WAS DISAPPOINTMENT. TERROR. ANGER.
"AND AS FAR AS I CAN TELL-- THIS PLACE--THIS BEAUTIFUL STRANGE PLACE, IT KNEW-- IT RECOGNIZED THAT, AND..."
WELL...
"IT REACHED OUT."
ARE YOU COMING?
"I MADE MY DECISION.
"I DOVE DEEP..."

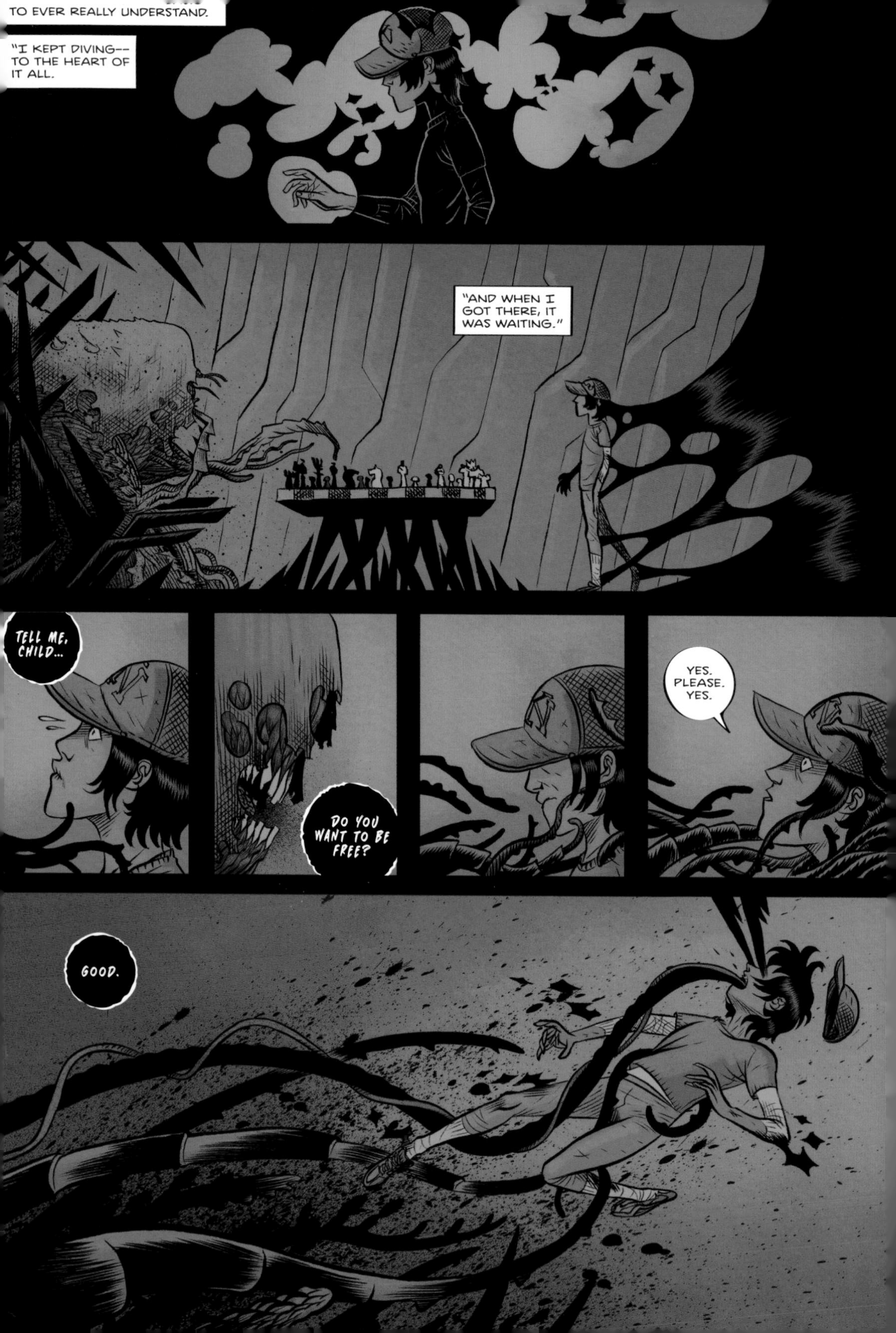
TO EVER REALLY UNDERSTAND.
"I KEPT DIVING-- TO THE HEART OF IT ALL.
"AND WHEN I GOT THERE, IT WAS WAITING."
TELL ME, CHILD...
DO YOU WANT TO BE FREE?
YES. PLEASE. YES.
GOOD.

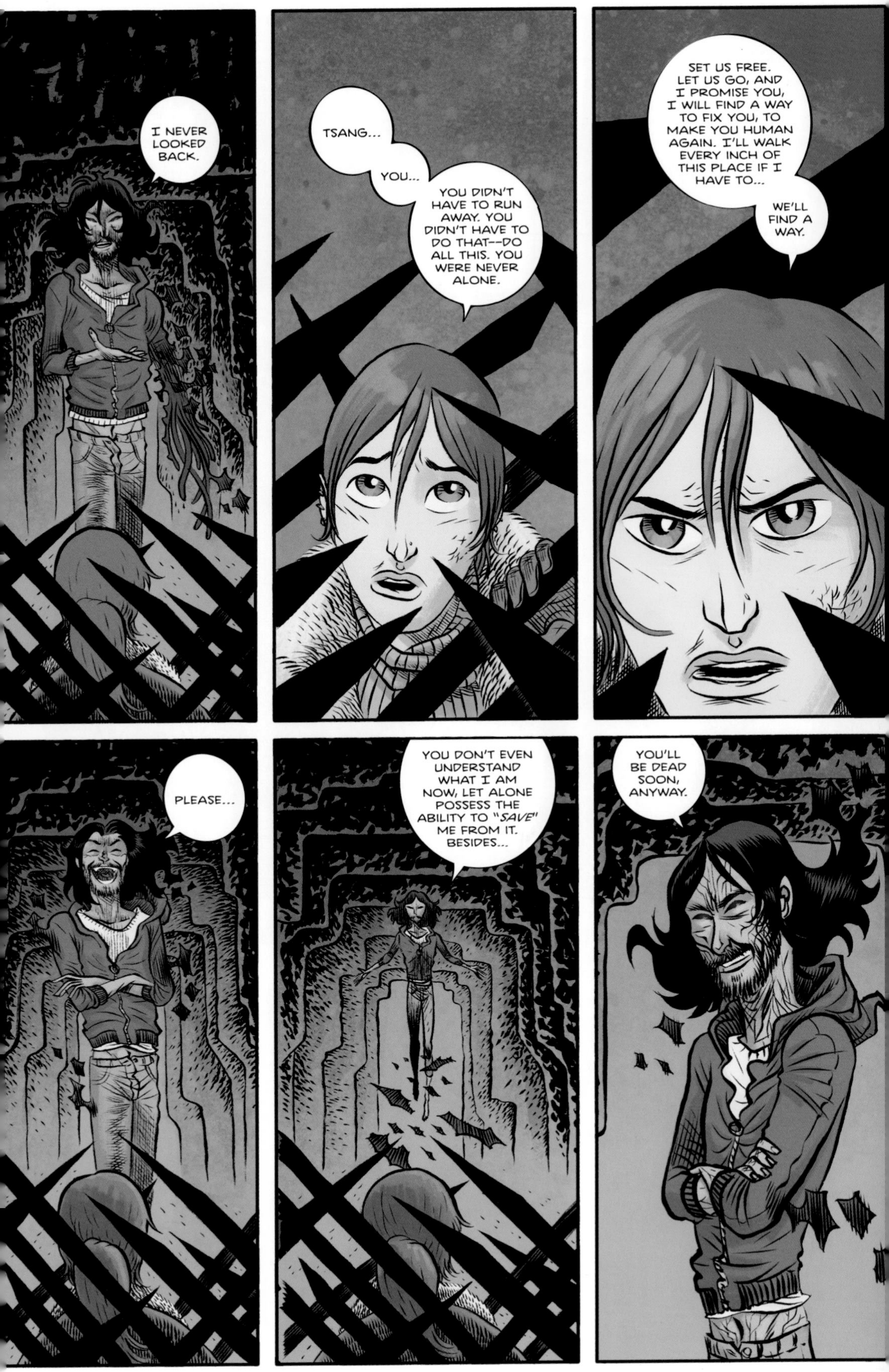
I NEVER LOOKED BACK.
TSANG...
YOU...
YOU DIDN'T HAVE TO RUN AWAY. YOU DIDN'T HAVE TO DO THAT--DO ALL THIS. YOU WERE NEVER ALONE.
SET US FREE. LET US GO, AND I PROMISE YOU, I WILL FIND A WAY TO FIX YOU, TO MAKE YOU HUMAN AGAIN. I'LL WALK EVERY INCH OF THIS PLACE IF I HAVE TO...
WE'LL FIND A WAY.
PLEASE...
YOU DON'T EVEN UNDERSTAND WHAT I AM NOW, LET ALONE POSSESS THE ABILITY TO "*SAVE*" ME FROM IT. BESIDES...
YOU'LL BE DEAD SOON, ANYWAY.

PICK
DAD
00-421-533
tut-
tut-
tut-
tut-
tut-
tut-
tut-
tut-
tut-
tut-
tut-
--
PICK
PICK
PICK
tut-
tut-
tut-
CRACK

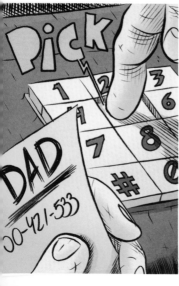

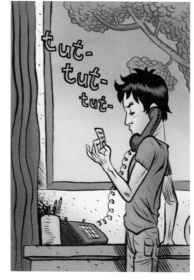

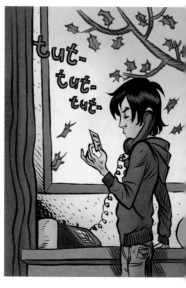

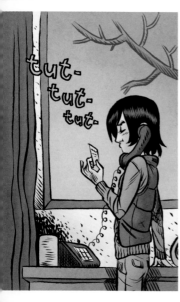

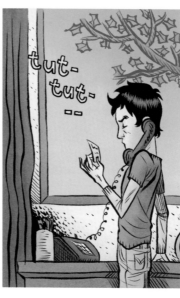

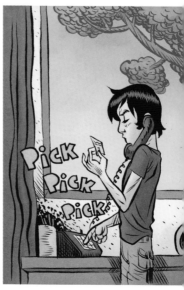

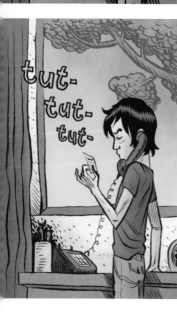

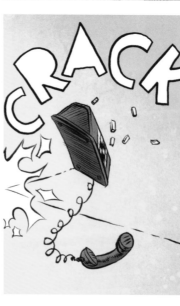

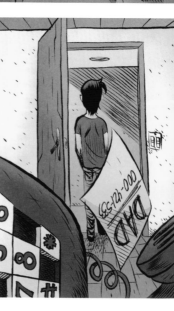

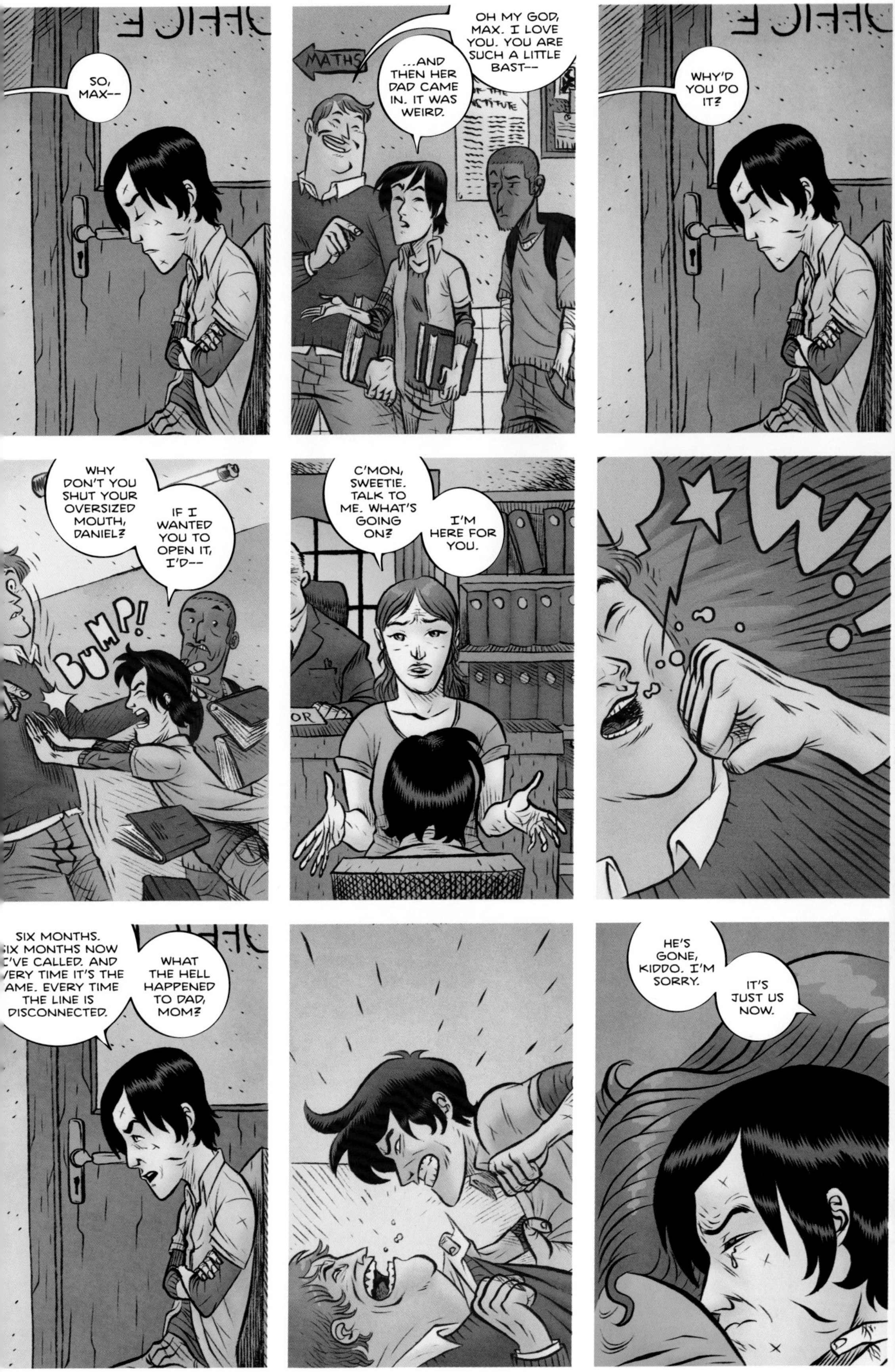
SO, MAX--
MATHS
...AND THEN HER DAD CAME IN. IT WAS WEIRD.
OH MY GOD, MAX. I LOVE YOU. YOU ARE SUCH A LITTLE BAST--
WHY'D YOU DO IT?
WHY DON'T YOU SHUT YOUR OVERSIZED MOUTH, DANIEL?
IF I WANTED YOU TO OPEN IT, I'D--
BUMP!
C'MON, SWEETIE. TALK TO ME. WHAT'S GOING ON?
I'M HERE FOR YOU.
SIX MONTHS. IX MONTHS NOW 'VE CALLED. AND VERY TIME IT'S THE AME. EVERY TIME THE LINE IS DISCONNECTED.
WHAT THE HELL HAPPENED TO DAD, MOM?
HE'S GONE, KIDDO. I'M SORRY.
IT'S JUST US NOW.

SO THE OTHER TWO HAVE BEEN CAPTURED?

YES. THEY CAME AFTER THE FIRST, JUST AS I THOUGHT THEY WOULD.

GOOD. LET'S HOPE THEIR DEATH--OR RATHER, THE POSSIBILITY OF-- IS ENOUGH TO LURE HIM OUT. HE ALWAYS WAS FOND OF HUMANS.

LISTEN TO ME. "HE."

HE. SHE. IT. TAKE YOUR PICK. IF THERE'S ONE THING I'M CERTAIN OF IN THIS GAME WE'VE BEEN PLAYING, IT'S THAT ALL SYSTEMS ARE FLUID.

ALL IDENTITY IS MALLEABLE. WHEN IT COMES DOWN TO IT...

TAP!!!

THE ONLY THING THAT POSSESSES MEANING IS THE INHERENT LACK OF MEANING ITSELF. AT THE CENTER OF EVERYTHING THERE IS NOTHING--A GAPING VOID IN THE CENTER OF FOREVER. THE ANTITHESIS OF EVERY NARRATIVE EVER ASSEMBLED.

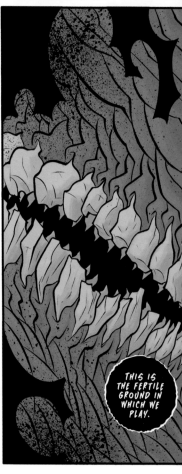

THIS IS THE FERTILE GROUND IN WHICH WE PLAY.

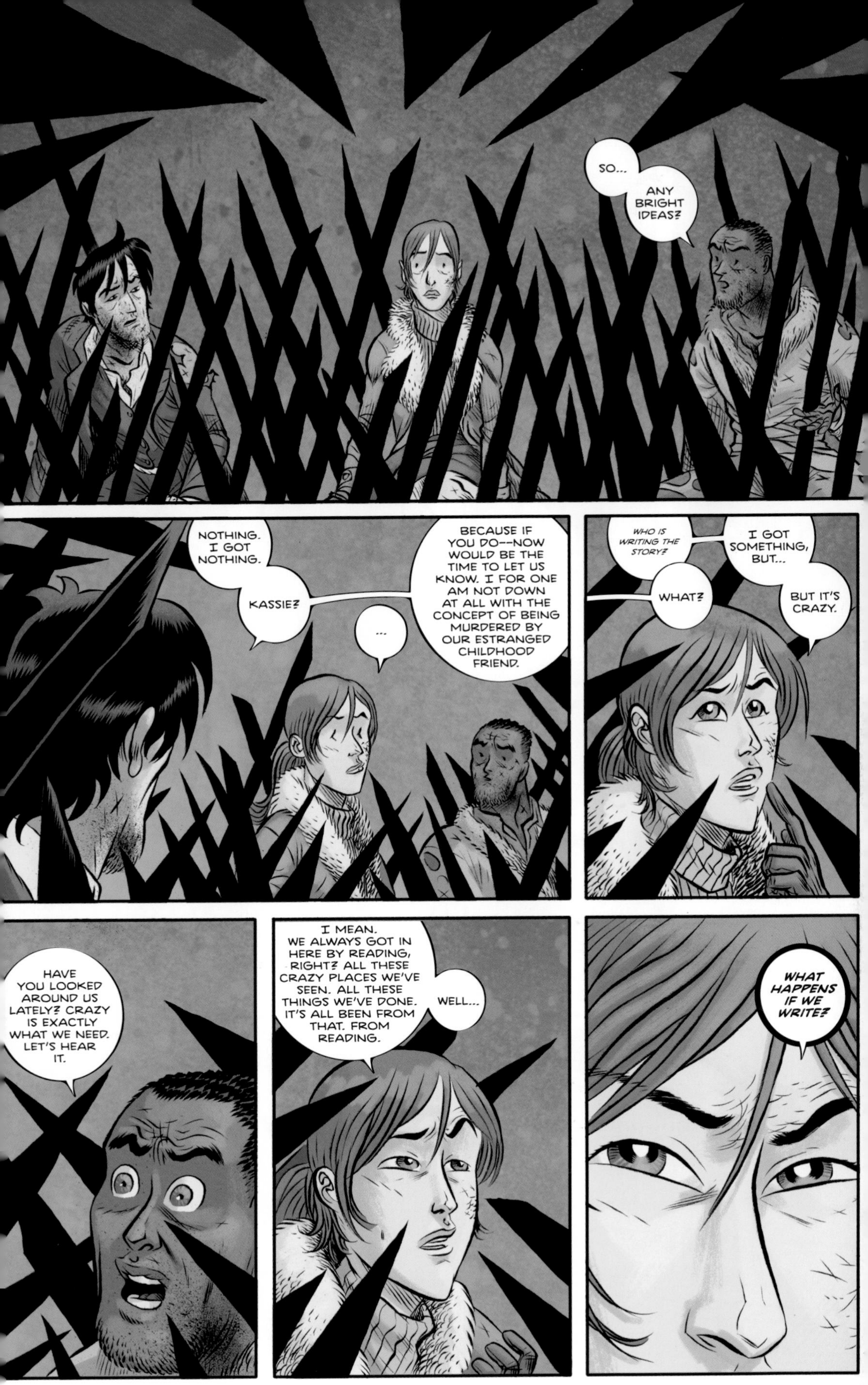
SO...
ANY BRIGHT IDEAS?
NOTHING. I GOT NOTHING.
KASSIE?
BECAUSE IF YOU DO--NOW WOULD BE THE TIME TO LET US KNOW. I FOR ONE AM NOT DOWN AT ALL WITH THE CONCEPT OF BEING MURDERED BY OUR ESTRANGED CHILDHOOD FRIEND.
...
WHO IS WRITING THE STORY?
I GOT SOMETHING, BUT...
WHAT?
BUT IT'S CRAZY.
HAVE YOU LOOKED AROUND US LATELY? CRAZY IS EXACTLY WHAT WE NEED. LET'S HEAR IT.
I MEAN. WE ALWAYS GOT IN HERE BY READING, RIGHT? ALL THESE CRAZY PLACES WE'VE SEEN. ALL THESE THINGS WE'VE DONE. IT'S ALL BEEN FROM THAT. FROM READING.
WELL...
WHAT HAPPENS IF WE WRITE?

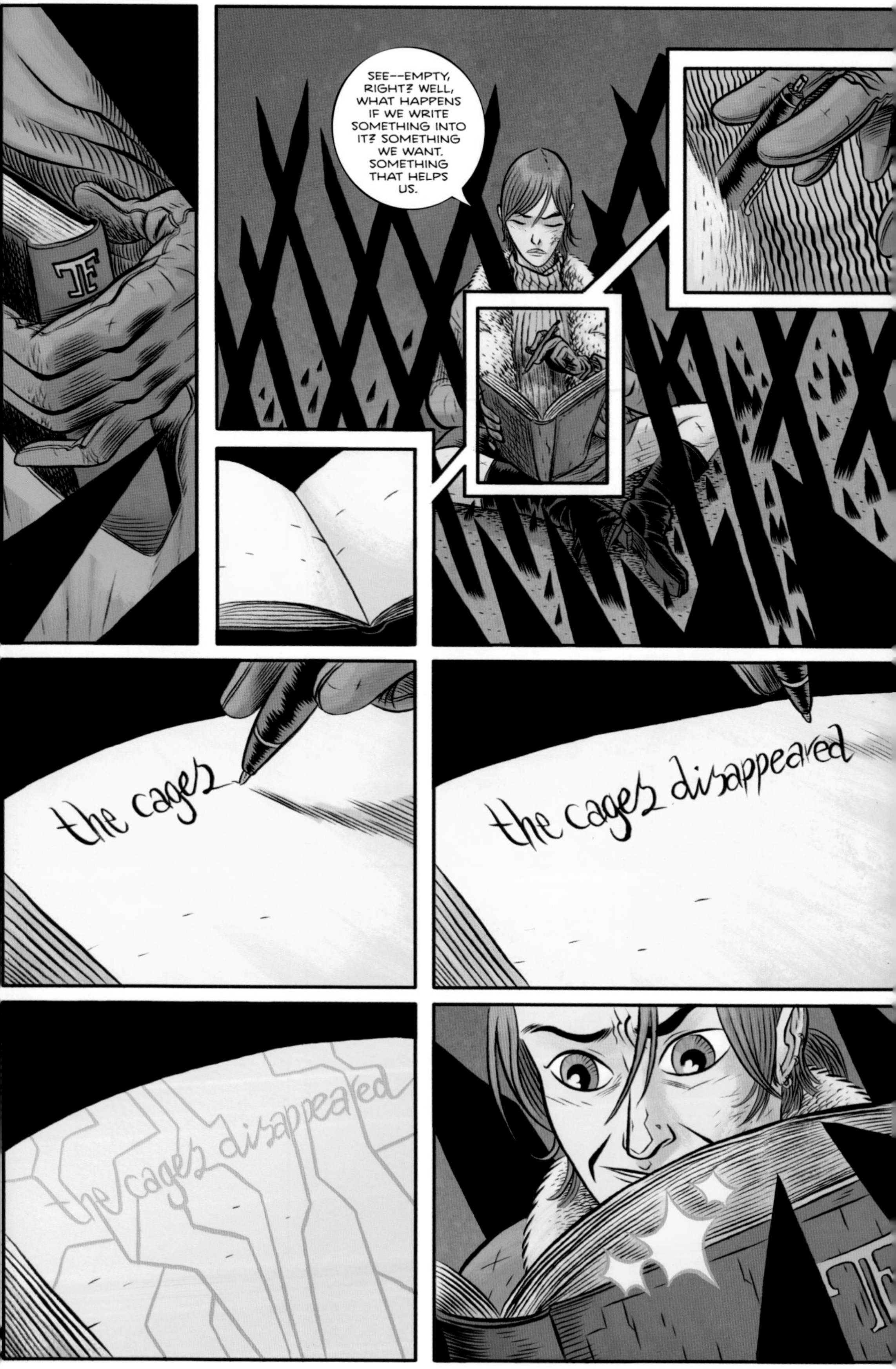
SEE--EMPTY, RIGHT? WELL, WHAT HAPPENS IF WE WRITE SOMETHING INTO IT? SOMETHING WE WANT. SOMETHING THAT HELPS US.
the cages
the cages disappeared
the cages disappeared

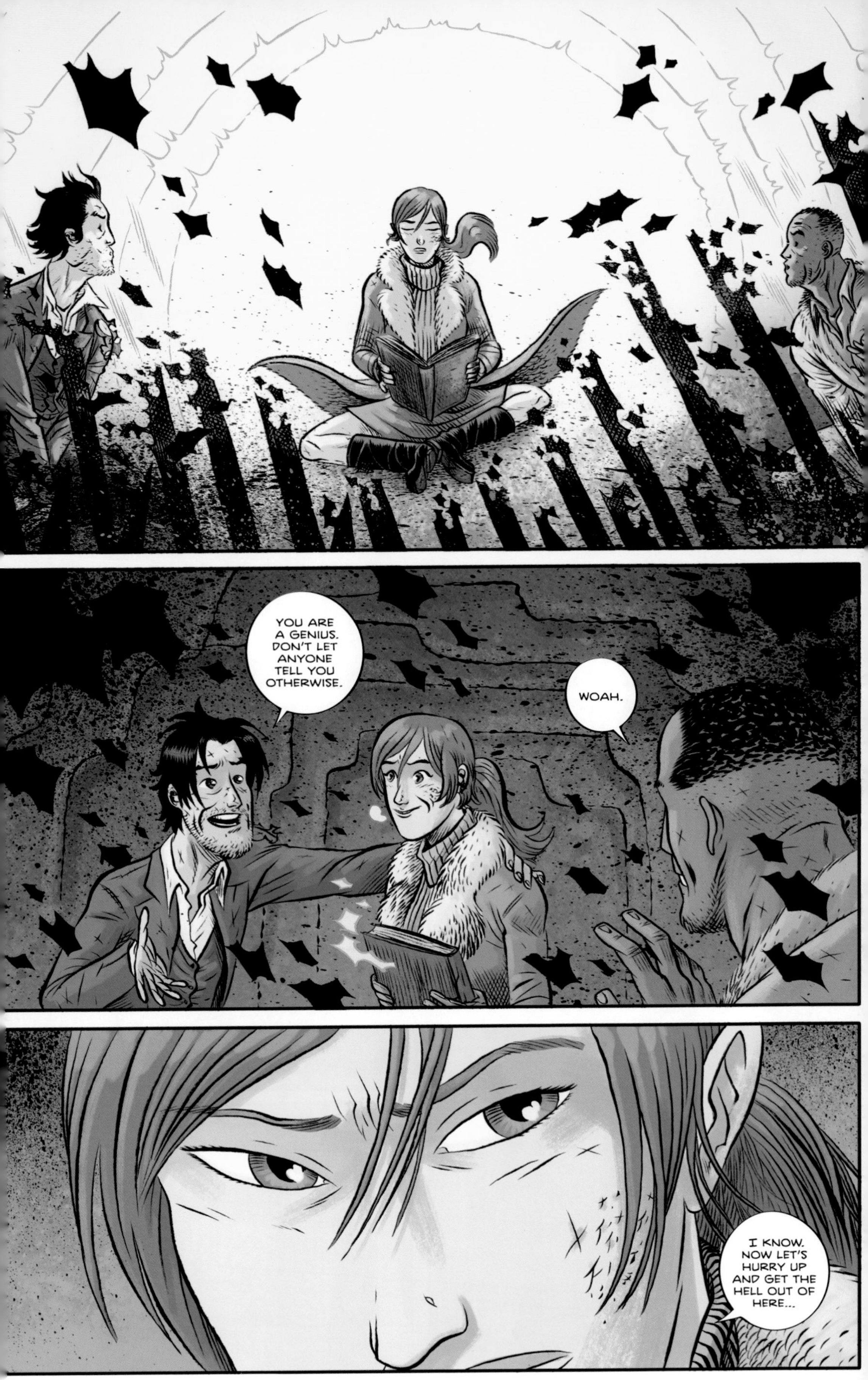
YOU ARE A GENIUS. DON'T LET ANYONE TELL YOU OTHERWISE.
WOAH.
I KNOW. NOW LET'S HURRY UP AND GET THE HELL OUT OF HERE...

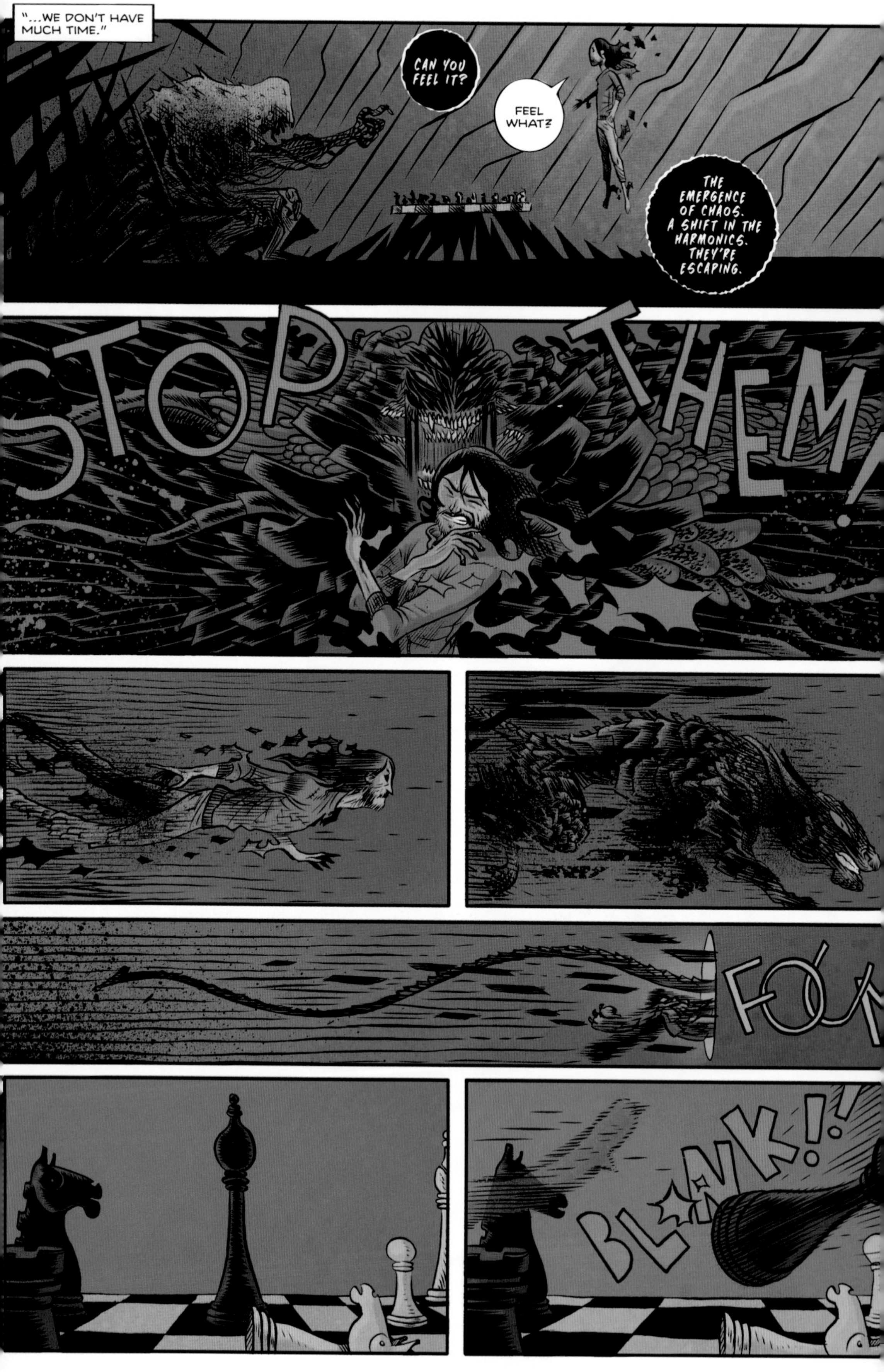
"...WE DON'T HAVE MUCH TIME."
CAN YOU FEEL IT?
FEEL WHAT?
THE EMERGENCE OF CHAOS. A SHIFT IN THE HARMONICS. THEY'RE ESCAPING.
STOP THEM!
BLANK!!

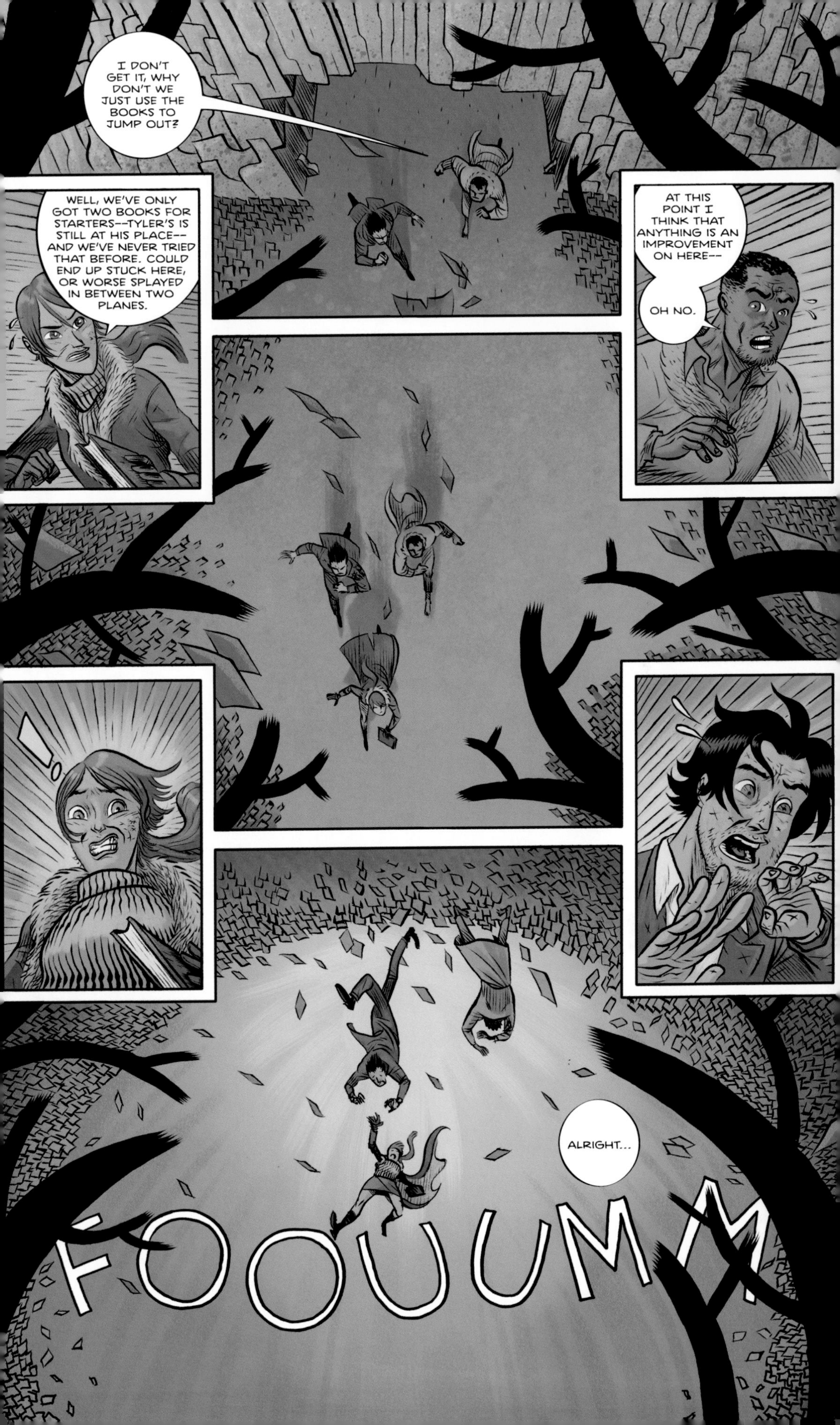
I DON'T GET IT, WHY DON'T WE JUST USE THE BOOKS TO JUMP OUT?
WELL, WE'VE ONLY GOT TWO BOOKS FOR STARTERS--TYLER'S IS STILL AT HIS PLACE--AND WE'VE NEVER TRIED THAT BEFORE. COULD END UP STUCK HERE, OR WORSE SPLAYED IN BETWEEN TWO PLANES.
AT THIS POINT I THINK THAT ANYTHING IS AN IMPROVEMENT ON HERE--
OH NO.
!
ALRIGHT...
FOOUUMM

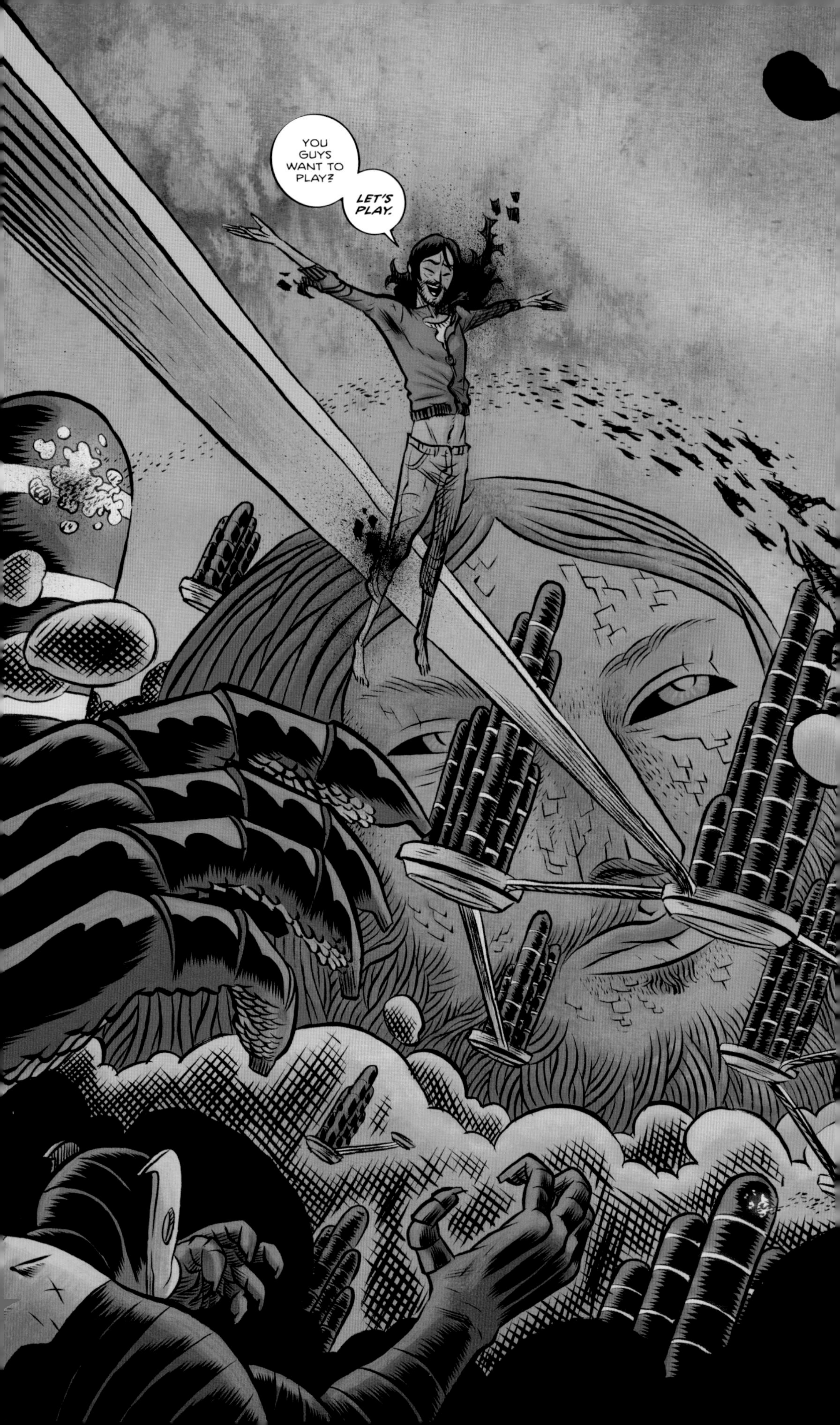
YOU GUYS WANT TO PLAY?
LET'S PLAY.

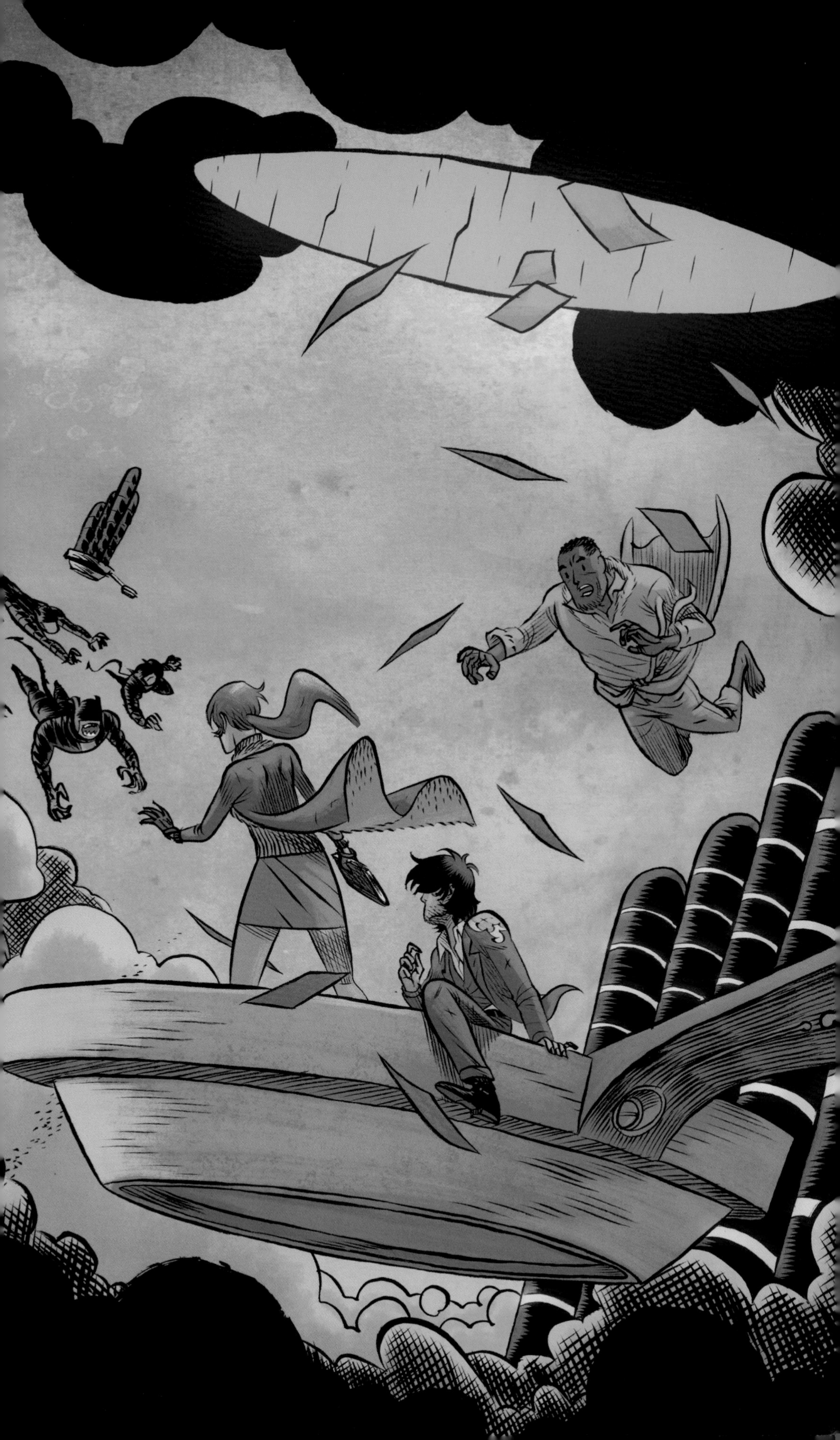

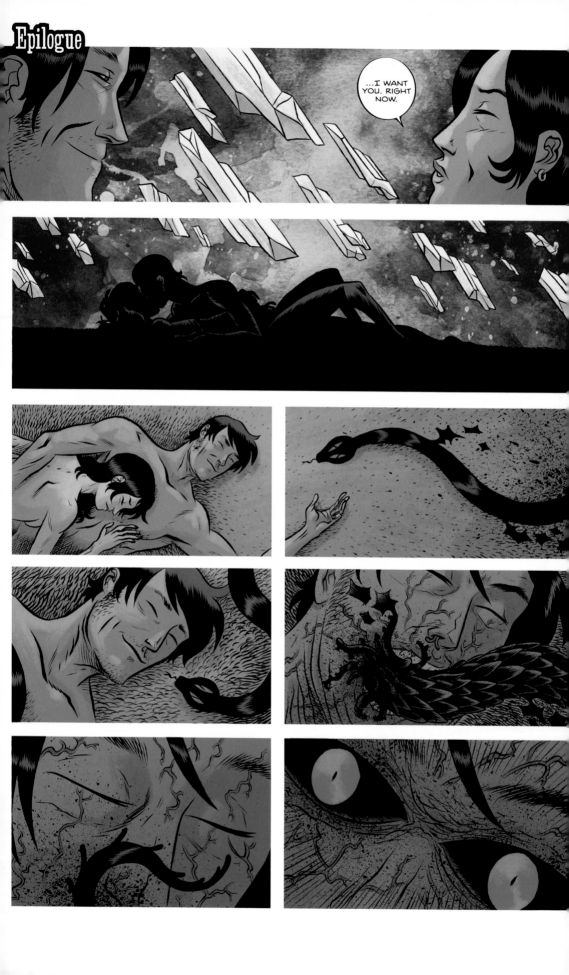

Epilogue

...I WANT YOU. RIGHT NOW.

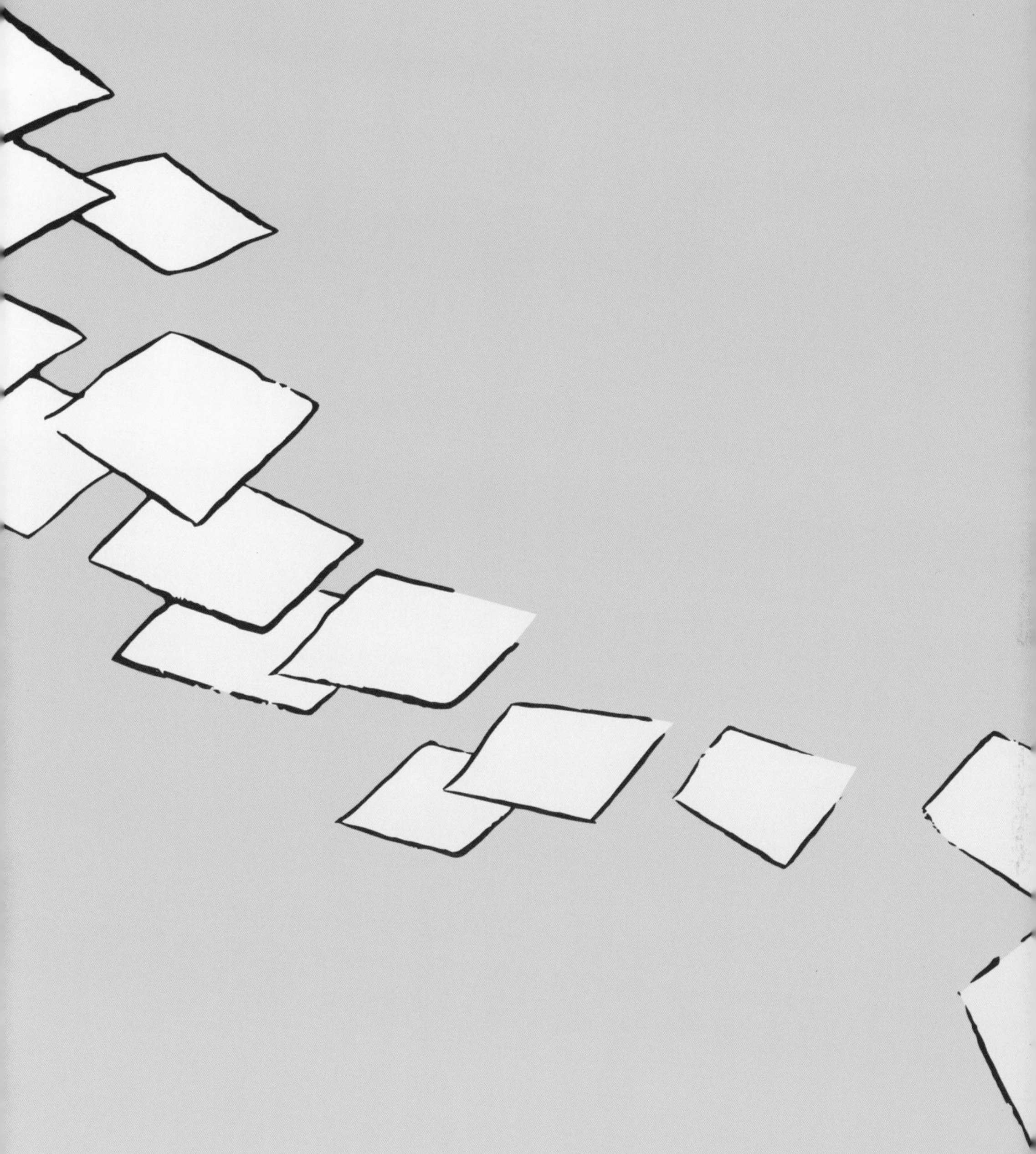

CHAPTER IV
Neverending
or
Until We Can't *(Let's Go)*

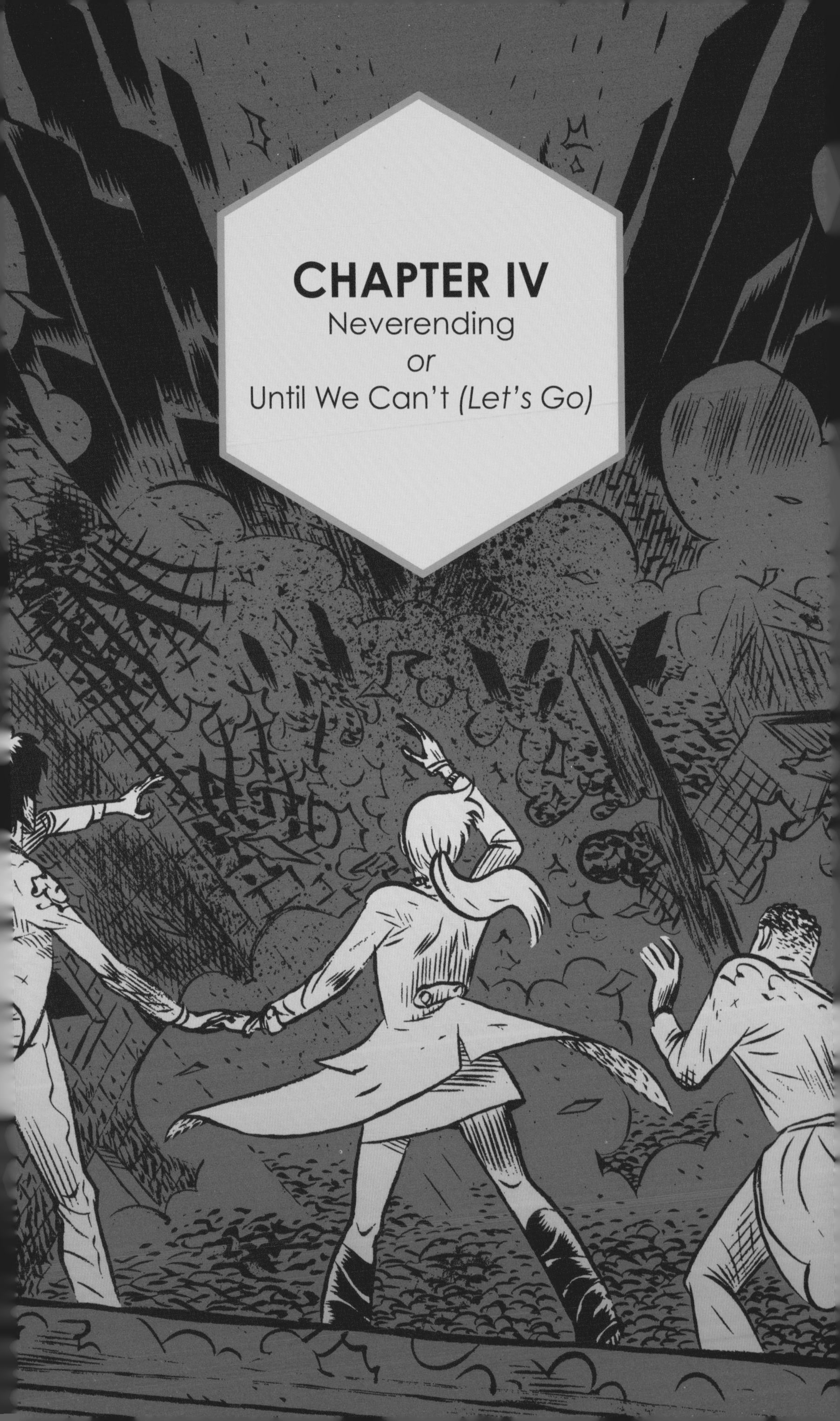

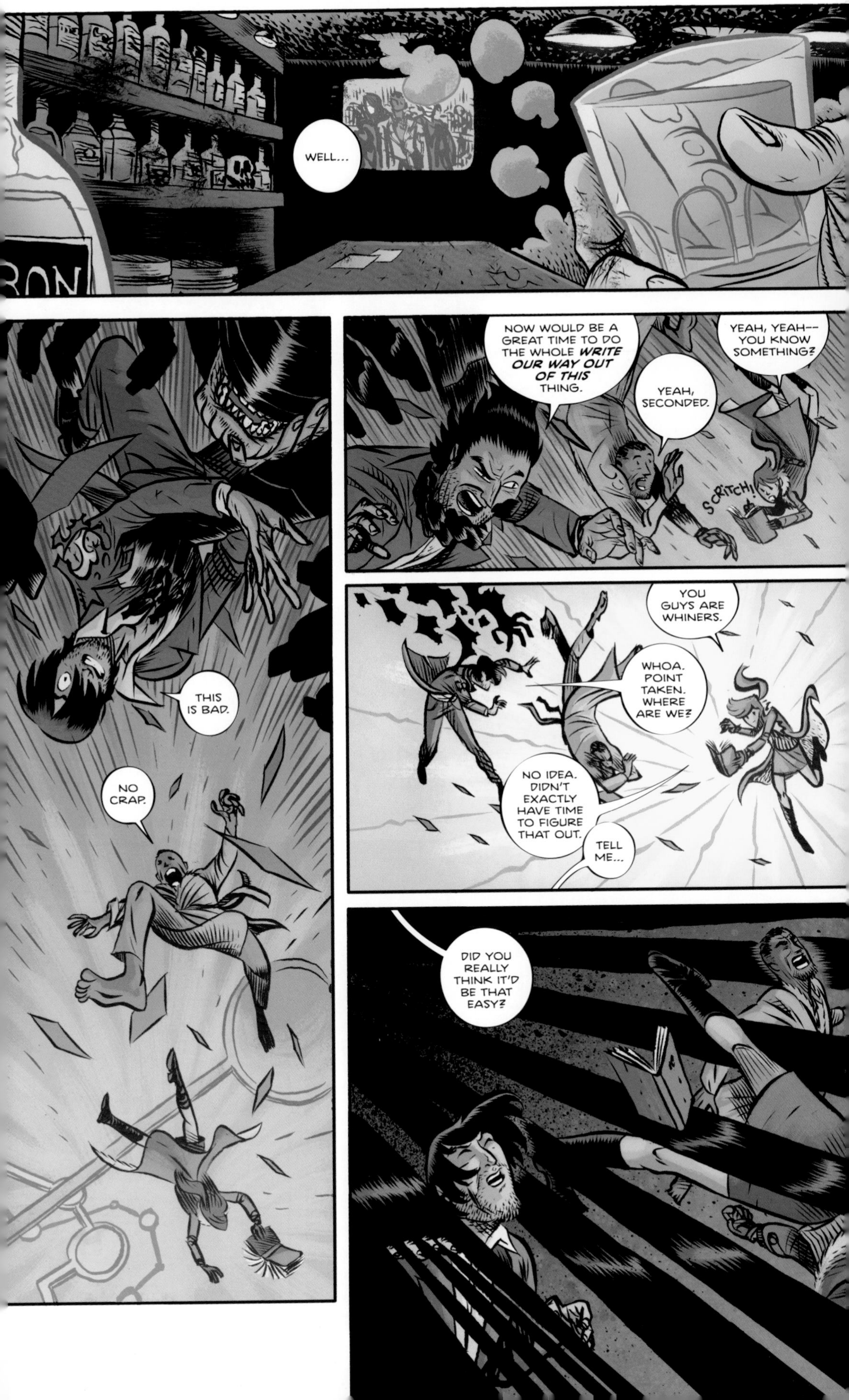

WELL...
THIS IS BAD.
NO CRAP.
NOW WOULD BE A GREAT TIME TO DO THE WHOLE ***WRITE OUR WAY OUT OF THIS*** THING.
YEAH, SECONDED.
YEAH, YEAH-- YOU KNOW SOMETHING?
SCRITCH!
YOU GUYS ARE WHINERS.
WHOA. POINT TAKEN. WHERE ARE WE?
NO IDEA. DIDN'T EXACTLY HAVE TIME TO FIGURE THAT OUT.
TELL ME...
DID YOU REALLY THINK IT'D BE THAT EASY?

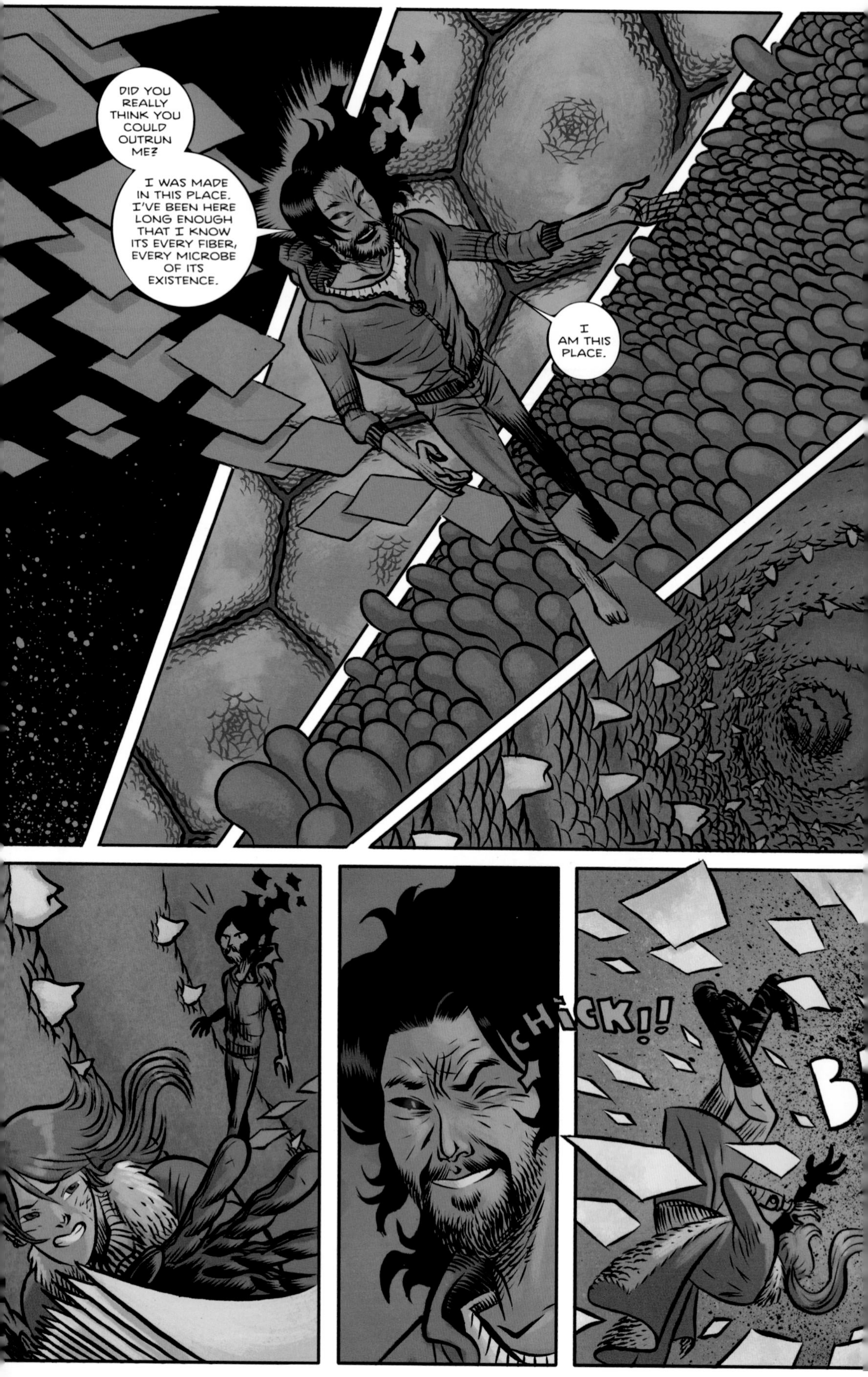
DID YOU REALLY THINK YOU COULD OUTRUN ME?
I WAS MADE IN THIS PLACE. I'VE BEEN HERE LONG ENOUGH THAT I KNOW ITS EVERY FIBER, EVERY MICROBE OF ITS EXISTENCE.
I AM THIS PLACE.
CHICK!!

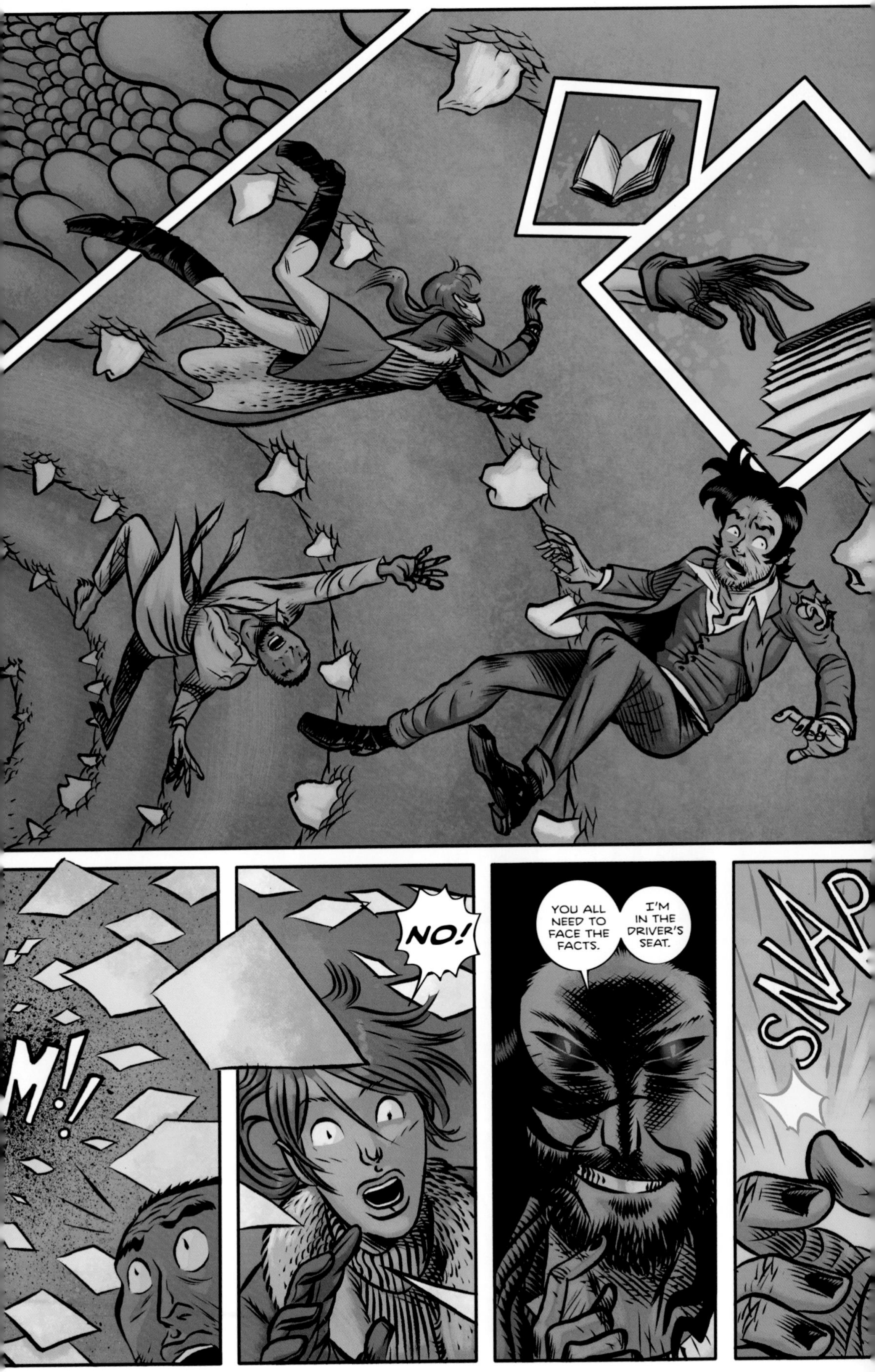

M!!
NO!
YOU ALL NEED TO FACE THE FACTS.
I'M IN THE DRIVER'S SEAT.
SNAP

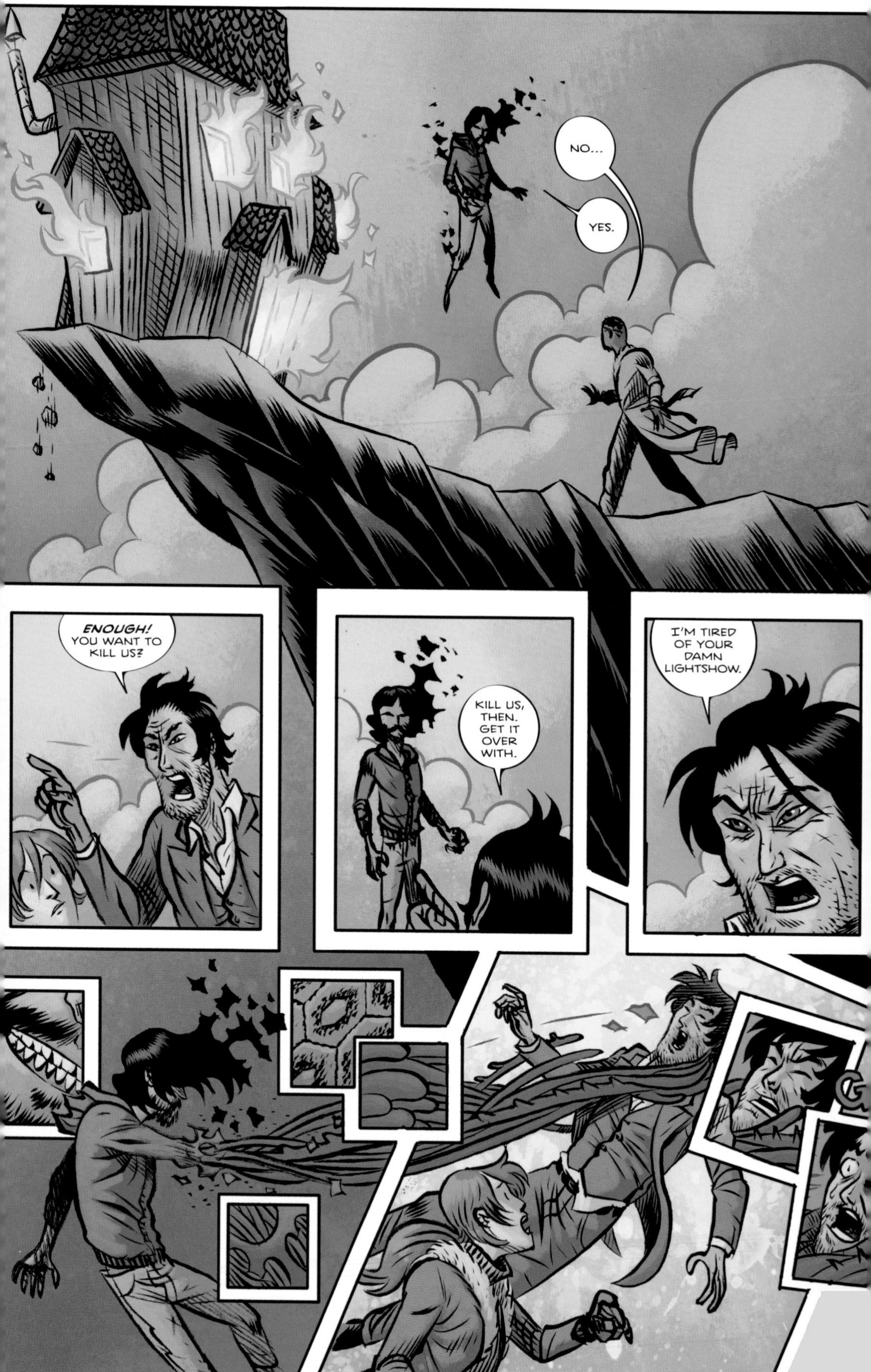

NO...
YES.
ENOUGH! YOU WANT TO KILL US?
KILL US, THEN. GET IT OVER WITH.
I'M TIRED OF YOUR DAMN LIGHTSHOW.

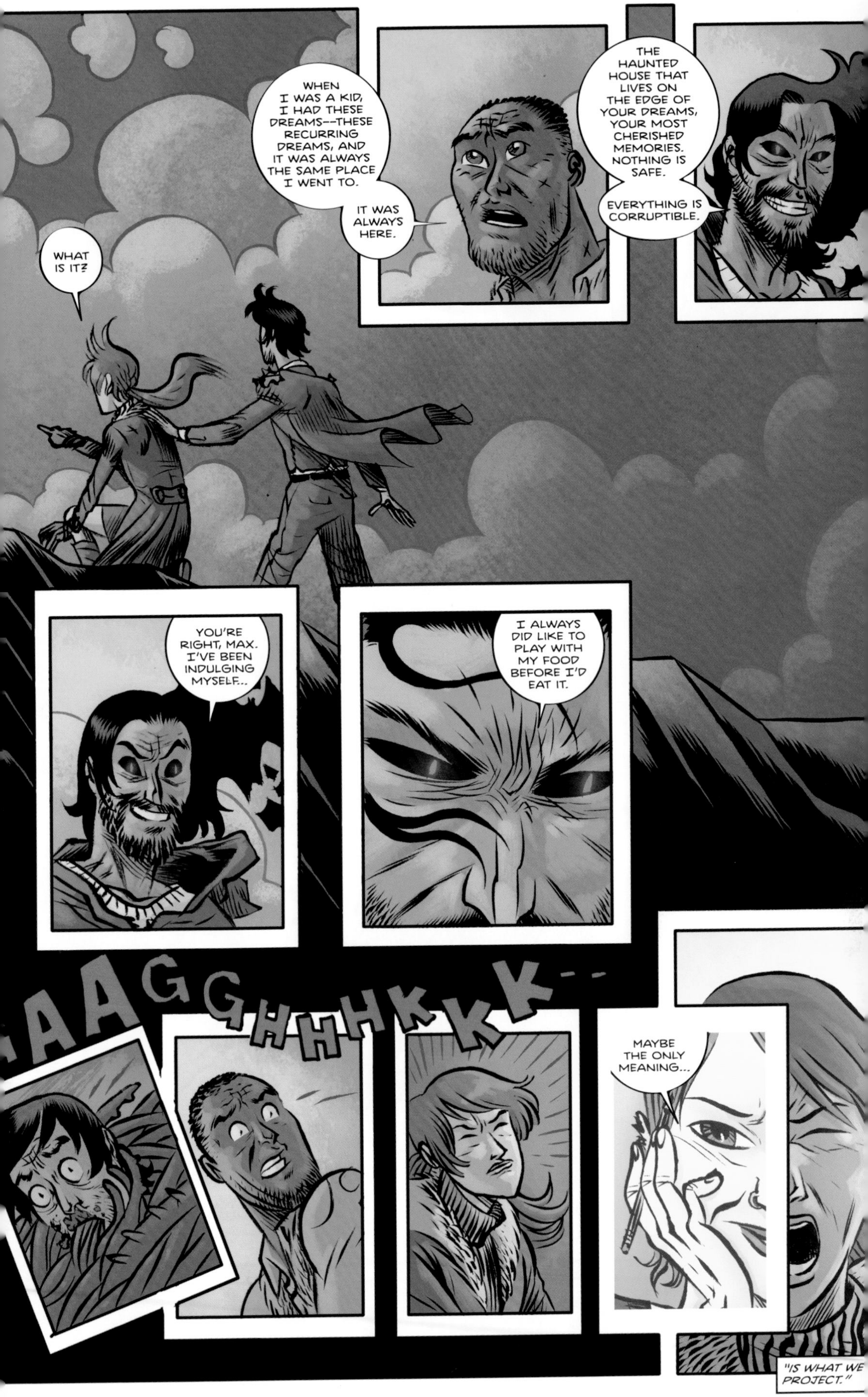

WHEN I WAS A KID, I HAD THESE DREAMS--THESE RECURRING DREAMS, AND IT WAS ALWAYS THE SAME PLACE I WENT TO.
IT WAS ALWAYS HERE.
THE HAUNTED HOUSE THAT LIVES ON THE EDGE OF YOUR DREAMS, YOUR MOST CHERISHED MEMORIES. NOTHING IS SAFE.
EVERYTHING IS CORRUPTIBLE.
WHAT IS IT?
YOU'RE RIGHT, MAX. I'VE BEEN INDULGING MYSELF...
I ALWAYS DID LIKE TO PLAY WITH MY FOOD BEFORE I'D EAT IT.
AAGGHHHKKK--
MAYBE THE ONLY MEANING...
"IS WHAT WE PROJECT."

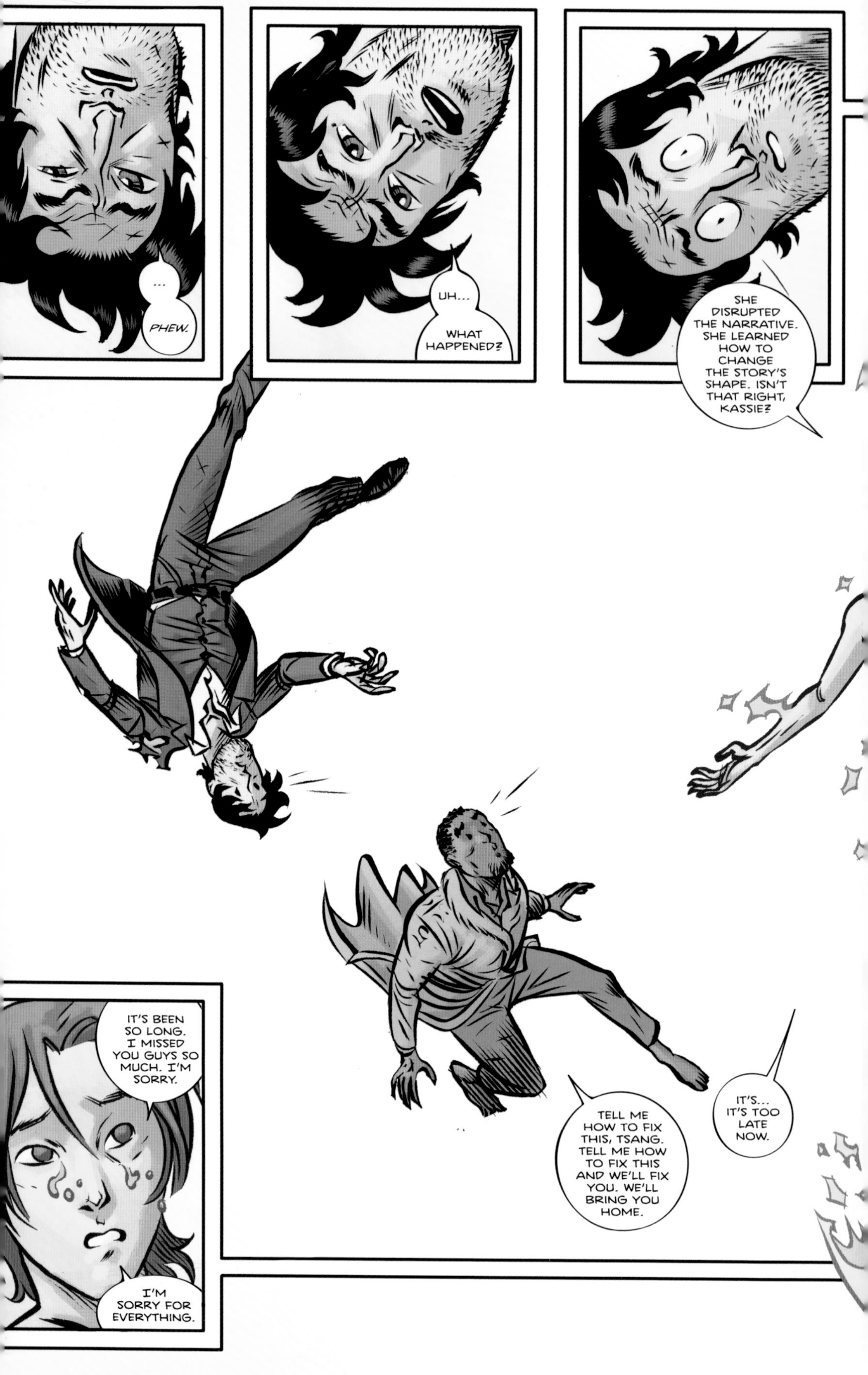
...
PHEW.
UH...
WHAT HAPPENED?
SHE DISRUPTED THE NARRATIVE. SHE LEARNED HOW TO CHANGE THE STORY'S SHAPE. ISN'T THAT RIGHT, KASSIE?
IT'S BEEN SO LONG. I MISSED YOU GUYS SO MUCH. I'M SORRY.
I'M SORRY FOR EVERYTHING.
TELL ME HOW TO FIX THIS, TSANG. TELL ME HOW TO FIX THIS AND WE'LL FIX YOU. WE'LL BRING YOU HOME.
IT'S... IT'S TOO LATE NOW.

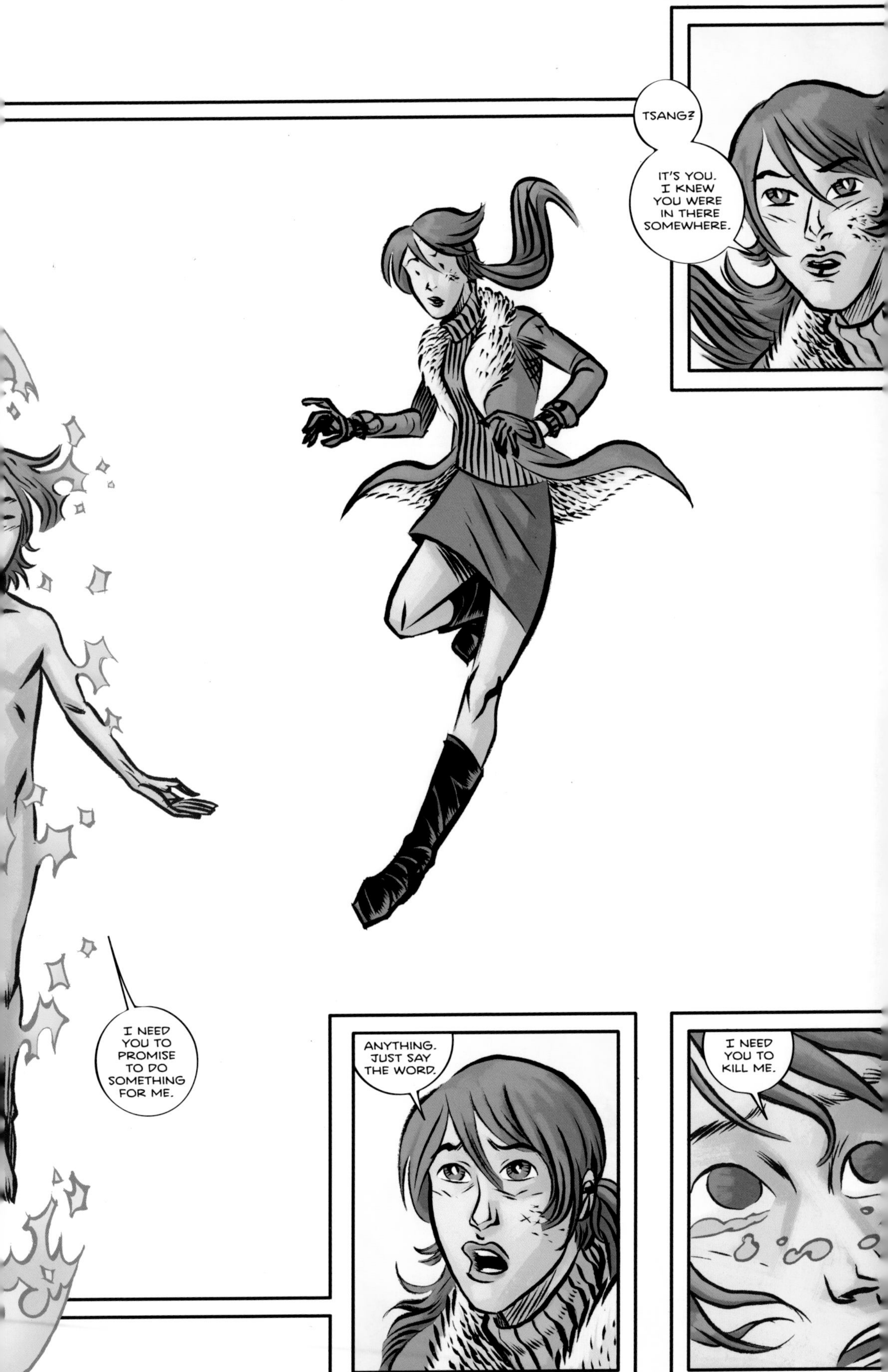
TSANG?
IT'S YOU. I KNEW YOU WERE IN THERE SOMEWHERE.
I NEED YOU TO PROMISE TO DO SOMETHING FOR ME.
ANYTHING. JUST SAY THE WORD.
I NEED YOU TO KILL ME.

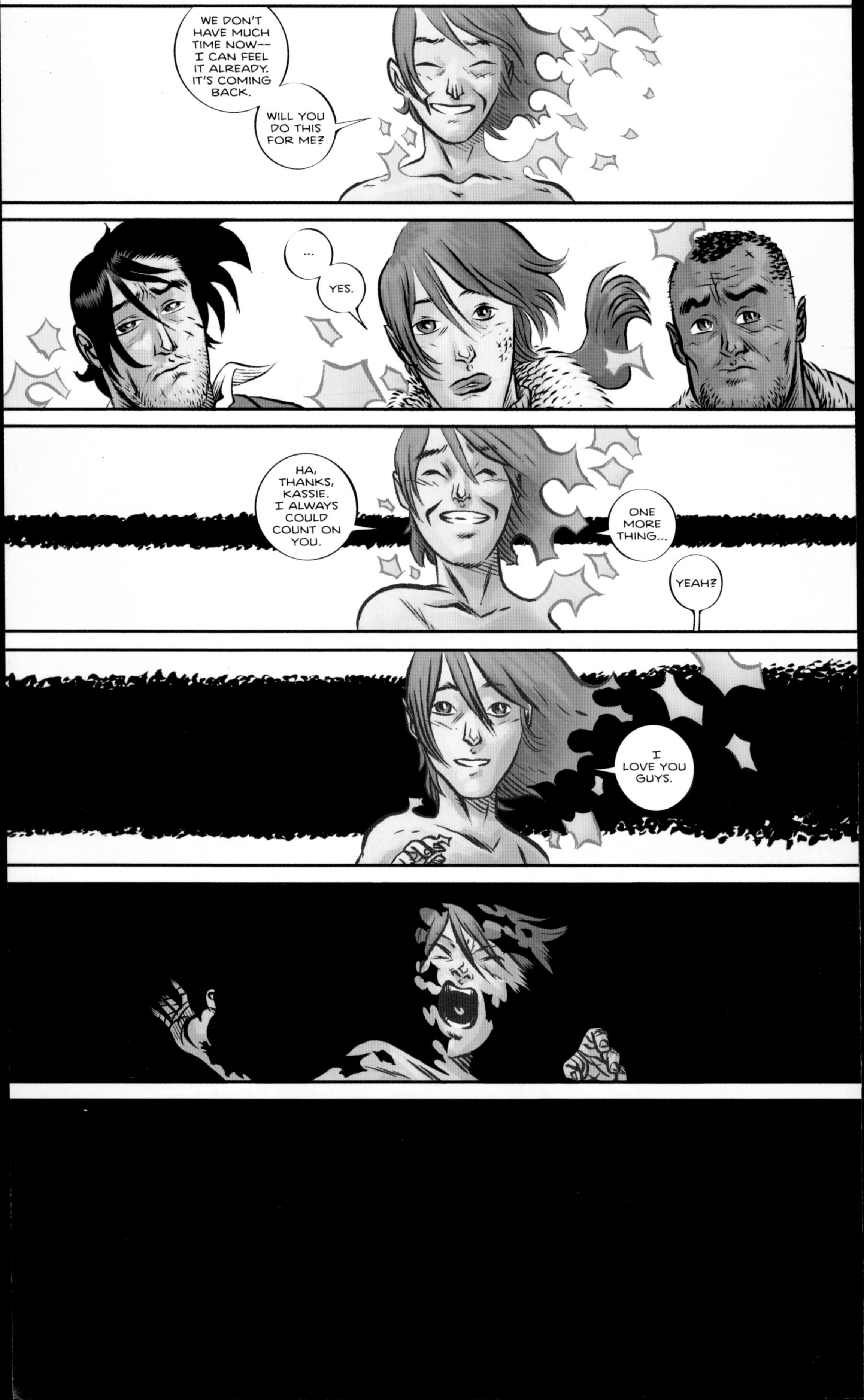
WE DON'T HAVE MUCH TIME NOW-- I CAN FEEL IT ALREADY. IT'S COMING BACK.
WILL YOU DO THIS FOR ME?
...
YES.
HA, THANKS, KASSIE. I ALWAYS COULD COUNT ON YOU.
ONE MORE THING...
YEAH?
I LOVE YOU GUYS.

FFOOUUUSSH!
TLANK!!

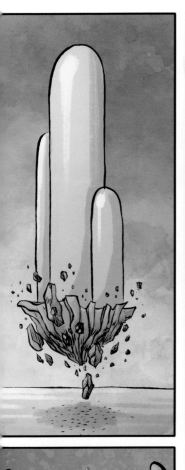

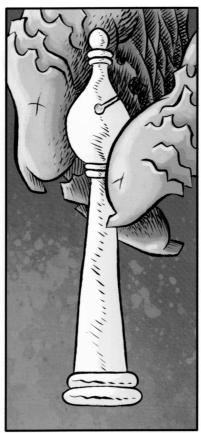

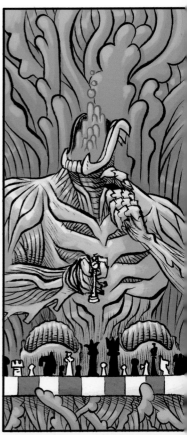

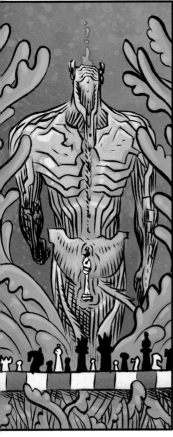

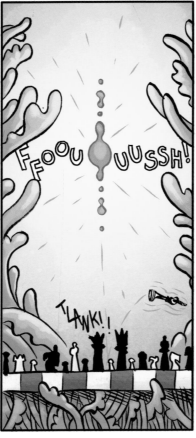

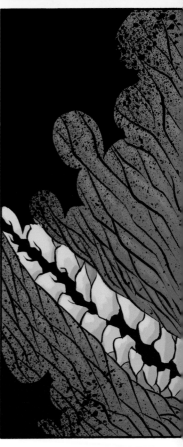

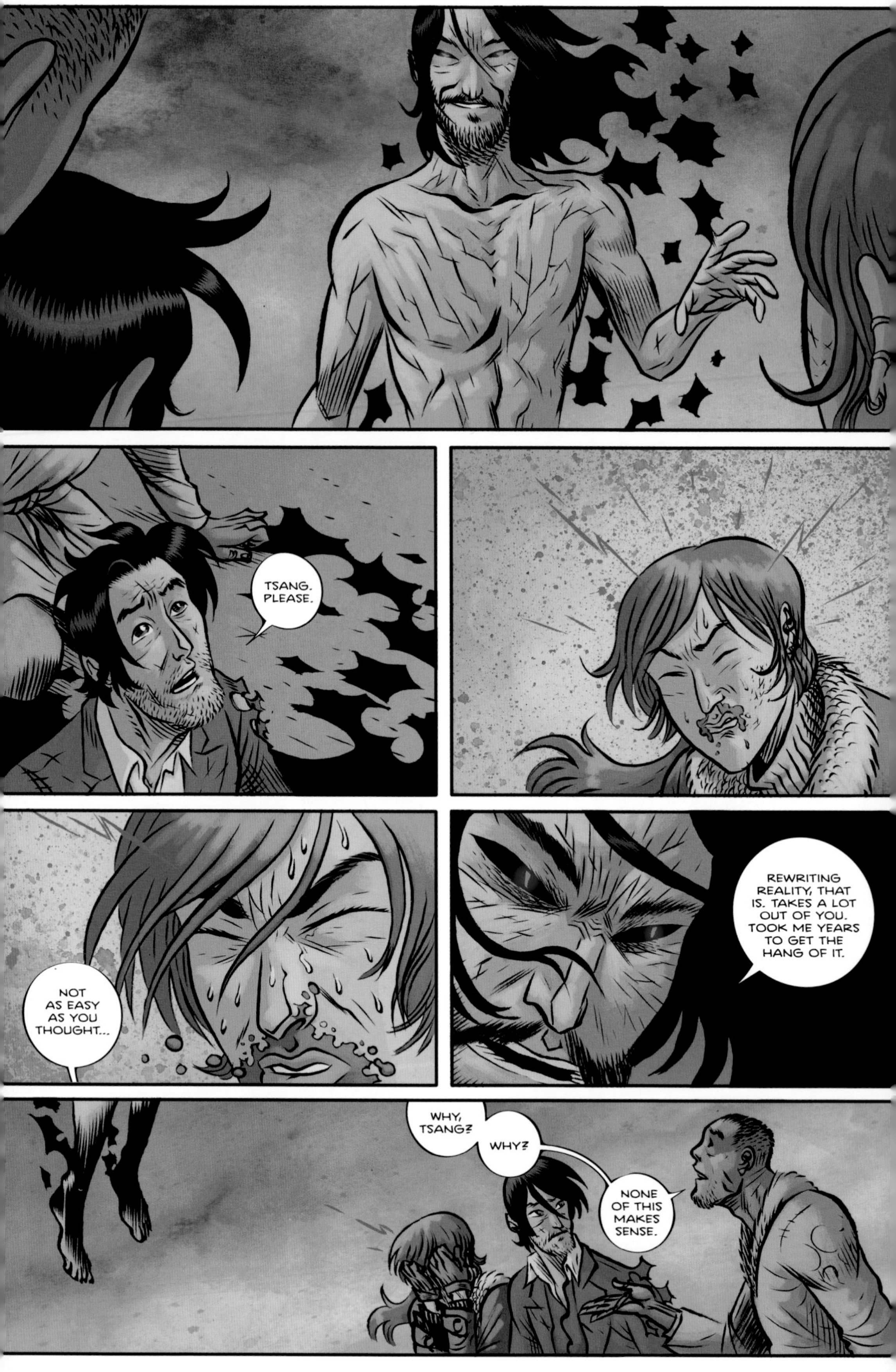
TSANG. PLEASE.
NOT AS EASY AS YOU THOUGHT...
REWRITING REALITY, THAT IS. TAKES A LOT OUT OF YOU. TOOK ME YEARS TO GET THE HANG OF IT.
WHY, TSANG?
WHY?
NONE OF THIS MAKES SENSE.

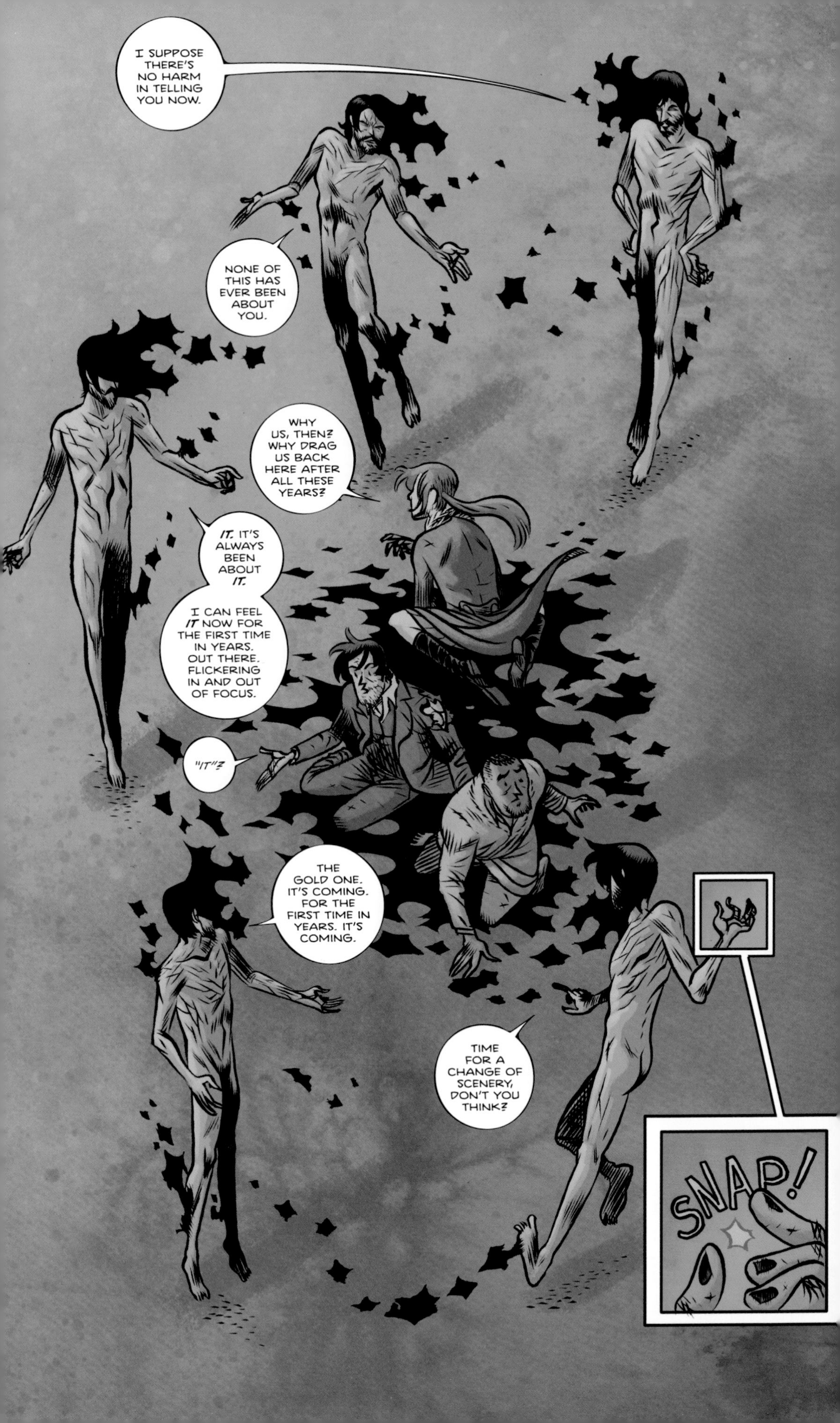
I SUPPOSE THERE'S NO HARM IN TELLING YOU NOW.
NONE OF THIS HAS EVER BEEN ABOUT YOU.
WHY US, THEN? WHY DRAG US BACK HERE AFTER ALL THESE YEARS?
IT. IT'S ALWAYS BEEN ABOUT *IT.*
I CAN FEEL *IT* NOW FOR THE FIRST TIME IN YEARS. OUT THERE. FLICKERING IN AND OUT OF FOCUS.
"IT"?
THE GOLD ONE. IT'S COMING. FOR THE FIRST TIME IN YEARS. IT'S COMING.
TIME FOR A CHANGE OF SCENERY, DON'T YOU THINK?
SNAP!

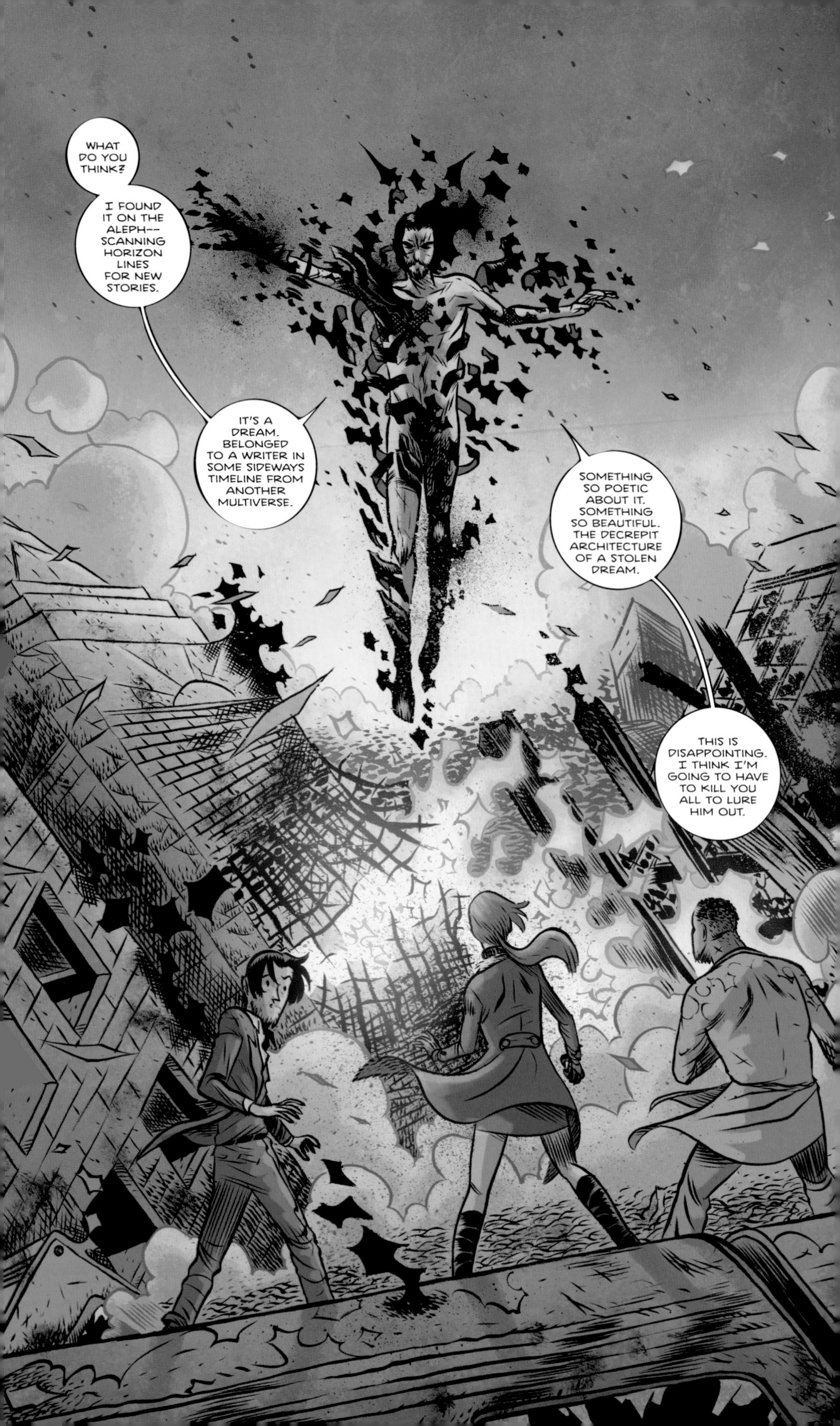
WHAT DO YOU THINK?
I FOUND IT ON THE ALEPH-- SCANNING HORIZON LINES FOR NEW STORIES.
IT'S A DREAM. BELONGED TO A WRITER IN SOME SIDEWAYS TIMELINE FROM ANOTHER MULTIVERSE.
SOMETHING SO POETIC ABOUT IT. SOMETHING SO BEAUTIFUL. THE DECREPIT ARCHITECTURE OF A STOLEN DREAM.
THIS IS DISAPPOINTING. I THINK I'M GOING TO HAVE TO KILL YOU ALL TO LURE HIM OUT.

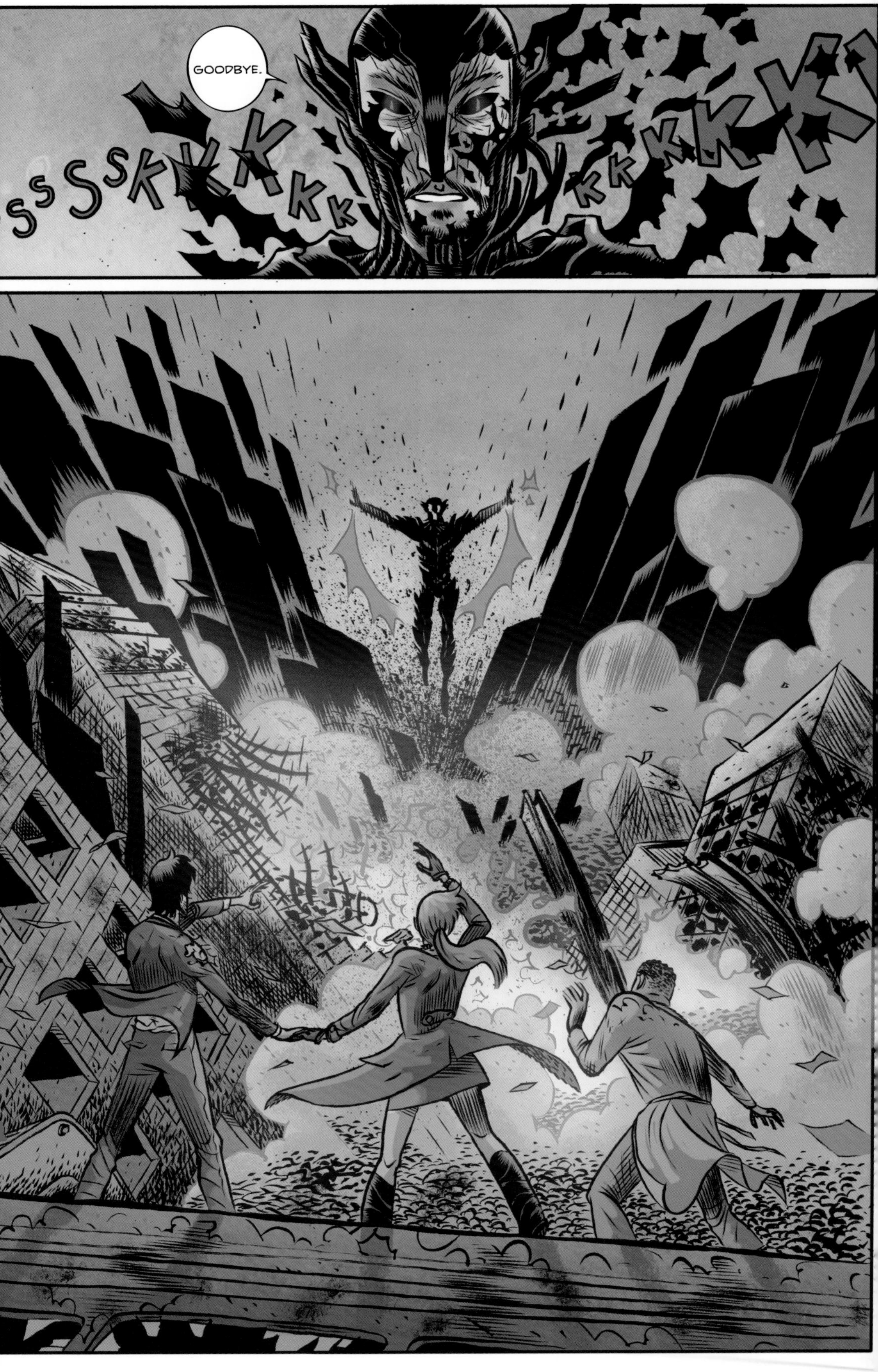
GOODBYE.
SSSSKKKKKKKKKKKK

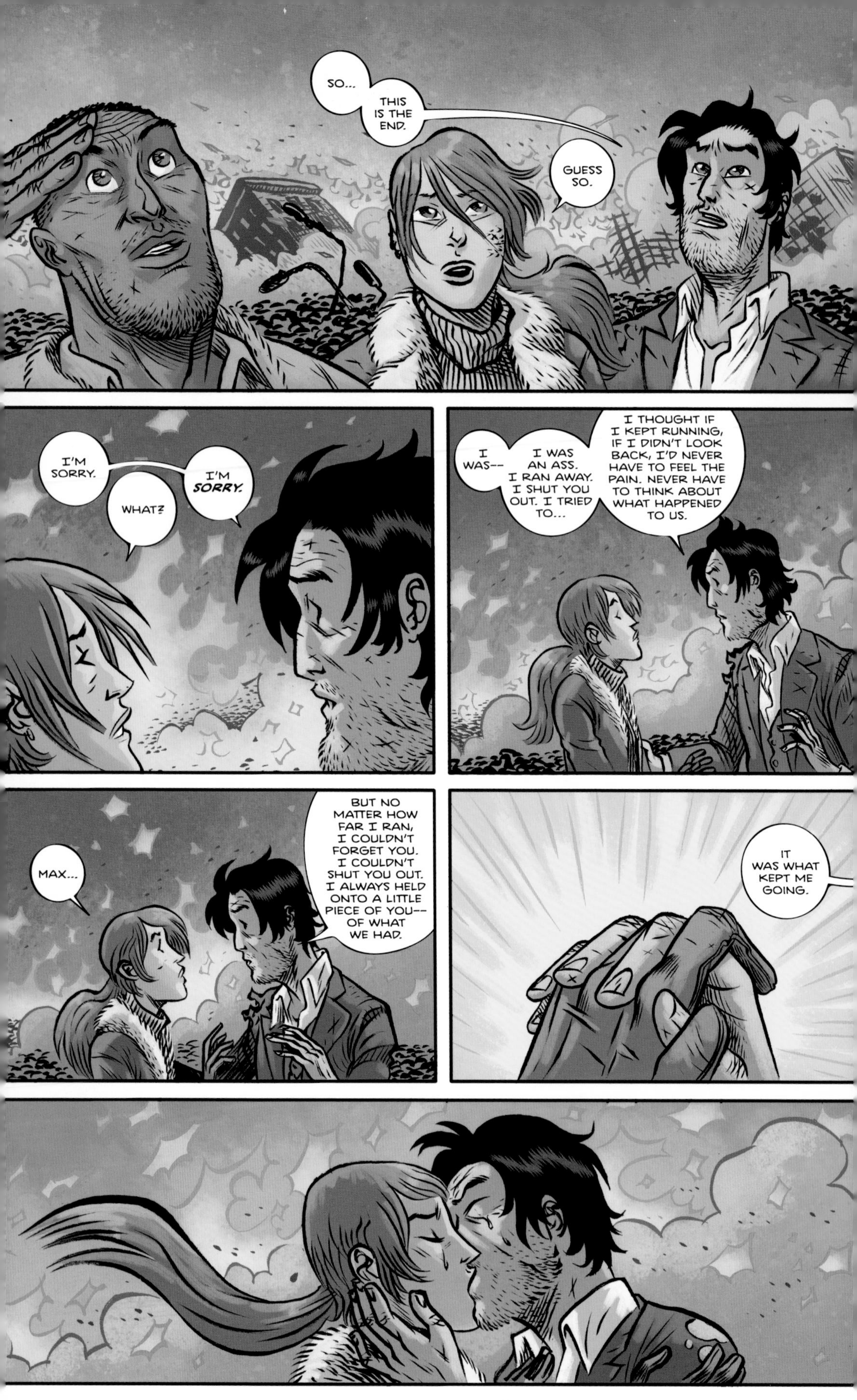
SO...
THIS IS THE END.
GUESS SO.
I'M SORRY.
WHAT?
I'M *SORRY.*
I WAS--
I WAS AN ASS. I RAN AWAY. I SHUT YOU OUT. I TRIED TO...
I THOUGHT IF I KEPT RUNNING, IF I DIDN'T LOOK BACK, I'D NEVER HAVE TO FEEL THE PAIN. NEVER HAVE TO THINK ABOUT WHAT HAPPENED TO US.
MAX...
BUT NO MATTER HOW FAR I RAN, I COULDN'T FORGET YOU. I COULDN'T SHUT YOU OUT. I ALWAYS HELD ONTO A LITTLE PIECE OF YOU-- OF WHAT WE HAD.
IT WAS WHAT KEPT ME GOING.

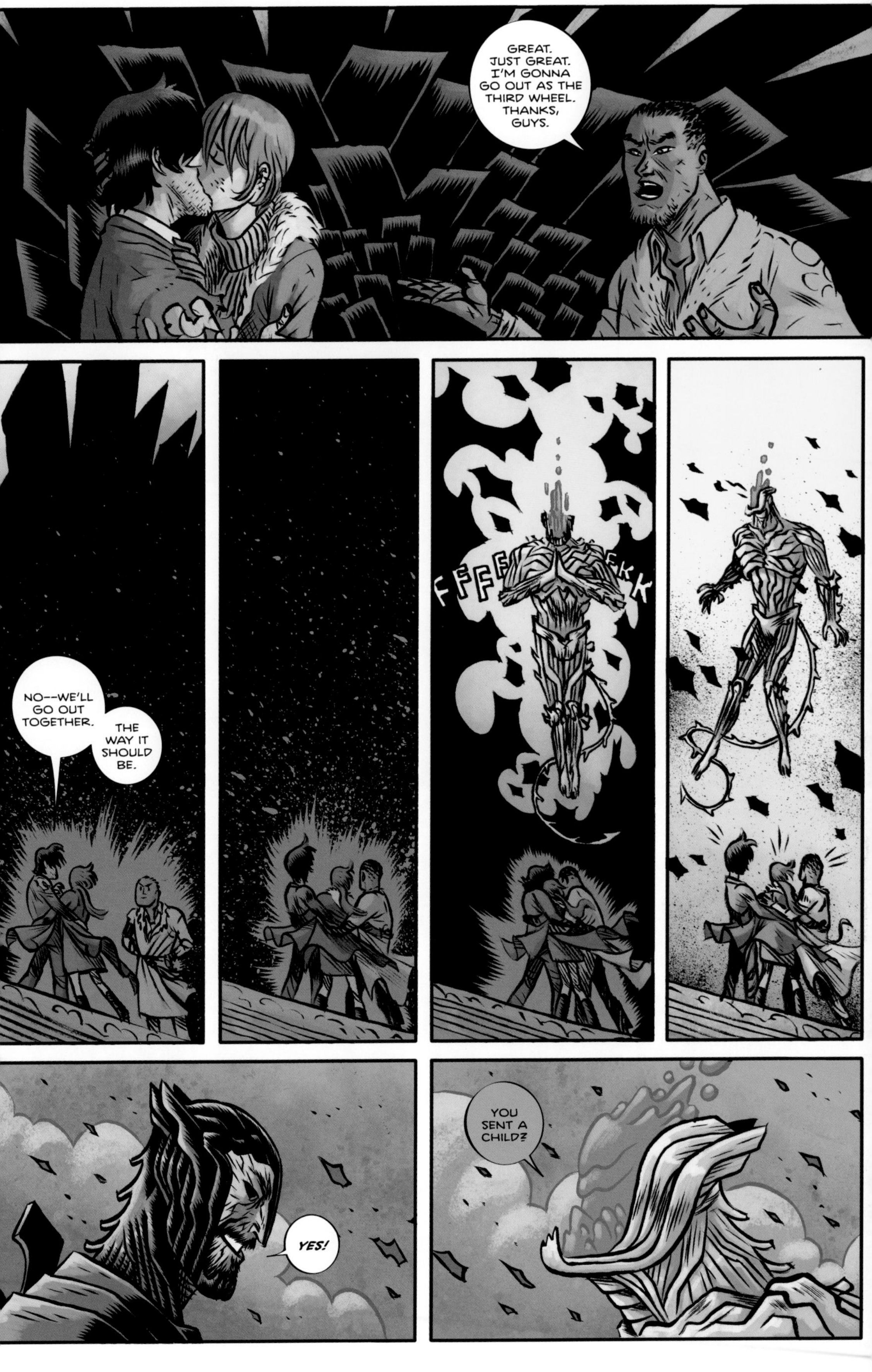
GREAT. JUST GREAT. I'M GONNA GO OUT AS THE THIRD WHEEL. THANKS, GUYS.
NO--WE'LL GO OUT TOGETHER.
THE WAY IT SHOULD BE.
FFFF
KK
YES!
YOU SENT A CHILD?

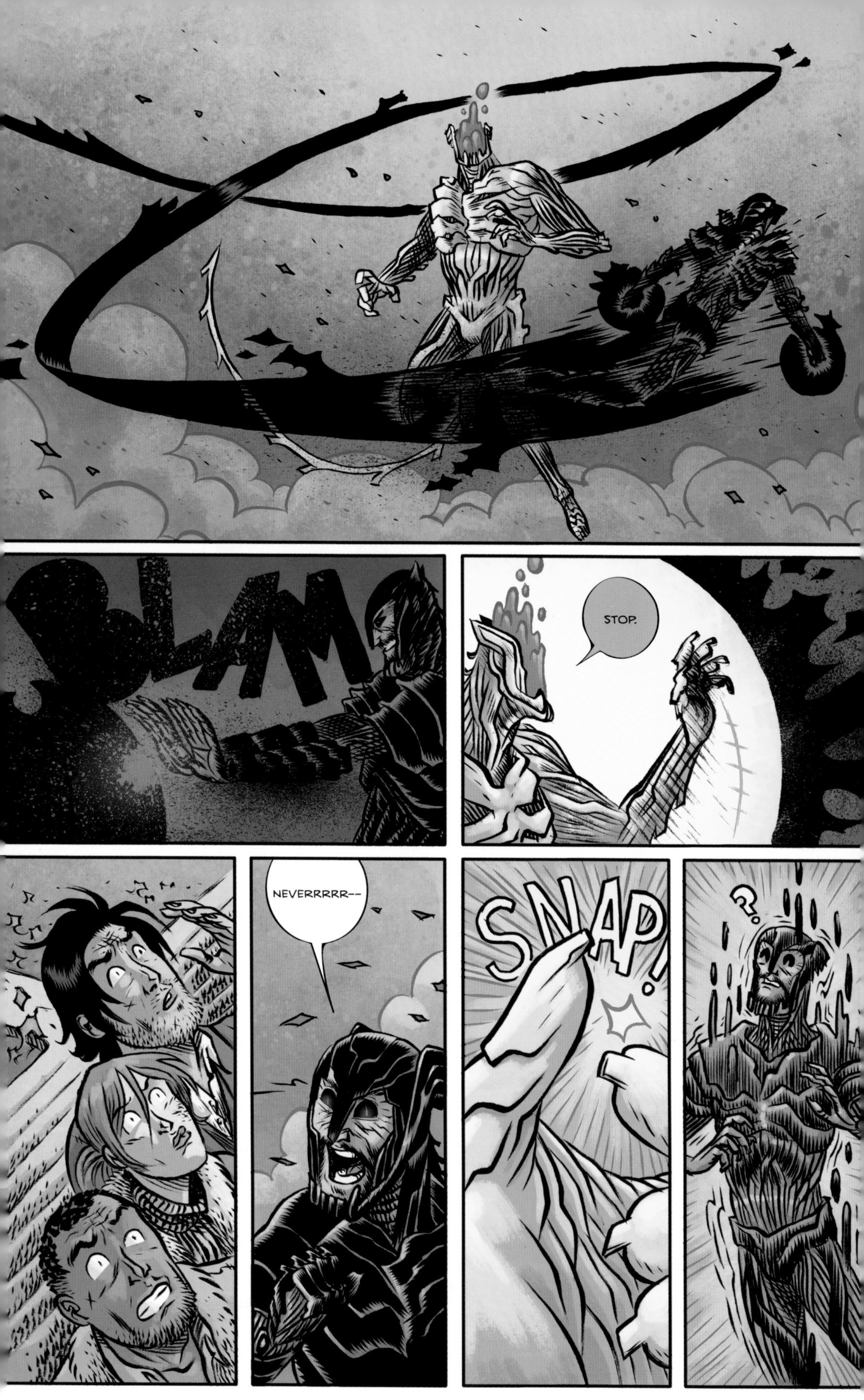
BLAM
STOP.
NEVERRRRR--
SNAP!
?

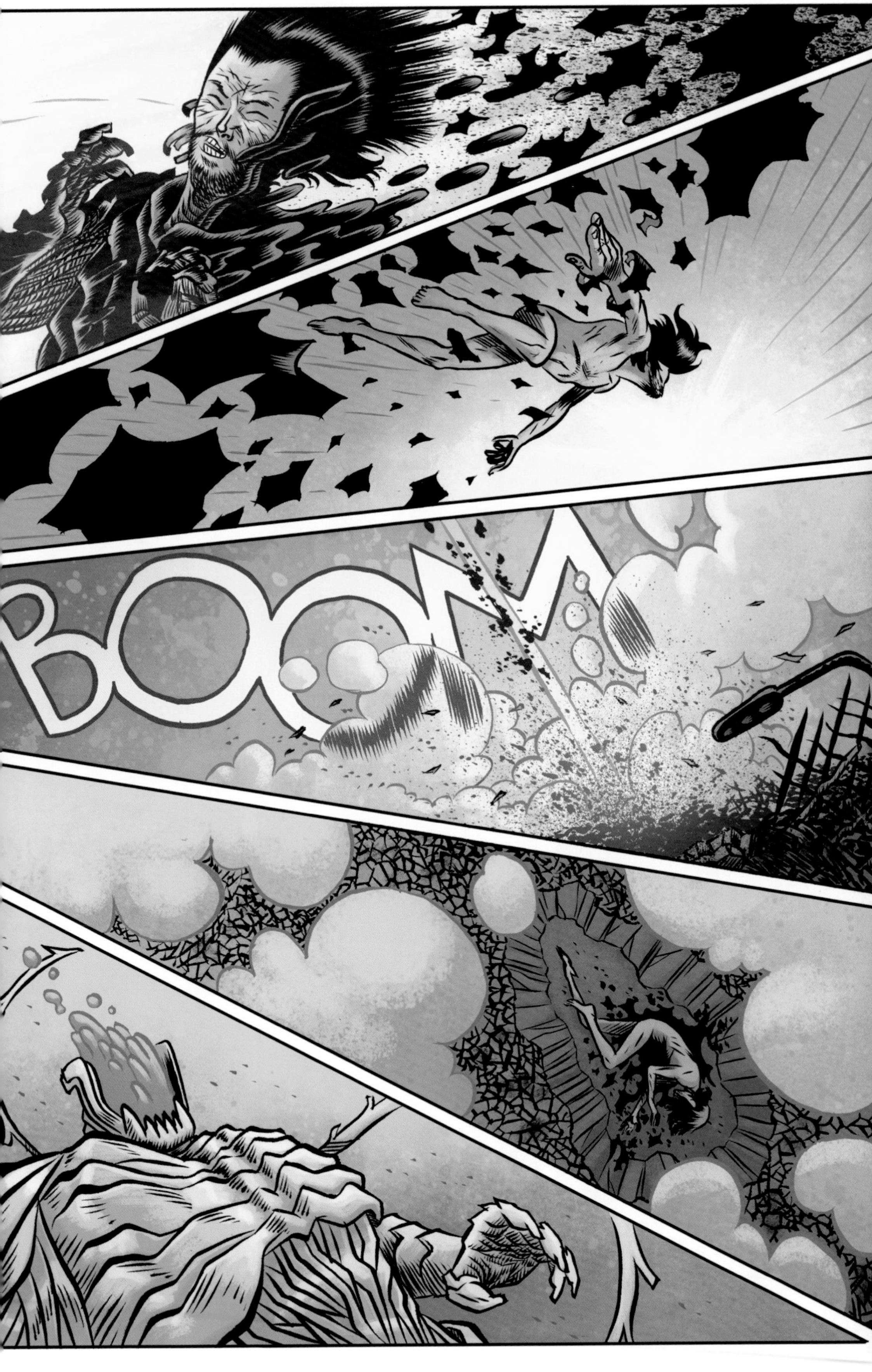
BOOM

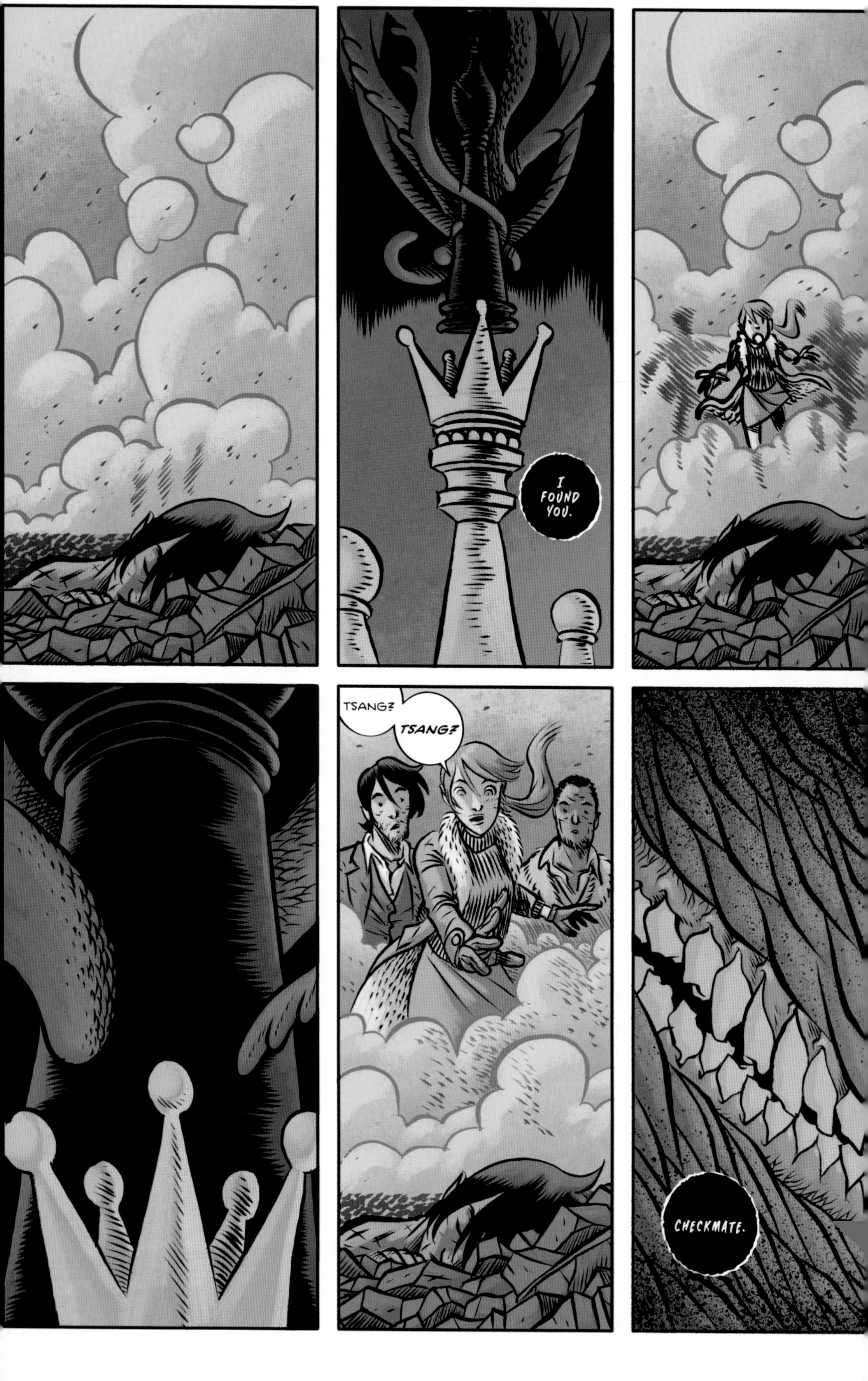
I FOUND YOU.
TSANG?
TSANG?
CHECKMATE.

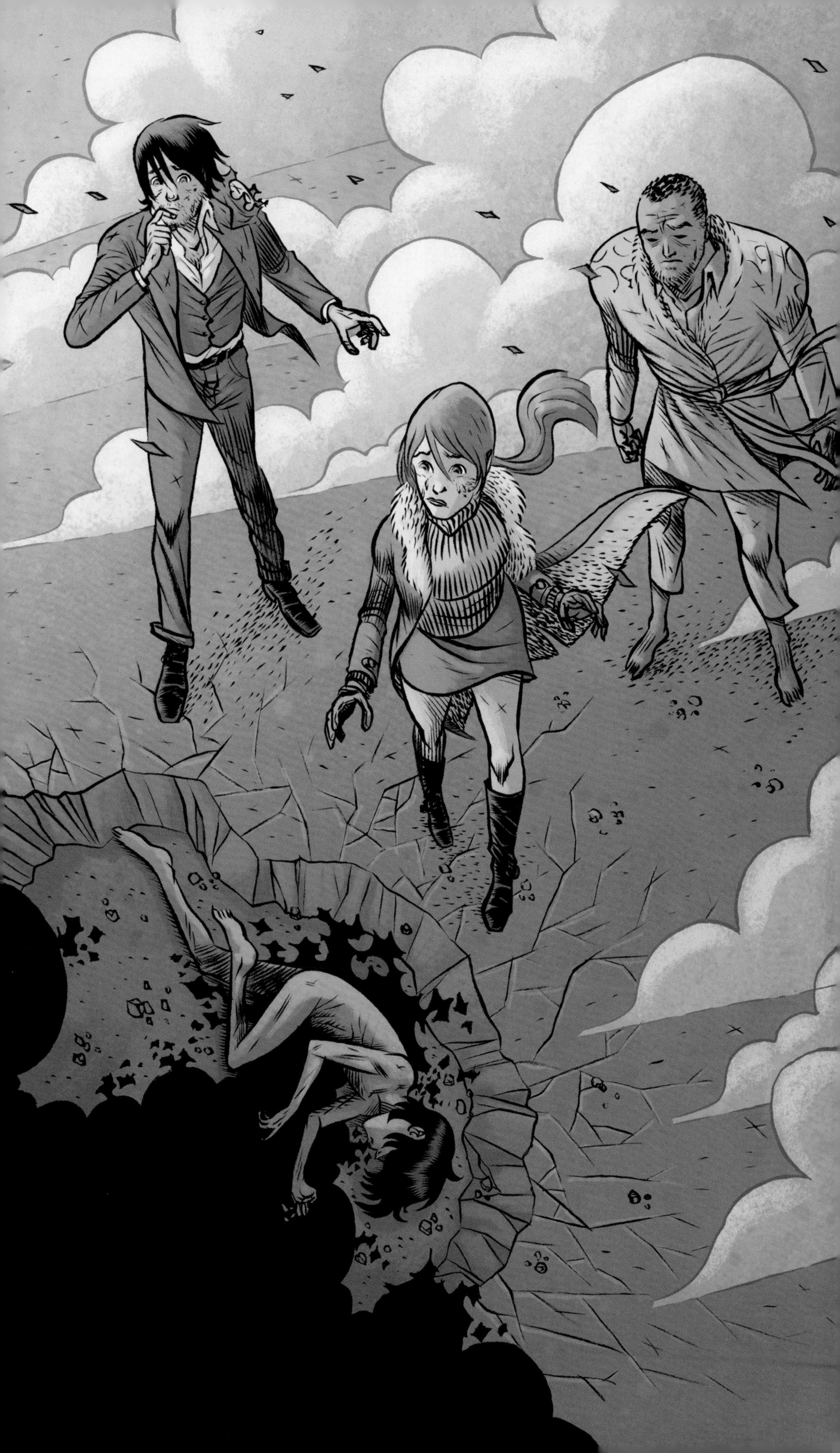

Epilogue

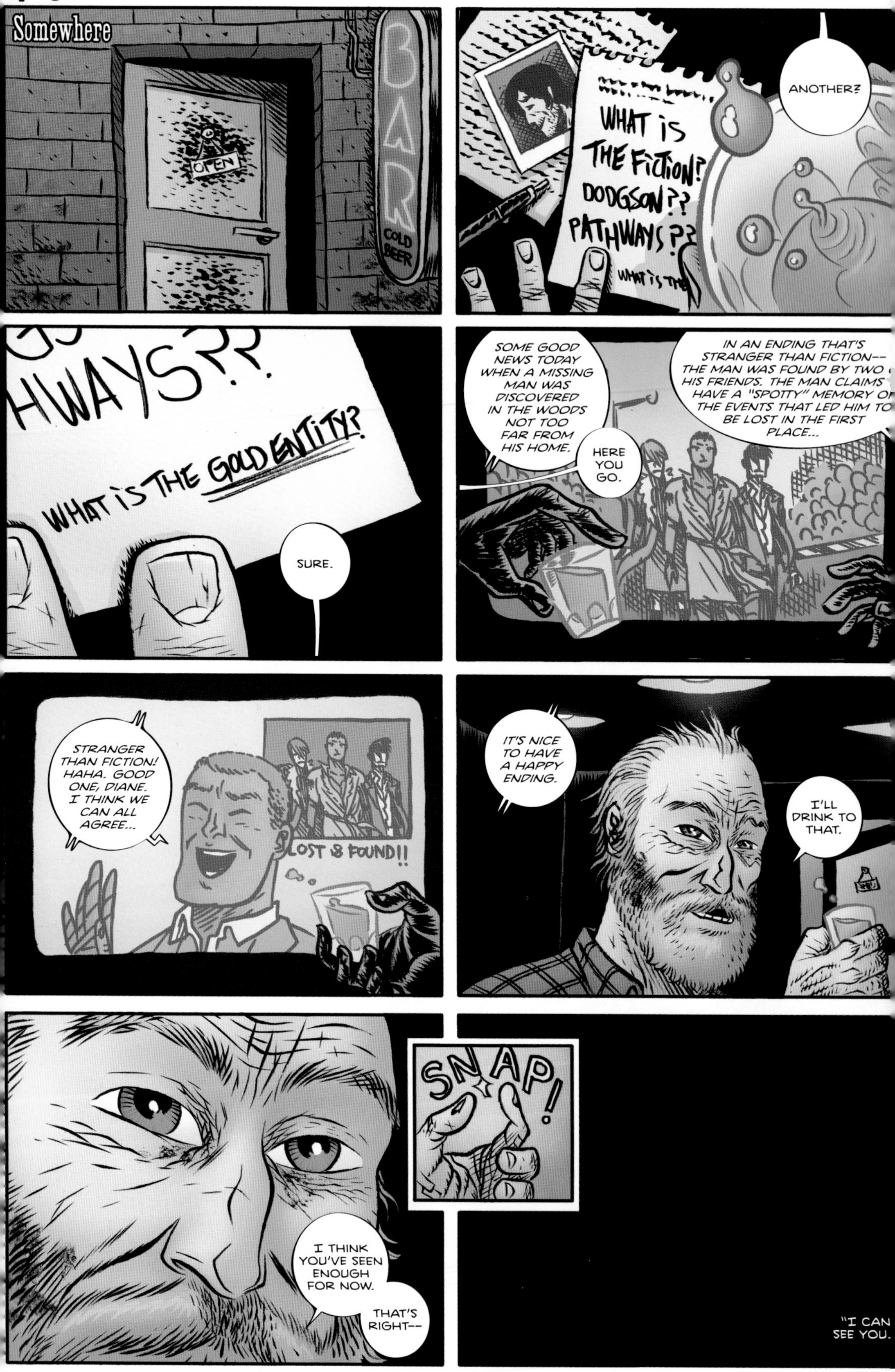

Somewhere
OPEN
BAR
COLD BEER
WHAT IS THE FICTION? DODGSON?? PATHWAYS??
ANOTHER?
HWAYS??
WHAT IS THE GOLD ENTITY?
SURE.
SOME GOOD NEWS TODAY WHEN A MISSING MAN WAS DISCOVERED IN THE WOODS NOT TOO FAR FROM HIS HOME.
HERE YOU GO.
IN AN ENDING THAT'S STRANGER THAN FICTION-- THE MAN WAS FOUND BY TWO HIS FRIENDS. THE MAN CLAIMS HAVE A "SPOTTY" MEMORY OF THE EVENTS THAT LED HIM TO BE LOST IN THE FIRST PLACE...
STRANGER THAN FICTION! HAHA. GOOD ONE, DIANE. I THINK WE CAN ALL AGREE...
LOST & FOUND!!
IT'S NICE TO HAVE A HAPPY ENDING.
I'LL DRINK TO THAT.
SNAP!
I THINK YOU'VE SEEN ENOUGH FOR NOW.
THAT'S RIGHT--
"I CAN SEE YOU.

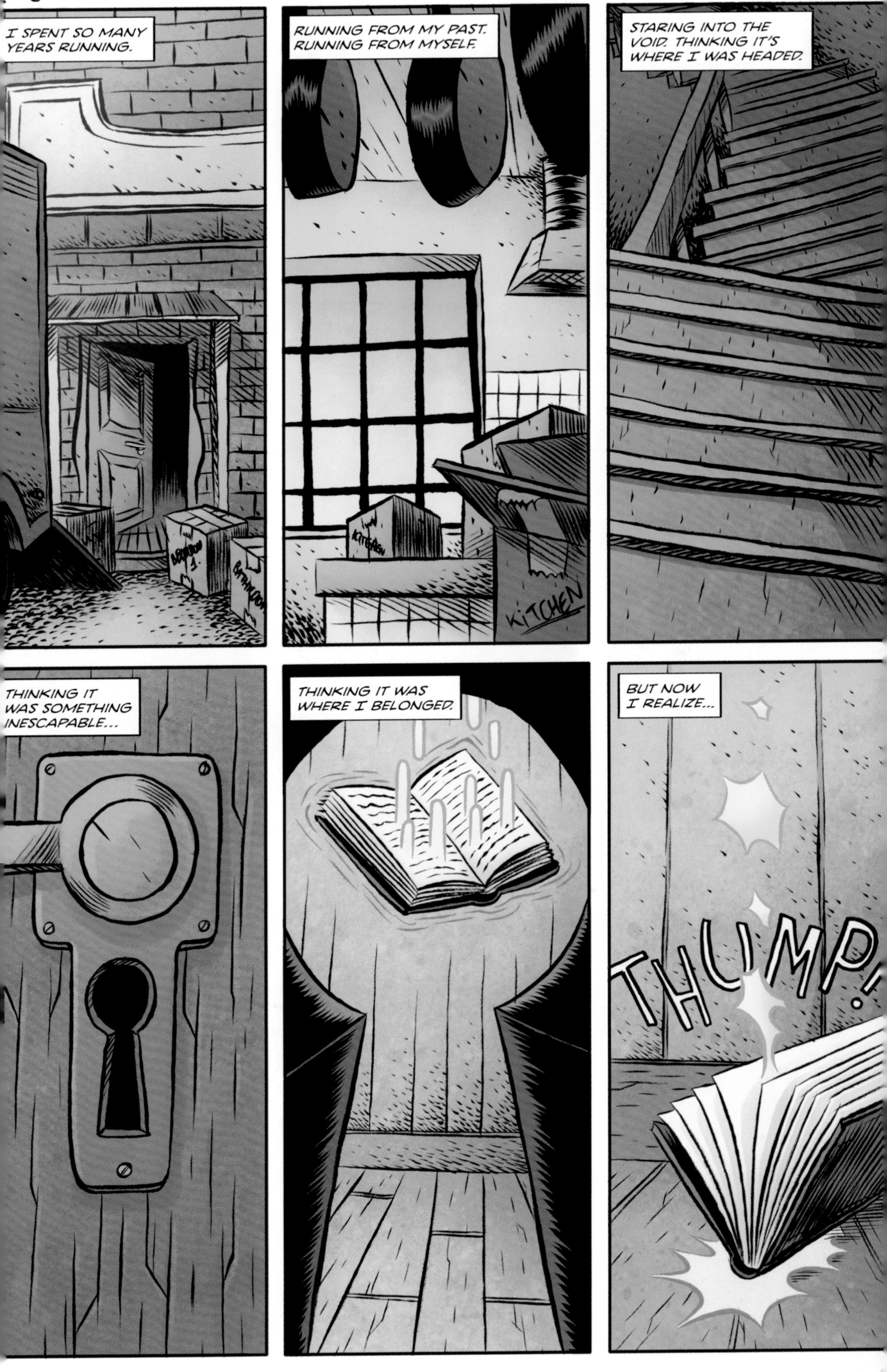
I SPENT SO MANY YEARS RUNNING.
RUNNING FROM MY PAST. RUNNING FROM MYSELF.
KITCHEN
STARING INTO THE VOID. THINKING IT'S WHERE I WAS HEADED.
THINKING IT WAS SOMETHING INESCAPABLE...
THINKING IT WAS WHERE I BELONGED.
BUT NOW I REALIZE...
THUMP!

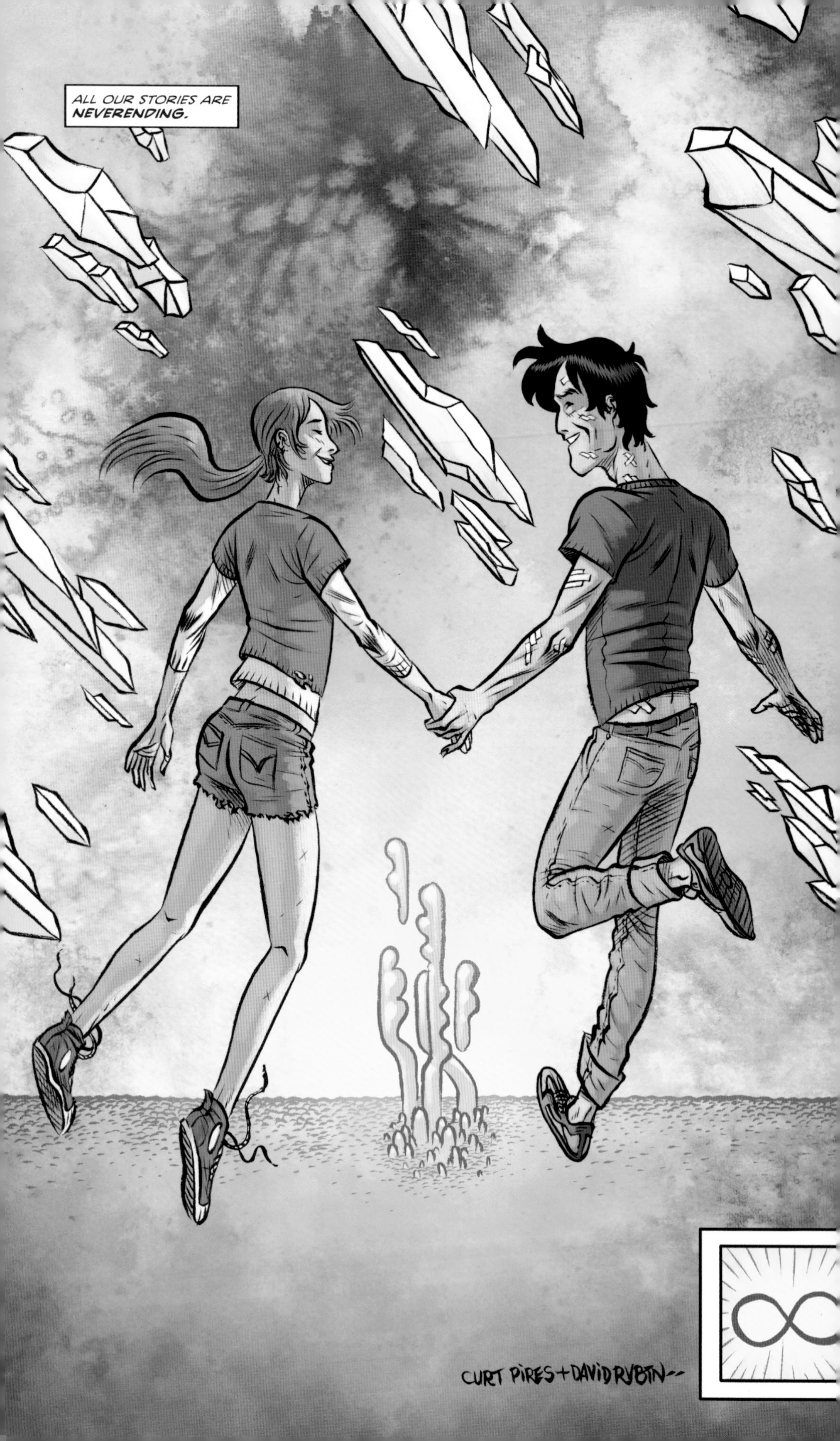
ALL OUR STORIES ARE NEVERENDING.
∞
CURT PIRES + DAVID RUBIN--

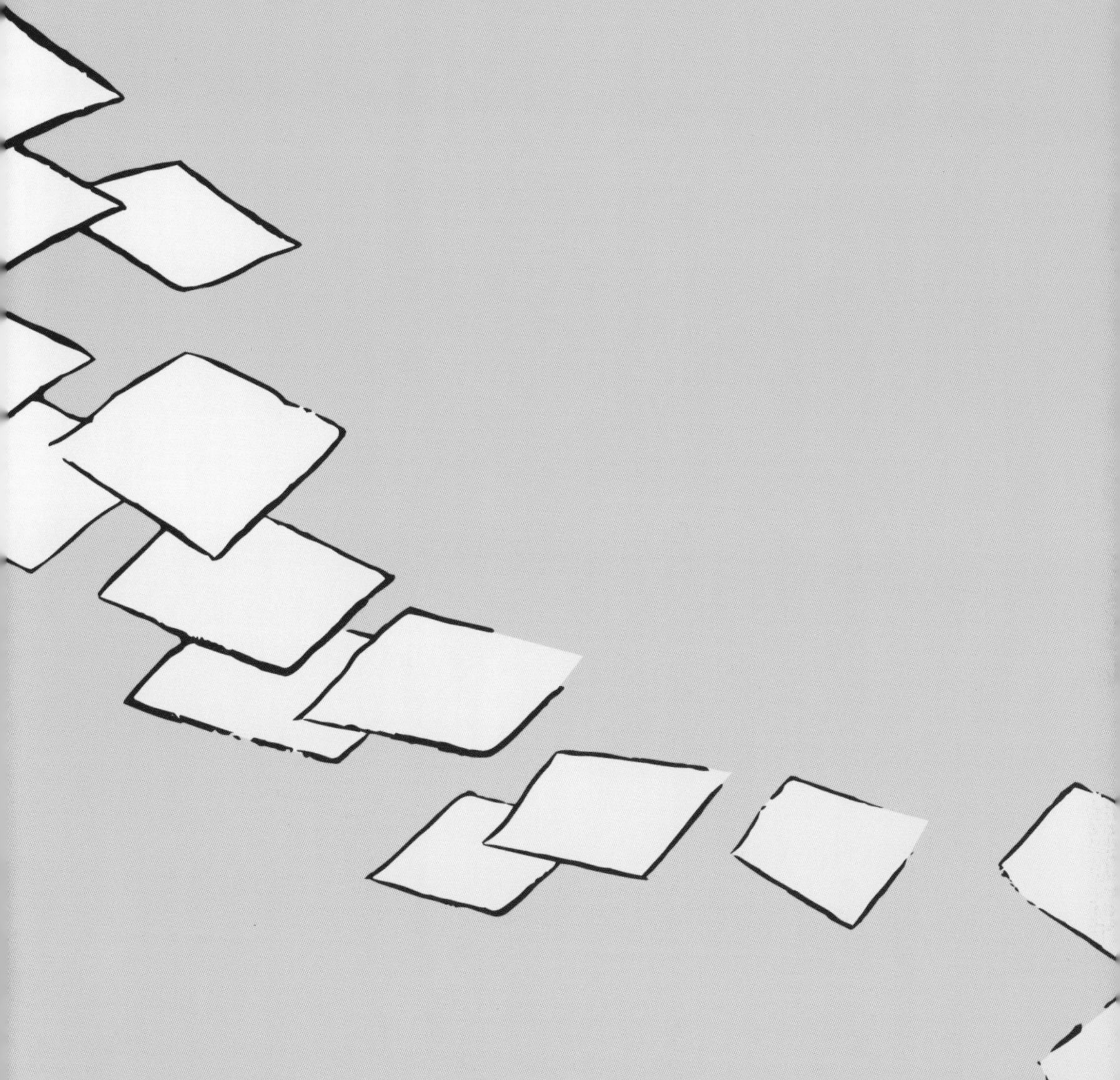

COVER GALLERY

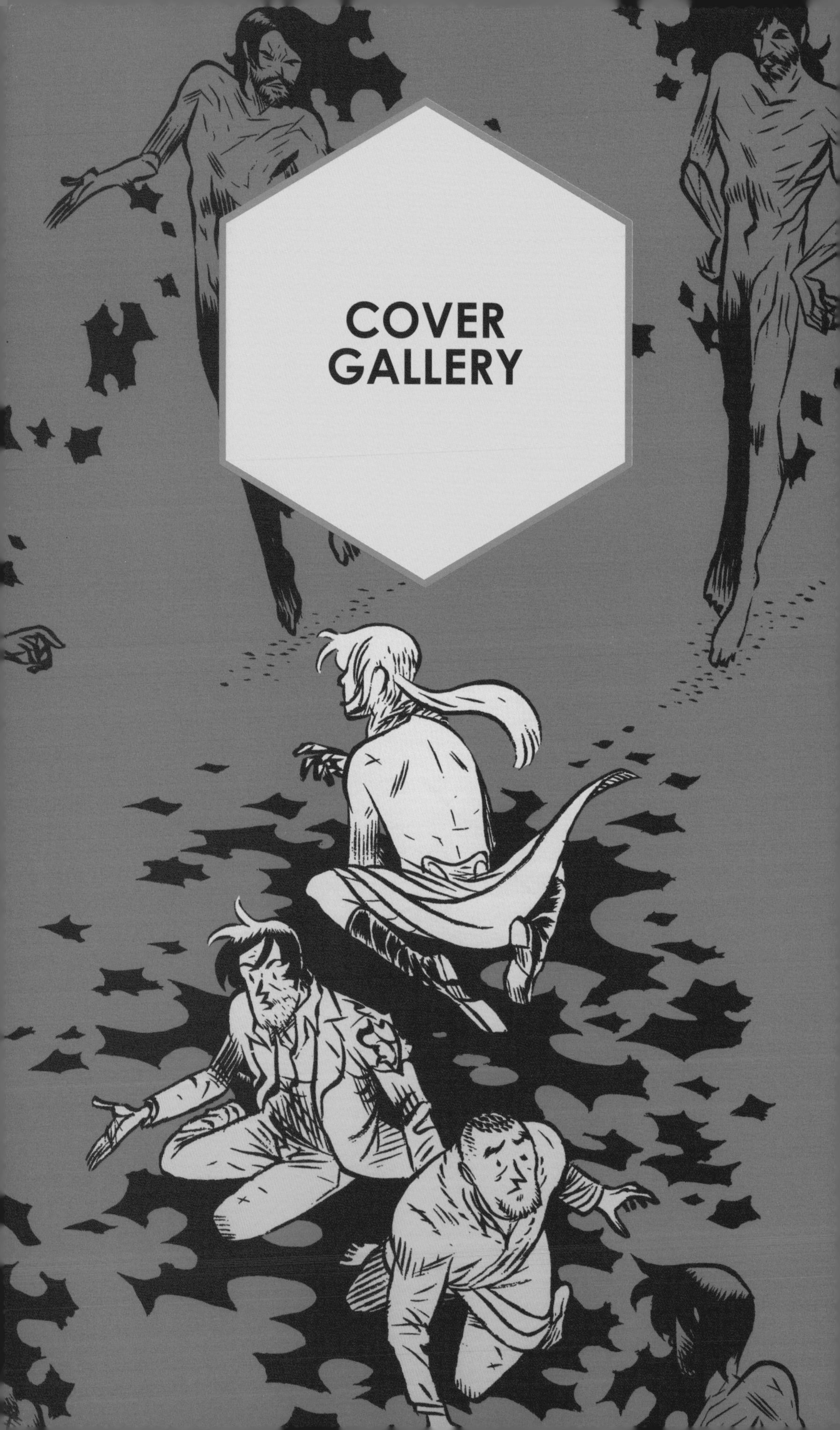

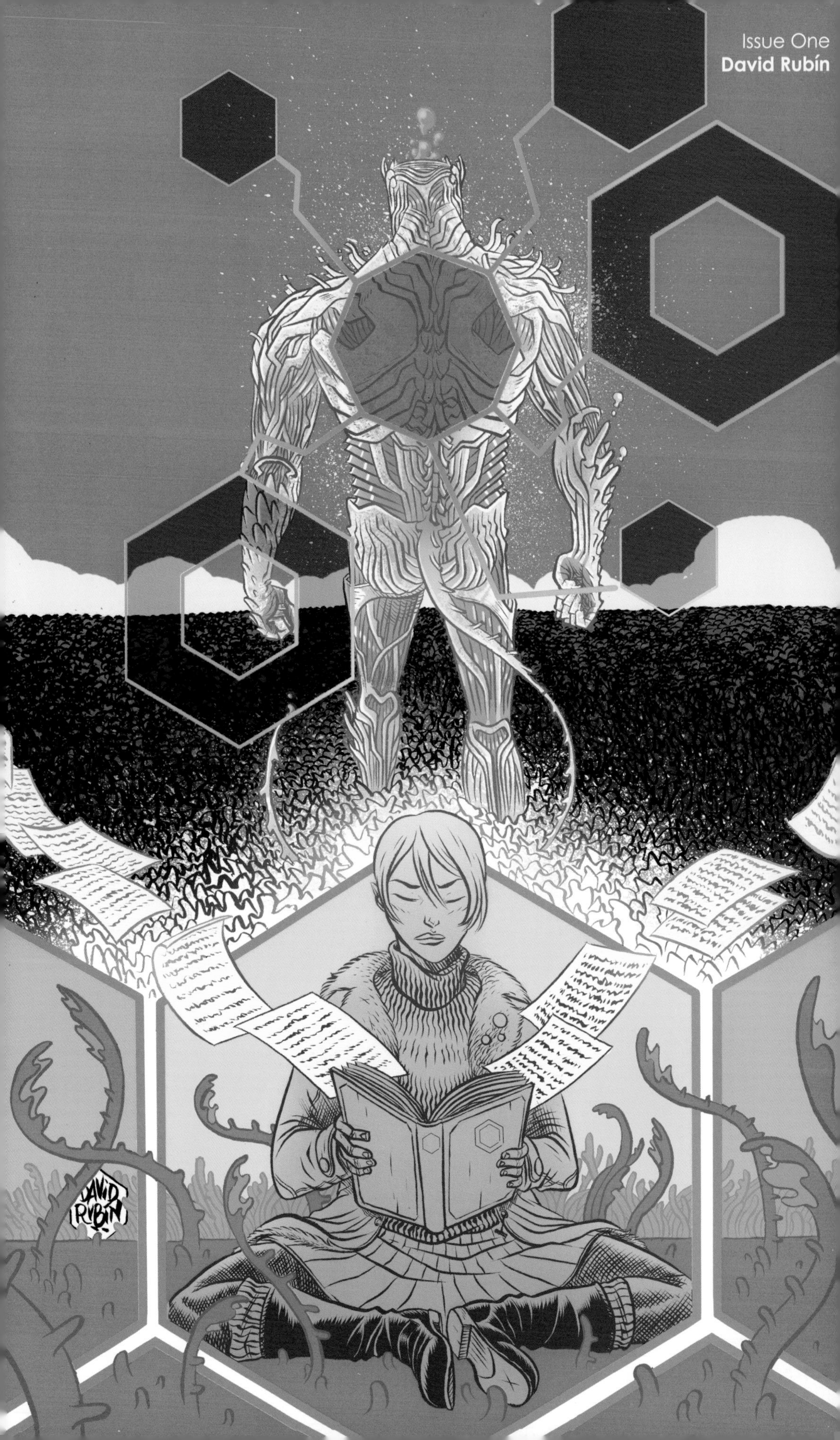
Issue One
David Rubín

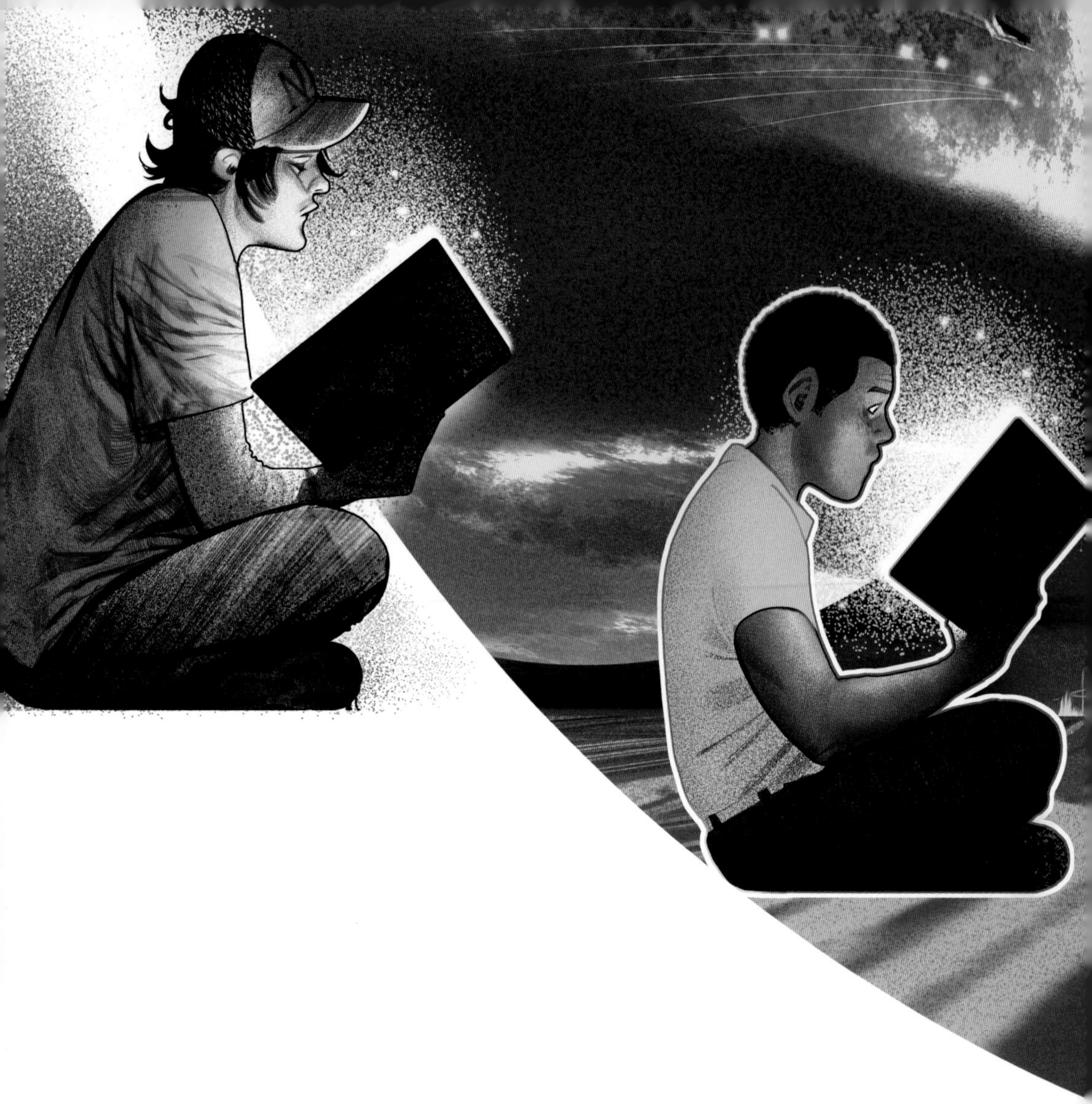

Issue One BOOM! Ten Years Variant
Frazer Irving

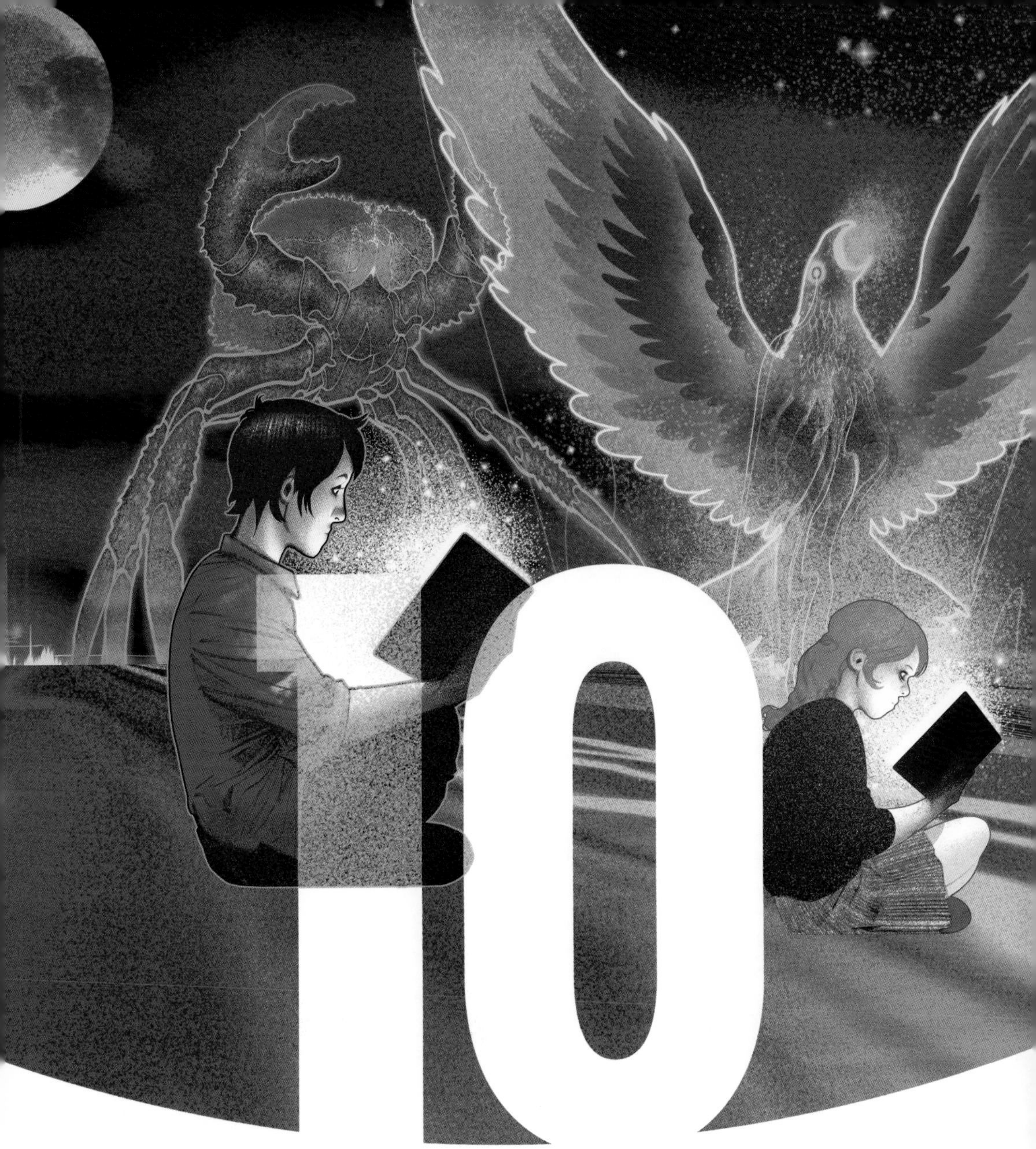
10

Issue One Variant
Tula Lotay

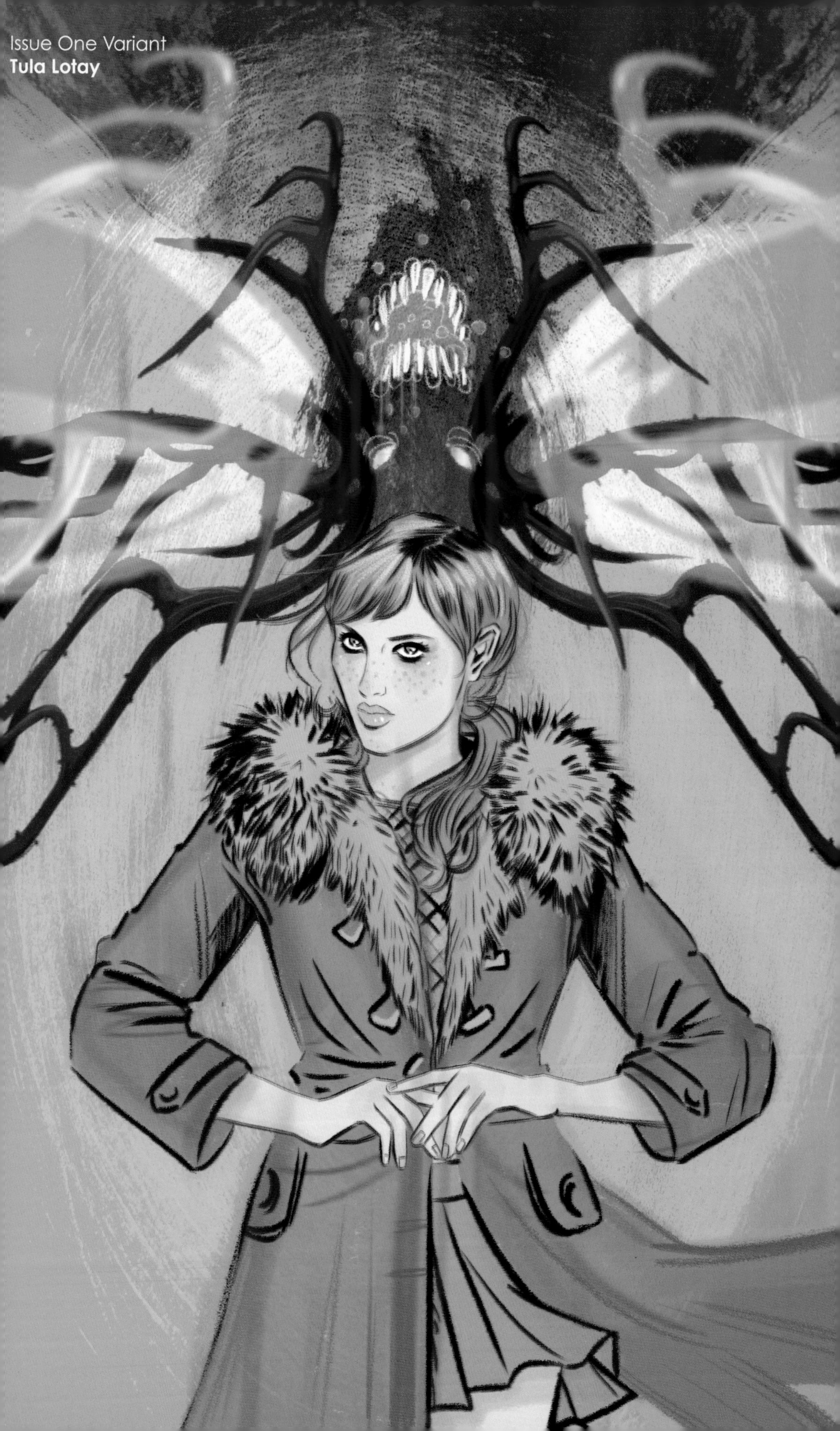

Issue Two
David Rubín

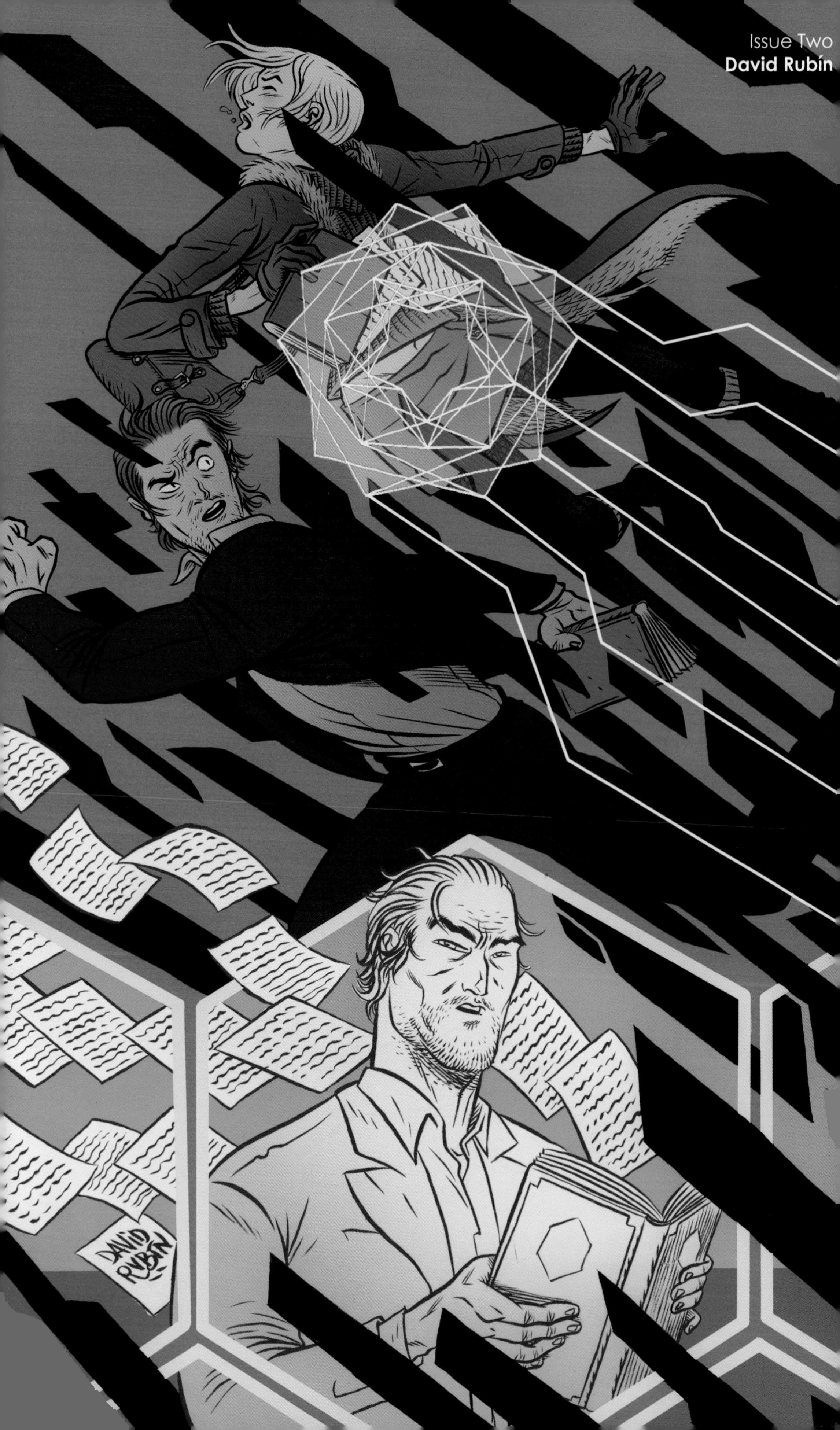
DAVID RUBÍN

Issue Three
David Rubín

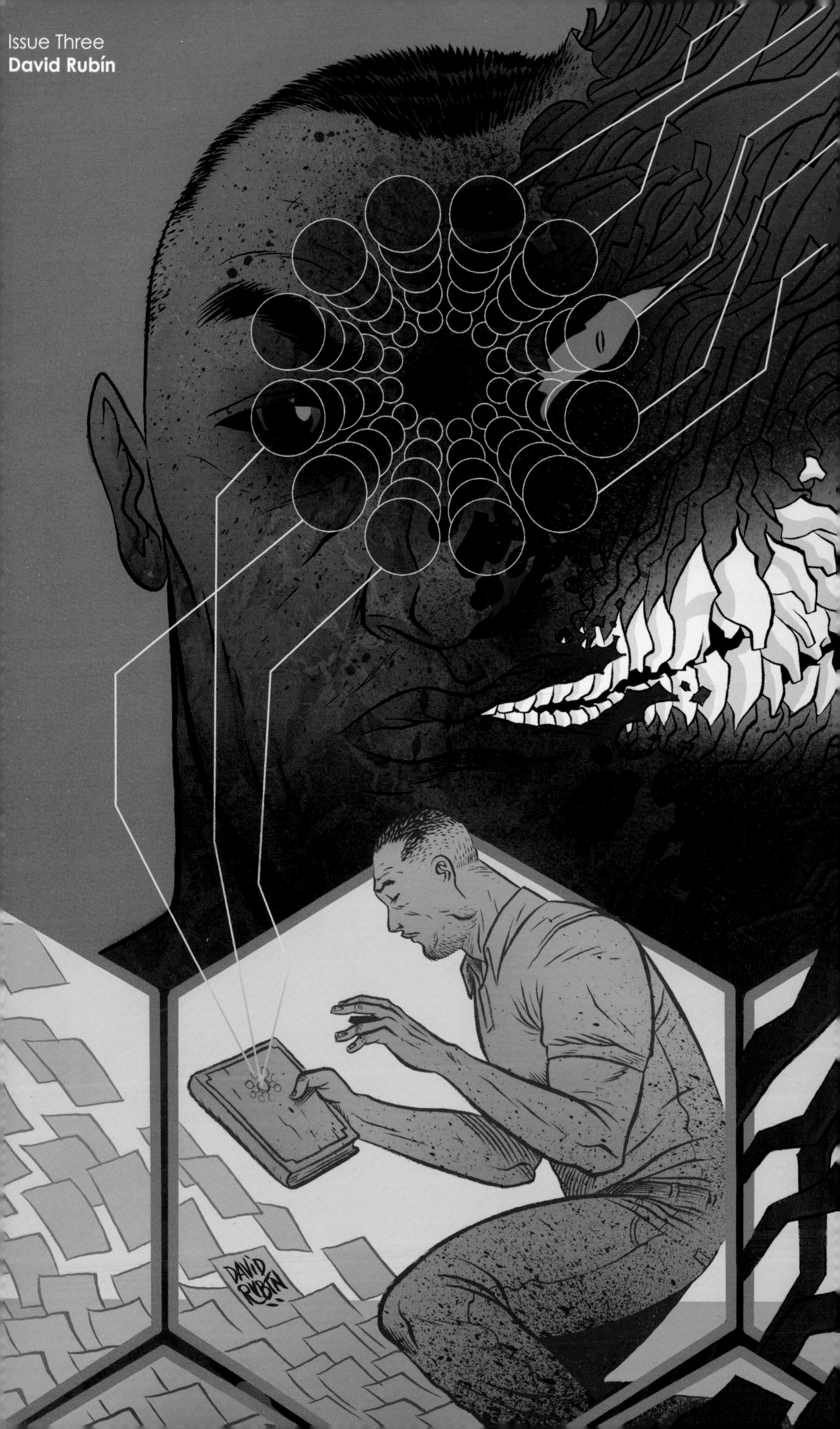
DAVID RUBÍN

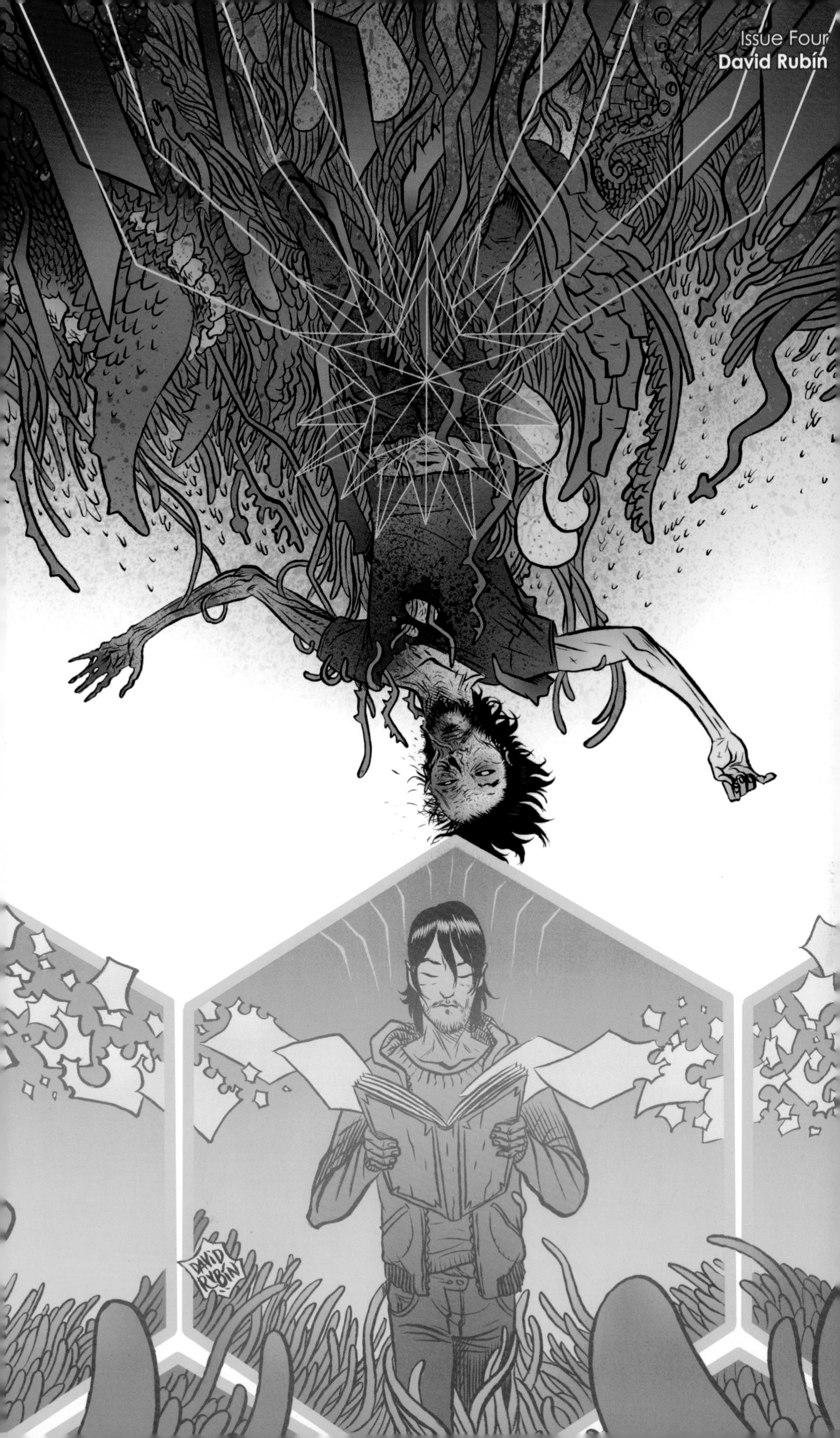
DAVID RUBÍN

Issue Four
David Rubín

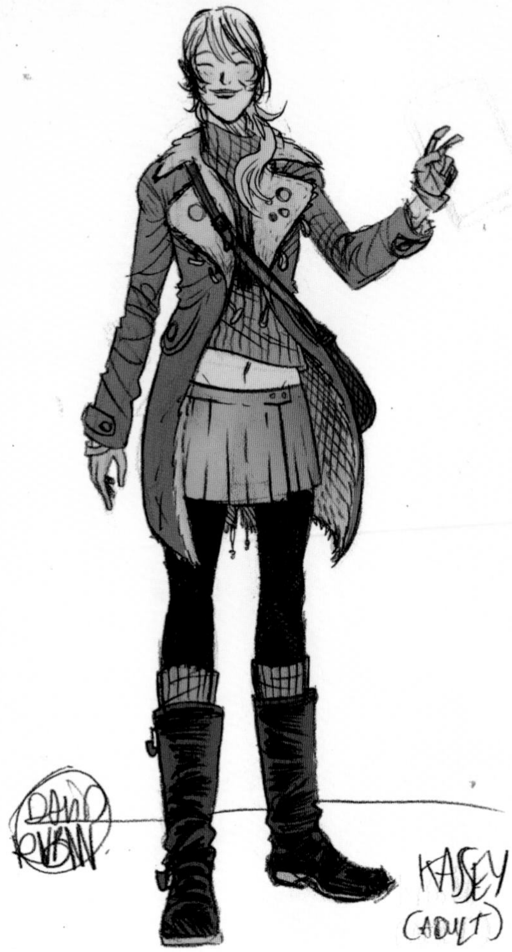
KASSEY
(ADULT)

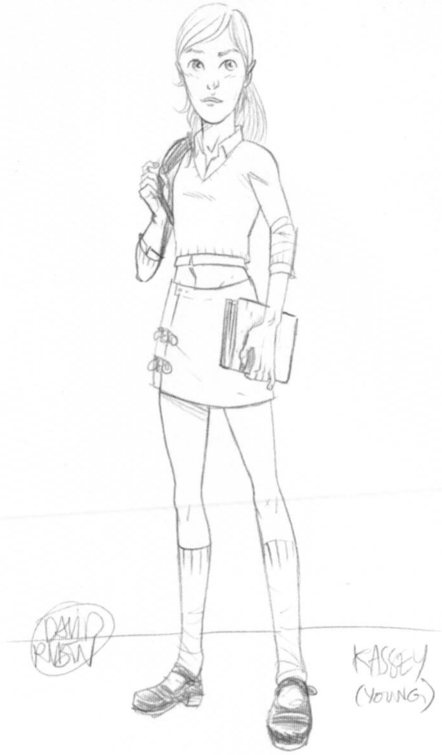
KASSEY
(YOUNG)

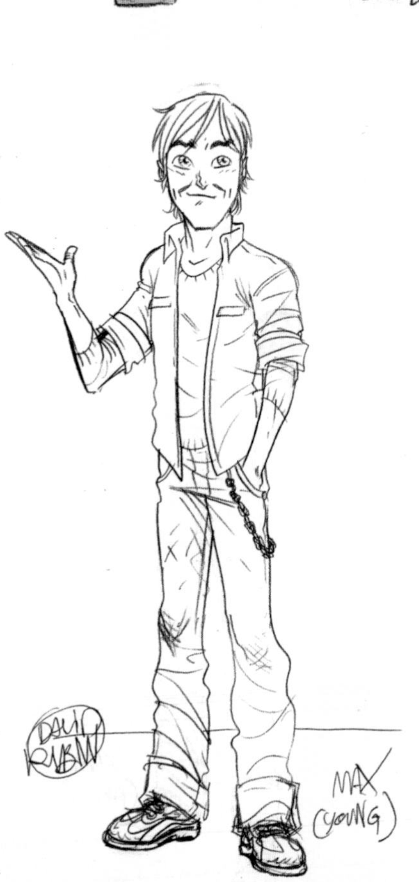
MAX
(YOUNG)

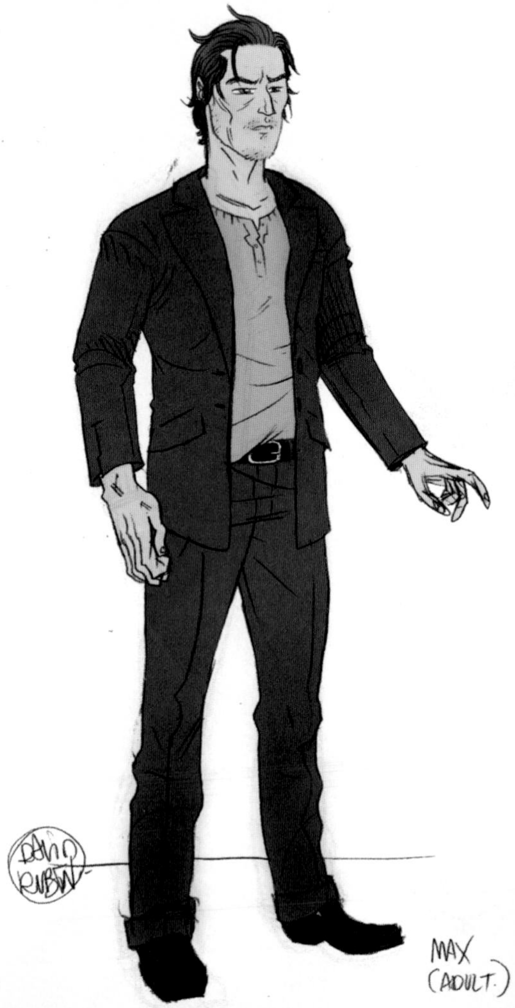
MAX
(ADULT.)

Character Sketches
David Rubín

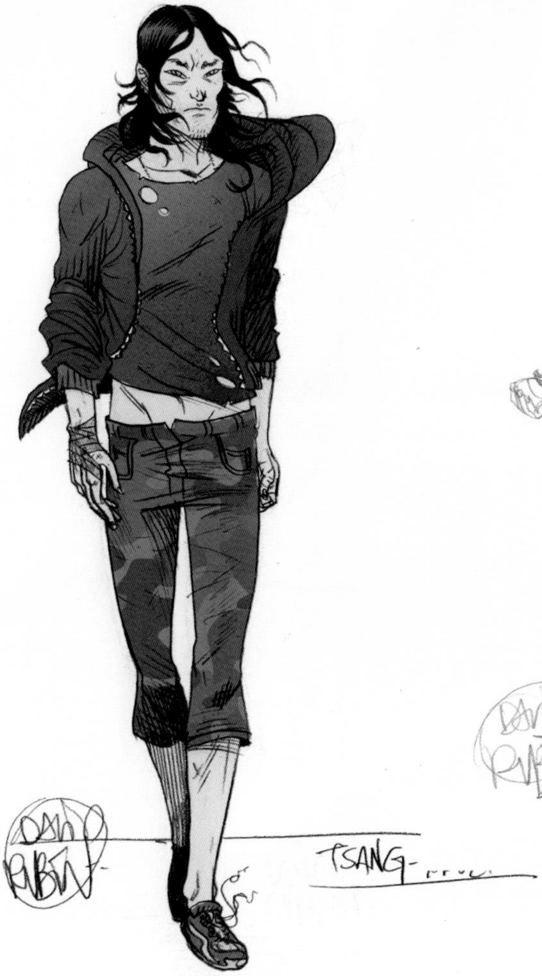
TSANG-

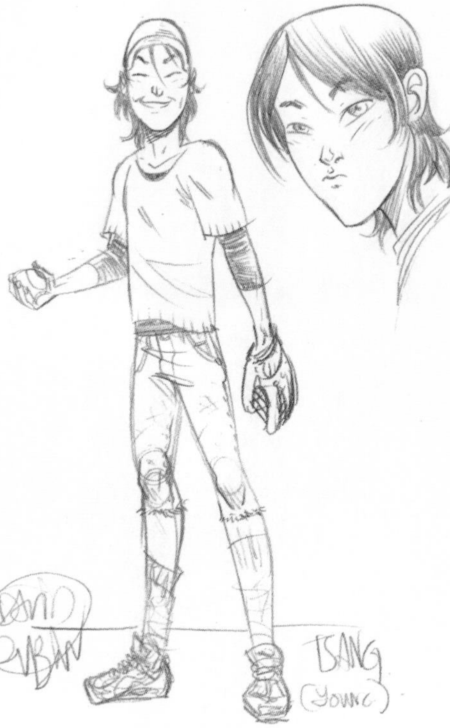
TSANG
(YOUNG)

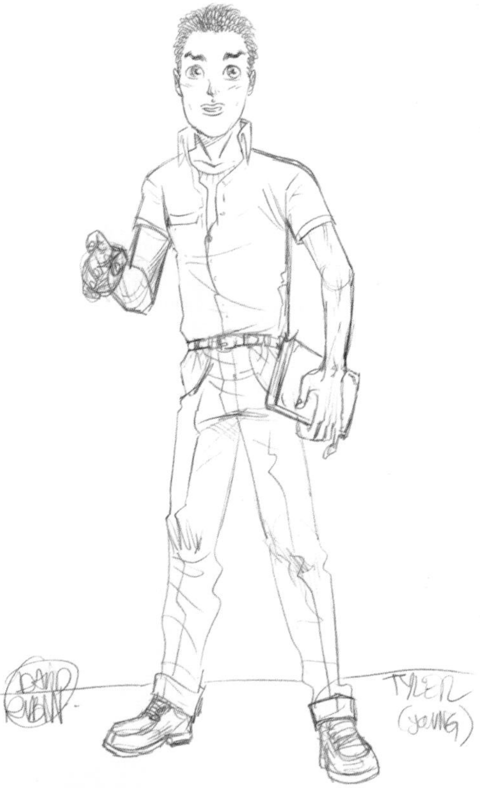
TYLER
(YOUNG)

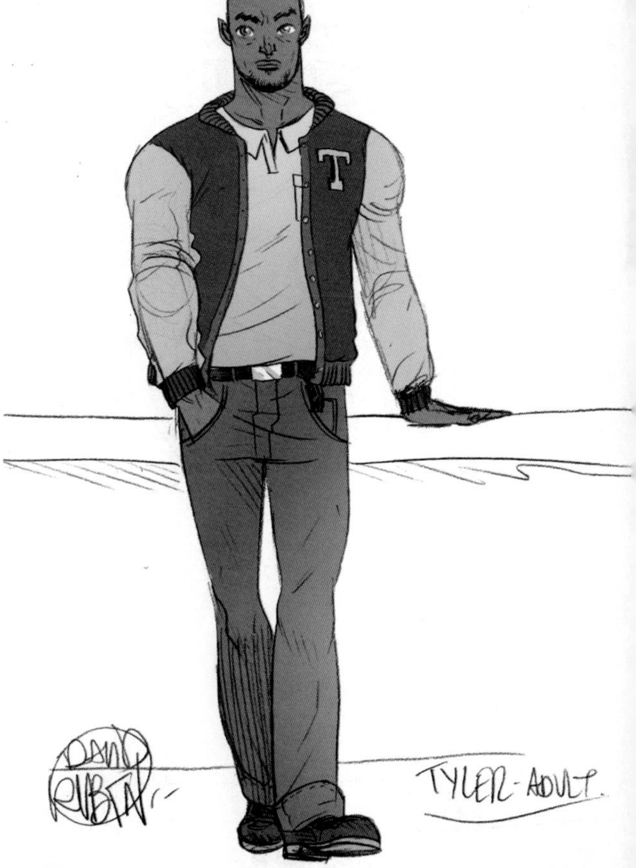
TYLER-ADULT.

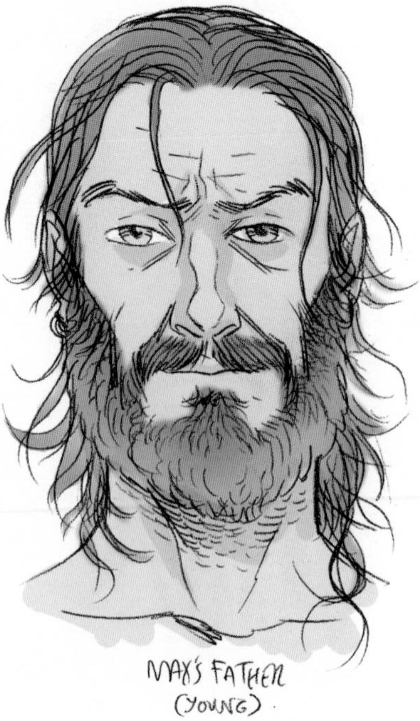
MAX'S FATHER
(YOUNG)

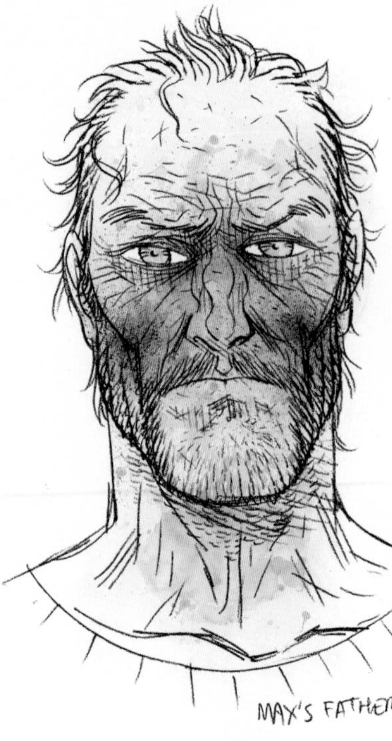
MAX'S FATHER

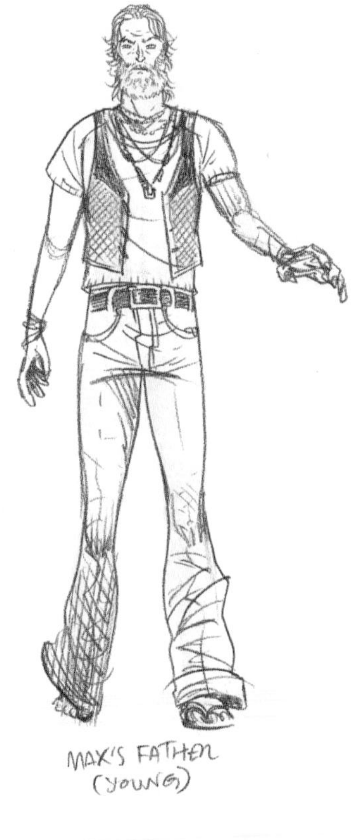
MAX'S FATHER
(YOUNG)

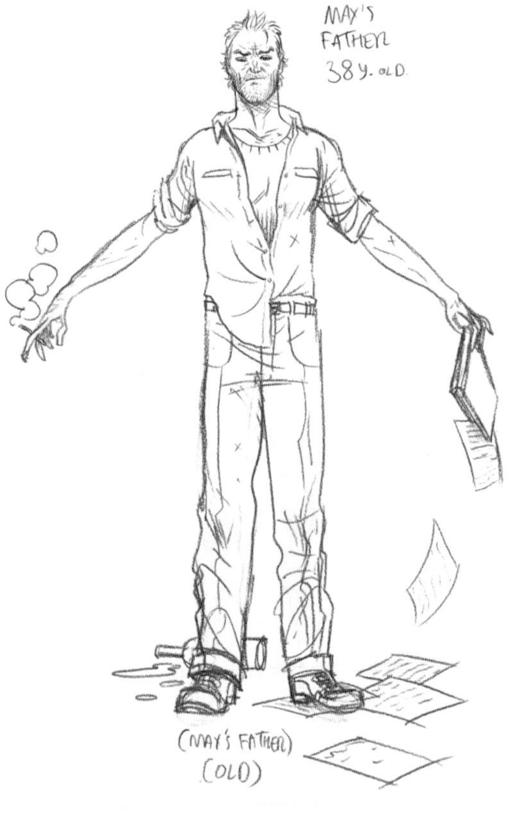
MAX'S
FATHER
38 Y. OLD
(MAX'S FATHER)
(OLD)

*NOTE: I NEED OTHER WAY FOR THIS DESIGN, I THINK, MAYBE....
"HUMAN" FORM
(BUT THE CORRUPTION IS A METAMORPHO, HE COULD CHANGE THE DENSITY, SIZE, AND FORM OF HIS BODY)
TAIL
BUGS AND OTHER INSECTS FLOATING ARROUND HIM.
WHERE THE CORRUPTION STEP EVERYTHING ROTS.
HE CAN MOVES LIKE A LIQUID, OR A PANTHER, OR A GORILLA, OR AN INSECT... ...etc...
THE CORRUPTION X DAVID RUBIN

LIGHT FLUID FLOATS OVER HIS HEAD
"FACE" MALEABLE SUBSTANCE, INFORM, IT COULD ADQUIRES DIFFERENTS FACES IF IS NECCESSARY.
LIKE WATCHMEN'S RORSCHORCH FACE BUT IN VOLUME (ABSTRACT)
HE CAN DEFORM HIS BODY, BUT NOT THE SAME WAY THAT THE CORRUPTION COULD.
(THE GOLDEN ENTITY IS MORE LIMITED THAN THE CORRUPTION)
THE GOLD ENTITY
X DAVID RUBIN--

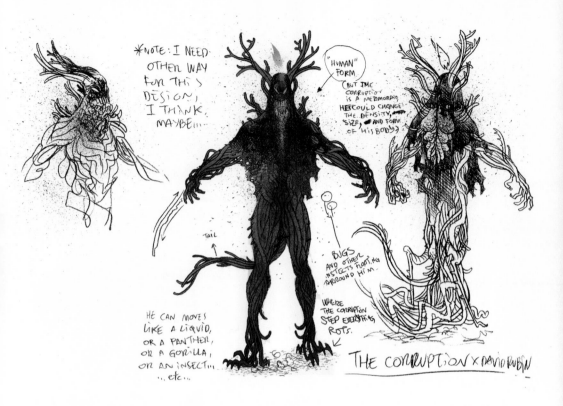

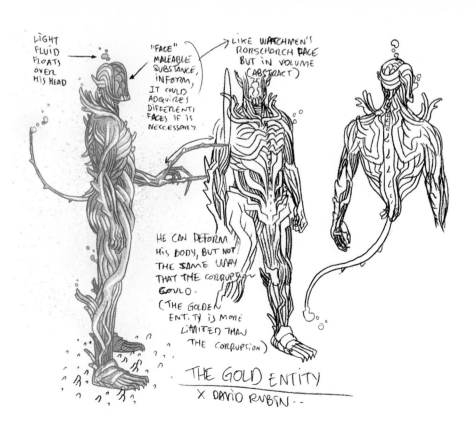